Frommer's®

YELLOWSTONE & GRAND TETON
NATIONAL PARKS

9th Edition

P9-CDH-414

By Elisabeth Kwak-Hefferan

FROMMER'S STAR RATINGS SYSTEM

Every hotel, restaurant, and attraction listed in this guide has been ranked for quality and value. Here's what the stars mean:

★ Recommended
★★ Highly Recommended
★★★ A must! Don't miss!

AN IMPORTANT NOTE

The world is a dynamic place. Hotels change ownership, restaurants hike their prices, museums alter their opening hours, and buses and trains change their routings. And all of this can occur in the several months after our authors have visited, inspected, and written about these hotels, restaurants, museums, and transportation services. Though we have made valiant efforts to keep all our information fresh and up-to-date, some few changes can inevitably occur in the periods before a revised edition of this guidebook is published. So please bear with us if a tiny number of the details in this book have changed. Please also note that we have no responsibility or liability for any inaccuracy or errors or omissions, or for inconvenience, loss, damage, or expenses suffered by anyone as a result of assertions in this guide.

Sunrise in Soda Butte Valley, Yellowstone.

CONTENTS

The slopes of Yellowstone's Mt. Washburn are known for their summer wildflowers.

A LOOK AT YELLOWSTONE & GRAND TETON

As flagships of the National Park System, Yellowstone and Grand Teton national parks are symbols of the great outdoors: magnificent, awe-inspiring monuments to unbridled nature and the American frontier as it once was. Join in the collective *"Ahh!"* at Old Faithful's timely gushes, or gaze in rapt wonder at the churning rainbow hues of the Grand Prismatic Spring. Fish, kayak, or canoe on Jenny Lake or the Snake River, or hike to jaw-dropping views of the Teton Range. Stay in a historic lodge, rough it in a log cabin, or sleep under the stars in a backcountry campground. Join a ranger-led trek, go horseback riding to a fireside cookout, or, in winter, discover the parks' pristine, snow-blanketed depths via snowcoach. However you choose to explore Yellowstone and Grand Teton, our EasyGuide will help you organize your trip and make the memories of a lifetime. Enjoy the adventure!

A herd of bison moves along Yellowstone's Firehole River near the Midway Geyser Basin.

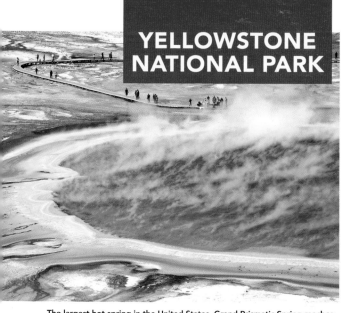

YELLOWSTONE NATIONAL PARK

The largest hot spring in the United States, Grand Prismatic Spring reaches temperatures of 160°F (70°C). Microbes that thrive in hot water give the spring its otherworldly colors.

The Grand Canyon of the Yellowstone and the Yellowstone River, downstream from the Lower Falls. Easy to strenuous hikes along the rim and down to the river afford the best views of the canyon.

A wolf pack in the Lamar Valley. After being hunted to extinction in the lower 48 states, wolves were reintroduced in Yellowstone in 1995. Today, there are an estimated 100 wolves in the park.

So-named because of its punctual eruptions, Old Faithful erupts every 60 to 110 minutes. Park facilities near the geyser include a visitor's center, boardwalks, accommodations, and dining.

A corral near the Roosevelt Lodge Cabins offers stagecoach rides, horseback riding, and cowboy-style cookouts.

An aerial boardwalk slated to open by 2018 will give visitors a bird's-eye view of the Grand Prismatic Spring.

Mountain goats—along with moose, bighorn sheep, and grizzlies— are frequently sighted on the Sepulcher Mountain Trail near Mammoth Hot Springs.

Palette Spring at Mammoth Hot Springs. Mammoth is a constantly shifting geological area, where old springs may dry up suddenly and new ones appear just as rapidly.

Visitors watch Old Faithful erupt from the porch of the Old Faithful Inn. Built in 1903–04, the rustic log inn is the park's most requested accommodation.

Winter in the park means fewer crowds, plus opportunities for cross-country skiing and snowshoeing. Park rangers lead free snowshoe walks from the Mammoth and West Yellowstone areas several times a week.

After most roads close in the winter, snowmobiles and strange-looking snowcoaches are the only ways to access many popular park areas.

Campgrounds in Yellowstone range from remote pack-in/out sites to enormous tent and RV villages with modern facilities.

GRAND TETON NATIONAL PARK

Despite being overshadowed by its more famous neighbor to the north, Grand Teton National Park offers shimmering lakes, towering peaks, and abundant wildlife, all on a more manageable scale than Yellowstone.

Fly-fishing in one of Teton's pristine lakes. Though strict limits are in place, anglers in the park can cast or troll for brook, brown, lake, and cutthroat trout, among other species.

Bison traverse the same roads as visitors to Grand Teton—and they have the right of way!

Grizzly bears are most active in the spring, when they emerge from hibernation. Human-grizzly encounters, although rare, are most likely to occur in the backcountry.

A hiker in Granite Canyon, Grand Teton. Even during the park's busiest periods, backcountry hikes allow visitors to quickly escape the crowds and reach isolated lakes, meadows, and streams.

Moose sightings are most frequent at the edges of ponds and valley bottoms, where they feed on willows and water plants, especially along the Moose-Wilson Road and near the Jackson Lake Lodge in Grand Teton.

A barn with a view: A few buildings still stand at Mormon Row, site of an 1890s Mormon homestead.

Autumn along the Snake River, with the Teton Range in the background.

Worth a stop before exploring the park, the Craig Thomas Discovery and Visitor Center offers information, displays, and ranger programs about the area's human history, ecology, and geology.

Canoeing on Jackson Lake, where the expansive shoreline holds a number of visitor facilities, marinas, hiking trails, restaurants, and campgrounds.

GATEWAYS TO YELLOWSTONE & GRAND TETON

A wolf dines on elk at the nonprofit Grizzly and Wolf Discovery Center at West Yellowstone, Montana.

Framed by four arches made of antlers, the Town Square in Jackson, Wyoming, is ringed by art galleries, restaurants, and souvenir shops.

The Old Trail Town in Cody, Wyoming, a frontier town founded by Old West showman Buffalo Bill Cody.

Horse-drawn sleds bring visitors close to the thousands of elk that graze every winter at the National Elk Refuge near Jackson.

Summer rafting trips on the Snake River range from peaceful float trips to challenging Class II and III rapids. Several top-notch outfitters are based in Jackson.

The spirit of the Wild West pervades Cody, where costumed interpreters stage gunfights on most summer evenings.

World-class downhill skiing and a large number of black diamond runs draw adrenaline seekers to Jackson's ski resorts.

Western dancing, live entertainment, and a raucous good time are on tap at the Million Dollar Cowboy Bar, Jackson's most famous watering hole.

INTRODUCING YELLOWSTONE & GRAND TETON

Yellowstone and Grand Teton National Parks are life-list destinations for millions of people—not just Americans—the world over. That's because you won't find places like these anywhere else on the planet: No other region combines rare geothermal fireworks, skyscraping mountains, glaciers, and a huge variety of wildlife such as grizzly bears, wolves, elk, and moose in one spot the way the Greater Yellowstone Ecosystem does. Here, you can spend days getting lost among the geysers and hot springs, gazing up at or down from towering peaks, marveling at incredible waterfalls, sniffing carpets of wildflowers, and scoping for that next thrilling wildlife sighting. There's something for everyone at these two exceptional parks—and as soon as you check this place off your life list, you're bound to start dreaming about your next visit.

Creatures great and small thrive in Yellowstone and Grand Teton National Parks. In the wilderness of Yellowstone's southern corners, grizzlies feed on cutthroat trout during their annual spawning run to the Yellowstone headwaters. In the soft blue depths of Octopus Pond, microbes of enormous scientific value are incubated and born; in the mountain ridges, gray wolves make their dens and mountain lions hunt bighorn sheep. Bald eagles and ospreys soar above the banks of the Snake River in Grand Teton, moose munch their way through meadows,

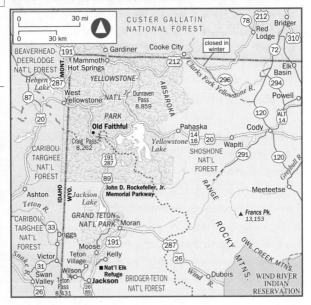

and elk and bison traverse the park on the same roads as visitors.

When John Colter, a scout for Lewis and Clark, first wandered this way in 1807, his descriptions of geysers, sulfurous hot pools, and towering waterfalls drew jeers and suspicion. No one doubts him now, but these are still places you should see for yourself. The explorers of today come in minivans and on bicycles, aboard snowmobiles and Telemark skis, and in such numbers that the parks sometimes seem to groan under the strain.

In the early days of Yellowstone, first established as a national park in 1872, visitors were so sparse that their unregulated activities—catching 100 trout at a time, washing their underwear in the hot pools—left few noticeable scars. Now, with millions of people visiting the parks annually, the strain on everything from sewer systems to fish populations is immense. Yet while there are problems, these parks still radiate extraordinary beauty: the jagged Tetons, the glassy surface of Jenny Lake, the awe-inspiring Grand Canyon of the Yellowstone, the towering Obsidian Cliff, the steamy meandering of the Firehole River. Wildlife that most Americans see only in zoos wanders freely here, from the grizzly to the river otter, the trumpeter swan to the rufous hummingbird. Aspen groves, fields of lupine, the howls of coyotes and wolves—all testify to the resilience and vitality of the Greater Yellowstone Ecosystem, which extends outside the borders of the park to Grand Teton and beyond.

This is not just a paradise for sightseers—it's a scientific preserve as well. The hot pools support a population of unique microbes known as thermophiles and extremophiles; studies of the elk herds and grizzlies have yielded crucial information on habitat needs and animal behavior; and the rocks of Yellowstone present the earth turned inside out—a treasure trove for geologists.

Most visitors will see or know little of this. They park in a pullout on U.S. 191/89/26 to pose in front of Grand Teton, or they sit on crowded benches to watch Old Faithful erupt. If you have more time, however, I suggest that you take little sections of these parks—just the Jenny Lake area in Grand Teton, say, or Yellowstone's northeast corner, the Lamar Valley—and savor them in all their fine detail, rather than embark on a madcap race to see every highlight.

Definitely get out of your car and away from the road, into the wild heart of the backcountry. These parks embody our country's beginnings: as a landscape of wilderness, of challenging and rugged extremes, and of extraordinary bounty and beauty. Use this guide as a set of footprints to help you find your way there.

A LOOK AT YELLOWSTONE

What other national park boasts an assortment of some 10,000 thermal features, including more than 300 geysers? Even when the rest of North America was still largely wilderness, Yellowstone was unique. Its collection of geothermal features is richer and more concentrated than any other in the world, with mud pots, geysers, and hot springs of all colors and sizes. Plus, there's a waterfall that's twice as tall as Niagara Falls and a canyon deep and colorful enough to be called "grand." Sure, other parks have great hiking trails and beautiful geologic formations—Grand Teton is pretty spectacular in its own right, as is Yosemite—but unlike many other parks, a sizable percentage of the geology in Yellowstone is reachable by visitors in average physical shape.

Ever focus your camera lens on an untamed grizzly bear, or a bald eagle? What about a wolf? Thousands of visitors have these experiences here every year. Protected from development by the national park and surrounding forests, Yellowstone is home to herds of bison and elk, packs of grizzly bears, flocks of trumpeter swans, schools of Yellowstone cutthroat trout, and subtler beauties such as wildflowers and hummingbirds.

And the park doesn't appeal solely to the visual senses; you'll smell it, too. Yellowstone has more than 1,100 species of native plants. When wildflowers cover the meadows in spring, their fragrances are overpowering. The mud pots and fumaroles have their own set of odors, though many are less pleasing than that of a wild lily.

Your ears will be filled with the sounds of geysers noisily spewing forth thousands of gallons of boiling water into the blue Wyoming sky. After sunset, coyotes break the silence of the night with their high-pitched yips.

You can spend weeks hiking Yellowstone's backcountry or fishing its streams, but the park's road system makes it easy to see its highlights from behind the windshield in a day or two. Roads lead past most of the key attractions and are filled with wildlife commuting from one grazing area to another, and many visitors to Yellowstone tour the park without hitting the trail. While there's no doubt that driving through the park yields vivid memories, those who don't leave their cars are shortchanging themselves.

Yellowstone closes in fall and then reopens as a winter destination come December, when cross-country skiing, snowshoeing, and snowmobiling are the prime pursuits. There's no cozier place than the lobby of the Old Faithful Snow Lodge, the only hotel in the park's interior that stays open during Yellowstone's long, cold, and snowy winter season. I highly recommend a visit when snow covers the ground. You often have the park to yourself, but dress appropriately (read: no fewer than three layers) and be ready to incur an extra expense in the form of snowcoach fare.

A LOOK AT GRAND TETON

Because the magnificent mountains of the Teton Range stand so tall, with the park curling snugly at their feet, visitors sometimes fail to appreciate the surrounding environment of rivers and high valley floor. The Tetons are a geologically young range of old pre-Cambrian granite, abrupt and sharp-edged as they knife up from the Snake River valley along a 40-mile-long fault sculpted over the course of the last 13 million years, with help from geological upheaval, retreating glaciers, and erosion (the Great Smoky Mountains, by comparison, uplifted some 270 million years ago). The result is a masterpiece. Many visitors regard Grand Teton National Park—with its shimmering lakes, thickly carpeted forests, and towering peaks blanketed with snow most of the year—as more dramatically scenic than its northern neighbor.

It's also a very accessible park. You can appreciate its breathtaking beauty on a quick drive-by, or take to the trails and waterways in search of backcountry lakes and waterfalls. The Tetons themselves are especially popular with mountain climbers, who scale them year-round.

There's a dynamic relationship between the Tetons and the valley below. The elk and other wildlife migrate from the high country down to the open grasslands to forage during the winter; in spring, snowmelt curls across the valley floor and west through a gap in the mountains, and the moraines and alluvial soils that slough off the mountains provide rich soil for the pastures below.

Visitors can float and fish the lively Snake River; visit the National Elk Refuge; hike in nearby ranges, such as the Wind River or the Gros Ventre; or play cowboy at one of the dude and guest ranches that dot the valley of Jackson Hole. Skiers and snowboarders have a blast on the slopes here, as well as at Grand Targhee on the other side of Teton Pass. And the chic town of Jackson, with its antler-arched square and its busy shops, offers everything from fly-fishing outfitters to classy art galleries to rowdy two-stepping crowds at cowboy bars.

1 | MAKING THE MOST OF YOUR TRIP

Yellowstone and Grand Teton are not just photo ops and zoos where the animals roam free. Both parks are works in progress; they are living, breathing wilderness areas. Plant your feet in a comfortable pair of walking or hiking shoes, find a trailhead, and set off into the woods with a sack lunch and a big bottle of water. Better yet, if you can afford the time, plan an excursion by boat around Shoshone Lake or to the south end of Yellowstone Lake, to areas few visitors ever see. There are isolated spots in Grand Teton, too—even on the far shore of popular Jenny Lake—where you'll be rewarded with a pristine, forested glade with nothing to distract you but wild moose and an awe-inspiring mountaintop.

If you're more adventurous, take a whitewater trip down Snake River Canyon, or let a guide take you up to Grand Teton's summit. In Yellowstone, sleep under the stars and listen to the wolves howl at Slough Creek Campground; or backpack for a week on the Thorofare Trail.

You'll never plumb the absolute depths of these parks—no one ever will. You could spend your whole life trying, though, and have a wonderful and illuminating time doing it.

THE best OF YELLOWSTONE & GRAND TETON

A "best of" list could never do justice to Yellowstone and Grand Teton National Parks. These are just starting points, the best of the excellent accommodations and dining the parks offer, as well as unique sightseeing and recreational opportunities. Some involve backcountry expeditions; others can be enjoyed from behind a windshield. In the wildly diverse environments of these two parks, you can be as adventurous as you want—climbing peaks and spending the night deep in the wilderness, or simply enjoying the more civilized side of the parks at grand lodges and enchanting roadside overlooks.

The Best Views

You'll never get it all in a camera lens, but you can try. Just don't get too caught up in Instagramming your trip: Compose some memorable shots, then put down the camera and take in the scenery with nothing between you and the view.

o **Grand Canyon of the Yellowstone** (Yellowstone): Here, plunging polychrome rock walls frame two of the most powerful waterfalls for hundreds of miles: 308-foot Lower Falls and 109-foot Upper Falls. Excellent views await along both the North and South Rims of the canyon, but **Artist Point,** at the end of South Rim Drive, offers a picture-perfect distant look at Lower Falls. For a closer look, brave the metal staircase of **Uncle Tom's Trail,** which dives deep into the canyon itself. On the North Rim, **Inspiration Point** delivers an equally impressive view. See "Yellowstone: The Extended Tour" in chapter 3.

o **Lamar Valley** (Yellowstone): If it's wildlife you seek, then make tracks to this expansive valley on the park's northeast side. Your chances of spotting at least some of Yellowstone's charismatic megafauna—including grizzly bears, wolves, elk, bison—are very high, especially if you visit at dawn and dusk. Multiple pullouts along the park road provide vantage points to set up your spotting scope or binoculars. See "Yellowstone: The Extended Tour" in chapter 3.

o **Mount Washburn** (Yellowstone): For one of the finest top-down views over Yellowstone, hike to the top of this 10,243-foot summit. From the windswept peak, you'll see the Grand Canyon of the Yellowstone slicing into the earth, the rolling Lamar and Hayden Valleys, and all the way to the Tetons. See "Day Hikes," chapter 4.

o **Yellowstone Lake** (Yellowstone): Sunrise over Yellowstone Lake is stunningly beautiful (especially if there's fog on the lake), whether you watch it from the sunroom at the **Lake Yellowstone Hotel,** the front porch at **Lake Lodge** or, even better, from a campsite along the southern wilderness shore. For an equally spectacular sunset view, drive 10 miles east of the hotels to **Lake Butte Overlook.** See "Yellowstone: The Extended Tour," in chapter 3.

o **Cathedral Group** (Grand Teton): The three central mountains of the Teton Range rarely disappoint, except on the unusual occasion when weather gets in the way—clouds tend to accent rather than obscure their majesty. A number of pullouts on both the inner and outer park roads grant a lovely view of them, but the **Cathedral Group Turnout** on the Jenny Lake Scenic Drive is particularly special. See "The Highlights," chapter 5.

o **Oxbow Bend** (Grand Teton): The view of 12,605-foot Mount Moran reflected in a wide bend of the Snake River is not to be missed—especially in fall, when the aspens and willows go golden. See "Touring Grand Teton," chapter 5.

The Best Thermal Displays

Yellowstone has more thermal features—geysers, mud pots, hot springs, and steam vents—than the rest of the world combined. When you're angling for a good shot of a colorful pool or a belching mud pot, obey the signs; otherwise, you could find yourself (quite literally) on shaky ground. For details on these steamy sights, see "Yellowstone: The Extended Tour," in chapter 3.

o **Upper Geyser Basin** (Yellowstone): Home to the mega-famous Old Faithful Geyser as well as enough other thermal features to form the largest concentration of geysers in the world, Upper Geyser Basin is a can't-miss destination. This is why you're here, isn't it?

o **Norris Geyser Basin** (Yellowstone): The park's oldest, hottest thermal area encompasses a dynamic collection of geysers, steaming hot springs, and hissing steam vents. Change is constant here, remaking this remarkable area year by year and day by day.

o **The Mammoth Hot Springs Terraces** (Yellowstone): Here you can observe Mother Nature going about the business of mixing and matching heat, water, limestone, and rock fractures to sculpt the landscape. This is one of the most colorful areas in the park; its tapestries of orange, pink, yellow, green, and brown, formed by masses of bacteria and algae, seem to change colors before your eyes. The mineral-rich hot waters that flow to the surface here do so at an unusually constant rate, roughly 750,000 gallons per day.

The Best Day Hikes

Just a few hundred yards off the road, things get a lot less crowded, and you'll have the views and the wildlife (almost) to yourself. Getting out of the car and into the wilds is always worthwhile, but these shorter trips are the best of the best for those not doing extended, multi-day hikes.

- **The Mount Washburn Trail** (Yellowstone): Starting at Dunraven Pass, south of Tower Junction, this walk to the fire lookout atop Mount Washburn offers unsurpassed views of both parks, plus the opportunity to see mountain wildlife, such as bighorn sheep. See p. 74.

- **The Lone Star Geyser Trail** (Yellowstone): This gentle, 5-mile hike along the Firehole River presents several places to stop and take in the scenery, go fishing, and—at the endpoint—view an active, medium-size geyser. It is also one of a few bicycle-friendly trails in Yellowstone, and in the winter, it's a popular cross-country skiing trail. See p. 78.

- **Upper Pebble Creek Trail** (Yellowstone): Explore the less-traveled, peak-heavy northeastern part of the park on this wildflower-filled ramble to cliff views and creekside hiking. See p. 73.

- **Amphitheater Lake Trail** (Grand Teton): Climbing the switchbacks up to this cirque-cradled, high-country lake is worth the effort, we promise. See p. 117.

The Best Backcountry Trails

To see the true heart of the parks, load up a backpack and spend a night or more in the wilderness. These remote areas make for unforgettable backpacking destinations, whether you're up for an overnight or a real multiday epic.

- **Thorofare Trail** (Yellowstone): This hike will take you deeper into road-free wilderness than you can get anywhere else in the lower 48 states. You'll spend a few nights on the trail, climbing up to the park's southern border and beyond to the Yellowstone River's headwaters, a high valley bursting with wildlife. Early in the summer, if the snow has melted, the cutthroat spawning run attracts grizzlies and coyotes. It's not for the faint of heart. See "Exploring the Backcountry," in chapter 4.

- **Bechler Area** (Yellowstone): The park's remote "Cascade Corner" features plentiful waterfalls, soakable hot springs, and riverside hiking. Several different out-and-back or loop options are possible, and you can even plan a long-haul hike from Bechler all the way to Old Faithful. See "Exploring the Backcountry," in chapter 4.

o **Cascade/Paintbrush Canyon Loop** (Grand Teton): Perhaps the most popular trail in Grand Teton, the Cascade/Paintbrush Canyon Loop, which starts on the west side of Jenny Lake, winds northwest 9.5 miles on the Cascade Canyon Trail to Lake Solitude and the Paintbrush Divide, then returns past Holly Lake on the 10-mile Paintbrush Canyon Trail. The payoff comes at the highest point, Paintbrush Divide, which offers marvelous views of Jackson Hole Valley and Leigh Lake. See "Exploring the Backcountry," in chapter 6.

The Best Campgrounds

If you stay in developed campgrounds in the parks, the outdoor life is pretty civilized. You'll have running water and, in most cases, flush toilets, plus there are opportunities to meet fellow campers.

o **Slough Creek & Pebble Creek Campgrounds** (Yellowstone): These two small, primitive campgrounds in the Lamar Valley are prized for their proximity to excellent trout fishing and wildlife-watching. Plus, they're much quieter than some of the other giant campgrounds in the park for a real away-from-it-all vibe. See p. 139.

o **Lewis Lake Campground** (Yellowstone): The park's southernmost campground has private-feeling sites tucked into the trees near the shores of Lewis Lake, making it great for paddlers or boaters. See p. 140.

o **Indian Creek Campground** (Yellowstone): Smallish, quiet, and with close to top-shelf fishing and elk and bison viewing, Indian Creek is another option that really makes you feel like you're getting off the beaten track. See p. 139.

o **Jenny Lake Campground** (Grand Teton): Situated near the edge of the lake from which it takes its name, Jenny Lake Campground is nestled among spruce and fir trees just a short walk away from the South Jenny Lake area. It's the perfect place to spend the night if you plan to hike around the lake to Hidden Falls or up Cascade Canyon the next day. Get there early, though: It's a highly desirable place to pitch a tent, and its first-come, first-serve sites fill quickly. See p. 152.

The Best Places to Eat in the Parks

The parks' restaurants aren't as much about five-star dining (with one notable exception) as they are about kicking back in a friendly, one-of-a-kind atmosphere to enjoy hearty fare. All of these options are detailed in chapter 7.

o **The Old Faithful Inn** (Yellowstone; ℂ **307/344-7311**): Don't miss a chance to linger over a meal under the soaring stone-and-timber architecture of the park's best hotel. The menu leans toward steak, seafood, and local favorites like bison. See p. 145.

o **The Lake Yellowstone Hotel** (Yellowstone; ℂ **307/344-7311**): A tinkling piano, Victorian details, and large picture windows over the lake give this restaurant Yellowstone's most elegant air. See p. 144.

o **Jenny Lake Lodge Dining Room** (Grand Teton; ℂ **307/543-3352**): This luxurious dining room stands head and shoulders above the rest with an expertly prepared, five-course prix-fixe dinner. Expect lots of local ingredients from the Jackson Farmers' Market, creative flavors, and impeccable service. Lodge guests get breakfast and dinner with the price of their room, but non-guests can also make reservations (top-quality dining means top dollar). See p. 156.

o **The Mural Room** (Grand Teton; ℂ **307/543-3463**): Jackson Lake Lodge's signature restaurant is known even more for its fantastic window views looking out over the Tetons than it is for its (quite good) food. See p. 154.

The Best Places to Sleep in the Parks

In-park lodging ranges from rustic old classics to sleek modern hotels, and some of them are true gems. All of these are detailed in chapter 7.

o **The Old Faithful Inn** (Yellowstone; ℂ **307/344-7311**): One peek into this 1904-era masterpiece, and you'll know why it's the most-requested hotel in the park. From its grand stone fireplace to its soaring timber-and-stone walls to its charmingly old-fashioned rooms, Old Faithful Inn is unlike any other hotel out there, in a national park or otherwise. See p. 136.

- **The Lake Yellowstone Hotel** (Yellowstone; ✆ 307/344-7311): If you're looking to do up your park vacation in style, this is your choice: Lovingly restored Colonial Revival details, a graceful sunroom with lake views, and carefully curated guest rooms make this the most upscale hotel at Yellowstone. See p. 135.

- **Roosevelt Lodge Cabins** (Yellowstone; ✆ 307/344-7311): Deluxe it isn't: This complex of very rustic cabins is as simple as it gets. But its authentic frontier feel, proximity to corrals for horseback rides, and prime location smack at the start of the Lamar Valley make this less-crowded lodge one of the most memorable places to bunk. See p. 134.

- **Jenny Lake Lodge** (Grand Teton; ✆ 307/543-3100): I challenge you find a better, more luxurious hotel in any national park than this one, where guests stay in fancy cabins, come together for A-list meals, and enjoy free perks like horseback rides and front-lawn yoga sessions. See p. 149.

The Best Places to Eat Outside the Parks

You might be practically in the wilderness out here, but the park's gateway towns boast some mighty fine dining choices. All of the establishments below are detailed in chapter 8.

- **In Jackson, Wyoming:** It's tough to pick just one favorite in the culinary capital of Wyoming, but **Snake River Grill** (✆ 307/733-0557; p. 188) has long been the preferred stop of locals and guests alike for its inventive, genre-blending dishes ranging from Asian-style noodles to quail. It's a splurge, but a worthy one.

- **In Cody, Wyoming: Cassie's Supper Club** (✆ 307/527-5500) is a brothel turned cowboy eatery, plating up some of the best steaks in the Rockies. After dinner, country bands hold court over the bustling dance floor. See p. 203.

- **Near Gardiner, Montana: Chico Dining Room** (✆ 406/333-4933), the restaurant at a beloved hot springs resort, offers a refined dining experience in the middle of nowhere. There's no better way to finish a day (or kick off an evening) of thermal relaxation than with a superb meal and a glass of wine from the extensive list here. See p. 166.

The Best Places to Sleep Outside the Parks

In high season, park rooms are at a premium and sell out quickly. These fine alternatives, located in the park gateways, are all detailed in chapter 7.

o **In Jackson, Wyoming:** The **Wort Hotel** (© 307/733-2190; p. 182) is a Jackson landmark with comfortable "New West"–style rooms and a town institution of a watering hole, the **Silver Dollar Bar.** The newish **Hotel Jackson** (© 307/733-2200;** p. 181) marries high design with comfortable Western touches.

o **In Gardiner, Montana:** The **Riverside Cottages** (© 406/848-7719) overlooking the Yellowstone River feel more like the artfully decorated guest cabin of a friend than a hotel, and the prices are reasonable, too. See p. 165.

o **In Cody, Wyoming:** Centered on a serene and green courtyard, the new-and-improved **Chamberlin Inn** (© 307/587-0202) features charming, historic rooms and apartments with serious literary cred: Ernest Hemingway once stayed here (and you can sleep in his room). See p. 200.

The Best Things to See & Do Outside the Parks

Don't assume that a Yellowstone and Grand Teton vacation must be confined to within park boundaries. Here are a few area attractions worth checking out. See chapter 8 for more information.

o **In Cody, Wyoming:** The **Buffalo Bill Historical Center** (© 307/587-4771) is the best museum in the region— make that five museums, as you can check out exhibits in wings dedicated to natural history, art, firearms, Native Americans, and Buffalo Bill Cody himself. See p. 197.

o **In Jackson, Wyoming:** Glimpse some of the finest artistic interpretations of the natural world at the fantastic **National Museum of Wildlife Art** (© 307/733-5771; p. 178), which houses 1,300 pieces within its red-sandstone walls. At the top of the **Jackson Hole Aerial Tram** (© 307/739-2753; p. 177), at Jackson Hole Mountain Resort, you can see the Tetons from an elevation of more than 10,000 feet. On busy summer days, the tram whisks sightseers and hikers up the mountaintop in just 12 minutes.

o **In West Yellowstone, Montana:** The **Grizzly and Wolf Discovery Center** (© **406/646-7001**), a nonprofit sanctuary for bears and wolves, lets you see the magnificent animals up close while learning about their lives, habitats, and the threats they face. It's no mere roadside wildlife park. See p. 158.

The Best Scenic Drives

Though we encourage you to get out and explore on foot whenever possible, the parks offer fantastic scenic drives for those disinclined or unable to hoof it. But do take your time, and take advantage of the many opportunities to pull over and gaze at the wonders before you.

o From the most beautiful part of Yellowstone (the northeast corner) through **Silver Gate** and **Cooke City,** up to the dizzying heights of **Beartooth Pass,** the **Beartooth Highway** (U.S. 212) drive is nothing short of spectacular. If that's not enough, you can extend the trip to **Red Lodge, Montana,** or head down to **Cody, Wyoming,** and connect to the East Entrance Road (see below). See chapter 3.

o The **East Entrance Road** is the second-most scenic way to approach Yellowstone (behind the Beartooth Highway, above). Wind through gorgeous Shoshone Canyon, top out on 8,530-foot **Sylvan Pass,** then cruise down from the high country to sweeping views over **Yellowstone Lake.** See chapter 3.

o A twisting, narrow road climbs Grand Teton's **Signal Mountain** to a fine 360-degree view of the valley and surrounding peaks. On the way up, you'll see wildflowers and birds; from the top, you can study the moraines and potholes left by retreating glaciers. See chapter 5.

THE PARKS IN DEPTH

In Yellowstone and Grand Teton National Parks, spectacular scenery combines with a genuine frontier history to create what we consider the real American West. The land is uncluttered and the setting is one of rugged beauty: the remote wilderness of Yellowstone's Thorofare country, the soaring peaks of the Teton Range, and the geothermal activity sprouting from below the surface of the Earth.

There's a little more modern civilization here than there was in years gone by, but this is still one of the few places in the U.S. where there are vast tracts of untouched wilderness. Make sure to take the time to experience it without the noise of cell-phones, cars, and other trappings of the 21st century: Your hiking boots and water bottle may be the most important items in your luggage.

YELLOWSTONE & GRAND TETON NATIONAL PARKS TODAY

The struggle to balance recreation and preservation is as old as the parks themselves, and it's an issue that continually rears its head in questions about the visitor experience, wildlife management, and what types of activities should be allowed within the parks. How can the park preserve the wilderness feel of the place while keeping its doors open to more than 4 million people every year? What's to be done about controversial populations of bison and wolves? Should snowmobiles be allowed in the park, and if so, how many? What about drones? These and other issues play out season after season, posing management challenges but also proving the parks are just as dynamic as they've ever been.

Bison, Bears & Wolves

In the frontier West—where bison seemed to be everywhere, grizzly bears were fearsome, and wolves regularly raided livestock—wildlife was treated as more of a nuisance than a national treasure. Eventually, the bison and grizzly populations around Yellowstone and Grand Teton were whittled down nearly to extinction, and ranchers and federal agents completely eradicated wolves by the 1930s.

It took some intensive management to bring grizzlies and bison back to reasonably healthy numbers in the area, and now the wolves, which were reintroduced from Canada in 1995, are reaping the benefits of the huge ungulate herds that have enjoyed a nearly predator-free environment for quite some time. But these high-profile species—called "charismatic megafauna" by biologists—are not out of the woods yet. Given the pressures of development around the parks, they might never be secure again.

There are now more than 5,500 bison in Yellowstone and Grand Teton, and, naturally, they pay no mind to the parks' invisible boundaries. In the winter, when the snow is deep, they leave the park to forage at lower elevations, sometimes in ranch pastures inhabited by domestic cattle. The ranchers fear that the bison will spread brucellosis, a virus that can be transmitted to cattle, causing infected cows to abort their unborn calves. There have been no documented cases of bison-cattle transmission, but the perceived threat to livestock still worries state officials and other stakeholders. Currently, federal, state, and tribal agencies slaughter some bison each winter as a population control measure. The practice is controversial, and park and state officials continue to search for some middle ground with animal-rights activists.

Wolves are another sore point with area ranchers, who worry that a booming wolf population threatens their livestock (and wolves do sometimes prey on cows and sheep). Wolf advocates, on the other hand, argue that restoring the natural wolf population returns the ecosystem to its original, balanced state. The reintroduction has been astonishingly successful.

Rapidly reproducing, feeding on abundant elk in Yellowstone's Lamar Valley, wolves now number about 100 in Yellowstone and about 530 in the Greater Yellowstone Ecosystem, and the packs have spread as far south as Grand Teton, where several have denned and produced pups. Gray wolves were delisted from the endangered species lists in Montana and Idaho in 2011 (and both states allow limited wolf hunting) but retain their endangered status in Wyoming.

Grizzly bears once teetered on the brink of extinction in the parks, but they've made a slow comeback, reaching an estimated population of more than 700 in the Yellowstone area. (Wolves have helped, because their hunting results in more carcasses to scavenge.) Because of this success, in 2007 the U.S. Fish and Wildlife Service removed the grizzly from the threatened species list for the Yellowstone area, a decision that was subsequently reversed in 2010. As of late 2016, the U.S. Fish and Wildlife Service has proposed delisting grizzlies again, a move supported by the Interagency Grizzly Bear Committee, but a final decision has not been reached.

A Burning Issue

After years of suppressing every fire in the park, Yellowstone, in 1988, was operating under a new "let it burn" policy, based on scientific evidence that fires were regular occurrences before the settlement of the West and part of the natural cycle of a forest. That philosophy faced the ultimate test the same year, when nearly one-third of Yellowstone was burned by a series of uncontrollable wildfires. These violent conflagrations scorched more than 700,000 acres, leaving behind dead wildlife, damaged buildings, injured firefighters, and ghostly forests of stripped, blackened tree trunks.

What you will see, as you travel Yellowstone today, is a park that may be healthier than it was before the 1988 fires. Saplings have sprouted from the long-dormant seeds of the lodgepole pine (fire stimulates the pine cones to release their seeds), and the old, tinder-dry forest undergrowth is being replaced with new, green shrubs, sometimes as thick as one million saplings per acre. Visitors who want to better understand the effects of the fires of 1988 should check out the exhibits at the Grant Village Visitor Center; the coverage there is the best in the park.

Snowmobiles: To Ban or Not to Ban?

Winter in Yellowstone is a time of silent wonder, with fauna descending from the high country in search of warmth and food. The only dissonance in this wilderness tableau is the roar of snowmobiles, which inhabit the park's snow-packed roads in ever-growing numbers. The noisy, pollution-heavy engines are not exactly ecologically friendly, but the gateway towns are staunch snowmobile proponents because the activity boosts their economies in the moribund winter.

Before President Clinton left office in 2001, he "ended" the ongoing controversy by establishing a ban on snowmobiles in Yellowstone, effective the winter of 2003–04. However, gateway communities and snowmobile manufacturers responded with lawsuits; and the Bush administration also voiced its opposition to a total ban, delighting the outfitters in West Yellowstone and Cody. In mid-2004, a judge overturned the ruling enforcing the ban.

The park reached a new snowmobile management plan in 2013, part of its Winter Use Adaptive Management Program. Under these rules, four non-commercially guided snowmobile "events" with up to five snowmobiles per event are allowed to access the park daily—one event per park entrance. All snowmobiles used must meet standards for noise and emissions under Best Available Technology rules, and all snowmobile drivers must complete a free online education course before their trips. Commercial snowmobile outfitters have different regulations to meet. If you're planning a private trip, check with the park for the most up-to-date info on regulations at www.nps.gov/yell.

LOOKING BACK: YELLOWSTONE & GRAND TETON HISTORY

Yellowstone National Park

Before the arrival of European settlers, the only residents on the plateau were small bands of Shoshone Indians known as "Sheepeaters," who lived on the southern fringe. Three other Native American tribes came and went: the Crows

(Apsáalooke), who were friendly to the settlers; the Black-feet, who lived in the Missouri Valley drainage and were hostile to both Europeans and other tribes; and the Bannocks, who largely kept to themselves. The nomadic Bannocks traveled an east-west route in their search for bison: from Idaho past Mammoth Hot Springs to Tower Fall, and then across the Lamar Valley to the Bighorn Valley, outside the park's current boundaries. Called the Bannock Trail, the route was so deeply furrowed that evidence of it still exists today on the Blacktail Plateau near the Tower Junction. (You'll see remnants of the trail if you take Blacktail Plateau Drive, described in chapter 3.)

The first explorer of European descent to lay eyes on Yellowstone's geothermal wonders was probably John Colter, who broke away from the Lewis and Clark expedition in 1806 and spent 3 years wandering a surreal landscape of mud pots, mountains, and geysers. When he described his discovery on his return to St. Louis, no one believed him. Miners and fur trappers followed in his footsteps, reducing the plentiful beaver population of the region to almost zero, and occasionally making curious reports of a sulfurous world still sometimes called "Colter's Hell."

The first significant exploration of what would become the park took place in 1869, when a band of Montanans, led by David Folsom, completed a 36-day expedition. The group traveled up the Missouri River and into the heart of the park, where they discovered the falls of Yellowstone, mud pots, Yellowstone Lake, and the Fountain Geyser. Two years later, an expedition led by U.S. Geological Survey director Ferdinand V. Hayden brought back convincing evidence of Yellowstone's wonders, in the form of astonishing photographs by William Henry Jackson.

A debate began over the potential for commercial development and exploitation of the region, as crude health spas and thin-walled "hotels" went up near the hot springs. There are various claimants to the idea of a national park—members of the Folsom party later told an oft-disputed story about thinking it up around a campfire in the Upper Geyser Basin—but the idea gained steam as Yellowstone explorers hit the lecture circuit back East. In March 1872, President Ulysses S. Grant signed legislation declaring Yellowstone the nation's first national park.

The Department of the Interior got the job of managing the new park. There was no budget for it and no clear idea of how to take care of a wilderness preserve; many mistakes were made. Inept superintendents granted favorable leases to friends with commercial interests in the tourism industry. Poachers ran amok, and the wildlife population was decimated. A laundry business near Mammoth went so far as to clean linens in a hot pool.

By 1886, things were so bad that the U.S. Army took control of Yellowstone; iron-fisted management practices resulted in new order and protected the park from those intent on exploiting it. (However, the military did participate in the eradication of the plateau's wolf population.) By 1916, efforts to make the park more visitor-friendly had begun to show results: Construction of the first roads had been completed, guest housing was available in the area, and order had been restored. Stewardship of the park was then transferred to the newly created National Park Service, which remains in control to this day.

Grand Teton National Park

Unlike Yellowstone, Grand Teton can't boast of being the nation's first park and a model for parks the world over. This smaller, southern neighbor was created as the result of a much more convoluted process that spanned 50 years.

The first sign of human habitation in the Grand Teton region dates back 12,000 years. Among the tribes who hunted here

DATELINE

18,000 B.C.	Earliest evidence of humans in Wyoming.
11,000 B.C.	Earliest evidence of humans in Montana.
1620s	Arrival of the Plains Indians.
1807	John Colter explores the Yellowstone area, going as far south as Jackson Hole.
1867	The Union Pacific Railroad enters Wyoming.

1869	A party led by David Folsom undertakes the first modern exploration of Yellowstone.
1871	The Hayden Expedition surveys Yellowstone.
1872	Yellowstone is established as the nation's first national park.
1876	Warriors from the Sioux, Lakota, and Cheyenne tribes defeat General George A. Custer and his troops at the Battle

in the warmer seasons were the Blackfeet, Crow, Gros Ventre, and Shoshone, who came over the mountains from the Great Basin to the west. They spent summers here hunting and raising crops, before heading to warmer climes for the winter.

Trappers and explorers, who first arrived in the valley in the early 1800s, were equally distressed by the harsh winters and short growing seasons, which made Jackson Hole a marginal place for farming and ranching. Among these early visitors were artist Thomas Moran and photographer William Henry Jackson, whose images awoke the country to the Tetons' grandeur. Early homesteaders quickly realized that their best hope was to market the unspoiled beauty of the area, which they began doing in earnest as early as a century ago.

The danger of haphazard development soon became apparent. There was a dance hall at Jenny Lake, hot dog stands along the roads, and buildings going up on prime habitat. In the 1920s, after some discussion about how the Grand Teton area might be protected, Yellowstone park officials and conservationists went to Congress. Led by local dude ranchers and Yellowstone superintendent Horace Albright, the group was able to protect only the mountains and foothills, leaving out Jackson Lake and the valley; Wyoming's congressional delegation—and many locals—were vehemently opposed to enclosing the valley within park boundaries.

Then, in 1927, something called the Snake River Land Company started buying ranches and homesteads at the base

of the Little Bighorn (Montana).

1877 Chief Joseph of the Nez Perce tribe surrenders to U.S. soldiers in the Bear Paw Mountains after a flight that took his tribe though Yellowstone.

1883 The Northern Pacific Railroad crosses Montana.

1889 Montana, on November 8, becomes the 41st state in the Union.

1890 Wyoming becomes the nation's 44th state.

1929 Grand Teton National Park is established, consisting of only the main peaks of the Cathedral Range.

1950 National forest and private lands are added to Grand Teton National Park, forming the park's current boundaries.

continues

of the Tetons. The company turned out to be a front for John D. Rockefeller, Jr., one of the richest men in the world, working in cahoots with the conservationists. He planned to give the land to the federal government and keep a few choice parcels for himself. But Congress wouldn't have it, and Rockefeller made noises about selling the land, about 35,000 acres, to the highest bidder. In the 1940s, President Franklin D. Roosevelt created the Jackson Hole National Monument out of Forest Service lands east of the Snake River. That paved the way for Rockefeller's donation, and in 1950, Grand Teton National Park was expanded to its present form.

WHEN TO GO

Summer, autumn, and winter are the best times to visit the Northern Rockies. The days are sunny, the nights are clear, and the humidity is low. A popular song once romanticized "Springtime in the Rockies," but that season lasts for about 2 days in early June. The rest of the season formally known as spring is likely to be chilly and spitting snow or rain. Trails are still clogged with snow and mud.

Typically, from mid-June on, you can hike, fish, camp, and watch wildlife—except in the higher elevations, which cling to snow well into July. If you come before July 4 or after Labor Day, you won't have to share the view all that much. Wildflowers bloom at the lower elevations in early

1988 Five fires break out around Yellowstone, blackening approximately one-third of the park.	bison are killed as they cross into Montana.
1995 Gray wolves are reintroduced into Yellowstone National Park.	**2008** The gray wolf population in the Northern Rockies hits 1,600; the species is no longer listed as endangered.
2007 The U.S. Forest Service removes the Greater Yellowstone grizzly bear population from the threatened species list.	**2009** Montana has its first legal wolf hunting season since reintroduction in 1995.
2007–08 Due to brucellosis fears, over 1,500 Yellowstone	**2010** A court ruling returns the grizzly bear to the threatened species list.

summer—beginning in May in the lower valleys and plains, while in the higher elevations they open in July.

Autumn is not just the time when the aspens turn gold, it's also the time when gateway motel and restaurant rates are lower and the roads are less crowded. That allows you to pay more attention to the wildlife, which is busy fattening up for the winter.

Winter is a glorious season here, although not for everyone. It can be very cold, but the air is crystalline, the snow is powdery, and the skiing is fantastic. If you drive in the parks' vicinity in the winter, *always* carry winter clothing, sleeping bags, extra food, flashlights, and other safety gear. Every local resident has a horror story about being caught unprepared in the weather.

The Climate

The region is characterized by long, cold winters and short, relatively mild summers. There is not a lot of moisture, winter or summer, and the air is dry, except for the brief wet season in March and April.

Don't expect the kind of spring you get in lower elevations. Cold and snow can linger into April and May—blizzards can even hit the area in mid-June—although temperatures are generally warming. The average daytime readings are in the 40s or 50s (4°–15°C), gradually increasing into the 60s or 70s (16°–26°C) by early June. So, during **spring,** a warm

2010 A court ruling returns the gray wolf to the endangered species list.

2011 The U.S. Congress returns gray wolf management to the states, effectively delisting the species again in Wyoming and Montana.

2011 A grizzly bear kills a visitor near the Grand Canyon of the Yellowstone, the first bear-related fatality in the park in more than 20 years.

2016 A young man dies after falling into an off-trail hot spring, and several visitors are fined for walking into Grand Prismatic Hot Spring, then posting the crime online.

2016 The Interagency Grizzly Bear Committee recommends that the grizzly bear be taken off the Endangered Species List.

jacket, rain gear, and water-resistant walking shoes could be welcome traveling companions.

The area is rarely balmy, but temperatures during the middle of the **summer** are typically 75° to 85°F (24°–29°C) in the lower elevations and are especially comfortable because of the lack of humidity. Remember, too, that the atmosphere is thin at this altitude, so sunscreen is a must. Nights, even during the warmest months, will be cool, with temperatures dropping into the low 40s (4°–9°C), so you'll want to include a jacket in your wardrobe. Because summer thunderstorms are common, you'll probably be glad you've included a waterproof shell or umbrella.

As **fall** approaches, you'll want to have an additional layer of clothing because temperatures remain mild but begin to cool. The first heavy snows typically fall in the valley by November 1 (much earlier in the mountains) and continue through March or April. Aspen trees turn bright yellow; cottonwoods turn a deeper gold.

During **winter** months, you'll want long underwear, heavy shirts, vests, coats, warm gloves, and thick socks. Temperatures can be anywhere from the single digits (negative teens Celsius) to the 30s (-1° to 4°C) during the day, and subzero overnight temperatures are common. Ultracold air can cause lots of health problems, so drink fluids, keep an extra layer of clothing handy, and don't overexert yourself.

For up-to-date weather information and road conditions, call ✆ **307/344-2117** (Yellowstone), ✆ **307/739-3614** (Grand Teton in summer), ✆ **307/739-3682** (Grand Teton in winter), or 511 (in-state mobile), or visit **www.wyoroad.info**.

Avoiding the Crowds

Between the Fourth of July and Labor Day, the Northern Rockies come to life. Flowers bloom, fish jump, bison calves frolic—and tourists converge. The park roads are crowded with trailers, with the well-known spots jammed with a significant portion of the millions who make their treks to Montana and Wyoming every year. Your best bet: Travel before June 15, if possible, or after mid-September. Labor Day used to represent a reliable slowdown in visitation, but in recent years, people have continued filling the park well into the fall season. If you can't arrange an off-season visit, then go to the major

SEASONAL ROAD openings & closings

In Yellowstone Traveling Yellowstone's roads during spring months can be a roll of the dice because openings can be delayed for days (sometimes weeks) at a time, especially at higher altitudes. There is always some section of road in Yellowstone under construction, so call ahead and get a road report (𝄞 **307/344-2117**). It's irritating, but don't take it out on the road workers; they often labor through the night to cause as little inconvenience as possible.

The only road open year-round in the area is the north entrance to **Mammoth Hot Springs.** From Mammoth, a winter access road to the northeast entrance and **Cooke City** is plowed throughout the winter. This service for Cooke City residents gives visitors a great opportunity to watch wildlife in winter in the Lamar Valley. Just be watchful of the weather; the road is often slick with ice.

Snowplowing begins in early March. In Yellowstone, the first roads open to motor vehicles (usually by the end of Apr) include **Mammoth-Old Faithful, Norris-Canyon,** and **West Yellowstone-Madison.** If the weather cooperates, the **East Entrance-Lake** and **Lake-Canyon** will open in early May, followed by the **South Entrance-Lake, Lake-Old Faithful,** and **Tower-Tower Fall** in mid-May. **Tower-Canyon** over Dunraven Pass typically opens last—by the end of May, unless there's a late-season snowfall.

The **Chief Joseph Highway,** connecting the entrances in Cooke City, Montana, and Cody, Wyoming, often opens by early May. The **Beartooth Highway,** between Cooke City and Red Lodge, Montana, is generally open by Memorial Day weekend.

Winter road closures typically begin in mid-October, when the Beartooth Highway closes. Depending upon weather, most other park roads remain open until the park season ends in early November.

In Grand Teton Because Grand Teton has fewer roads and they're at lower elevations, openings and closings are more predictable. **Teton Park Road** opens to conventional vehicles and RVs around May 1. The **Moose-Wilson Road** opens to vehicles about the same time. Roads close to vehicles on November 1, although they never close for nonmotorized use.

attractions at off-peak hours when others are eating or sleeping. Or, as I suggest over and over, abandon the pavement for the hiking trails—a foolproof way to shake the hordes.

Whenever you come, give these parks as much time as you can; you'll experience more at an unhurried pace.

Yellowstone's Average Monthly Temperatures (High/Low)

	JAN	FEB	MAR	APR	MAY	JUNE	JULY	AUG	SEPT	OCT	NOV	DEC
°F	29/10	34/13	40/17	49/26	60/34	70/41	80/47	78/45	69/37	56/29	39/19	31/12
°C	-2/-12	1/-11	-1/-8	9/-3	16/1	21/5	27/8	26/7	21/3	13/-2	4/-7	-1/-11

Grand Teton's Average Monthly Temperatures (High/Low)

	JAN	FEB	MAR	APR	MAY	JUNE	JULY	AUG	SEPT	OCT	NOV	DEC
°F	26/1	31/3	39/12	49/22	61/31	71/37	81/42	80/40	70/32	56/23	38/14	27/2
°C	-3/-17	-1/-16	4/-11	9/-6	16/-1	22/3	27/6	27/4	21/0	13/-5	3/-10	-3/-17

Holidays

Banks, government offices, post offices, and many stores, restaurants, and museums are closed on the following legal national holidays: January 1 (New Year's Day), the third Monday in January (Martin Luther King Jr. Day), the third Monday in February (Presidents' Day), the last Monday in May (Memorial Day), July 4 (Independence Day), the first Monday in September (Labor Day), the second Monday in October (Columbus Day), November 11 (Veterans Day/ Armistice Day), the fourth Thursday in November (Thanksgiving Day), and December 25 (Christmas Day). The Tuesday after the first Monday in November is Election Day, a federal government holiday in presidential-election years (held every 4 years, and next in 2020). The parks are always open on holidays, but visitor centers are often closed.

RESPONSIBLE TRAVEL

Heavy summer auto traffic and the annual impact of millions of human beings have raised questions about the sustainability of these national parks. But a visit to Yellowstone and Grand Teton can be a relatively green vacation. In Yellowstone, concessionaire **Xanterra Parks & Resorts** (✆ **307/344-7311;** www.yellowstonenationalparklodges.com) has implemented numerous environmental initiatives, including a recycling and composting program, sourcing food for its restaurants locally and sustainably, and taking numerous measures to reduce water and energy use. The Old Faithful Snow Lodge, the newest lodging in the park, was built in part from reclaimed wood from the sawmill that cut the timber for the Old Faithful Inn, and the new gift shop at Mammoth has all sorts of green mementoes, as well as a kiosk for visitors to determine their personal carbon footprint and other interactive exhibits. Campgrounds have recycling bins near their entrances. In Grand Teton, the **Grand Teton Lodge Company** (© **307/543-2811;** www.gtlc. com) has also implemented very successful sustainability programs to lessen the human impact on the park. The company encourages hotel guests to take a "sustainable stay pledge" in return for several perks, such as a reusable water bottle and a slight discount on a room. A 2015 remodel of Jackson Lake Lodge added water- and energy-conserving fixtures and incorporated recycled materials, and GTLC cooperated with a 2016 park effort to dramatically reduce landfill waste.

But perhaps the best way to look at sustainability is to go off the grid on an overnight backpacking trip. The website of the outdoor-ethics organization **Leave No Trace** (www.lnt. org) provides useful tips for backpackers on how to leave a campsite in the same condition—or better—than they found it. Backpacking is a refreshing counterpoint to modern life that will give perspective on the issues of sustainability and personal energy dependence. For more on backpacking, see "Special Permits," in chapter 10, and the sections on each park's backcountry, in chapters 4 and 6.

TOURS
Academic Trips

One of the best ways to turn a park vacation into an unforgettable experience is to join an educational program. There are no finals in these courses; they're just a relaxed, informative way to spend time outdoors.

Yellowstone Forever ★★★, P.O. Box 117, Yellowstone National Park, WY 82190 (© **406/848-2400;** www.yellow stone.org), formerly the Yellowstone Association Institute, operates at the historic Lamar Buffalo Ranch, in the northeast part of the park, and at other locations in the vicinity. It typically offers several hundred courses a year, covering everything from winter wildlife tracking to wilderness medicine to the history of fur trappers on the plateau. Prices are reasonable (around $125–$145 per day for tuition), and some classes are specifically targeted to families and youngsters. To make the most of a class, you'll want to stay at the ranch or the Gardiner Yellowstone Overlook Field Campus, where

GENERAL RESOURCES FOR green TRAVEL

In addition to the resources for Yellowstone and Grand Teton listed above, the following websites provide valuable wide-ranging information on sustainable travel.

o **Responsible Travel** (www.responsibletravel.com) is a great source of sustainable travel ideas; the site is run by a spokesperson for ethical tourism in the travel industry.

o **Sustainable Travel International** (www.sustainabletravel international.org) promotes ethical tourism practices and manages a directory of sustainable tourism properties and tour operators around the world.

o **Carbonfund.org** (www.carbonfund.org), **TerraPass** (www. terrapass.com), and **Cool Climate Network** (http://cool climate.berkeley.edu) provide info on "carbon offsetting," or offsetting the greenhouse gas emitted during flights.

o The **"Green" Hotels Association** (www.greenhotels.com) recommends green-rated member hotels around the world that fulfill the association's stringent environmental requirements. **Environmentally Friendly Hotels** (www. environmentallyfriendlyhotels.com) offers more green accommodation ratings.

o For information on sustainable outdoor recreation, visit **Tread Lightly!** (www.treadlightly.org).

shared cabins are available for $37 to $40 a night per student. Customizable hiking, geology, and wildlife-watching **private tours** with an experienced naturalist run about $610 per day for groups of up to five people, including transportation. The institute has also teamed with Xanterra Parks & Resorts to offer 4- to 5-night **Lodging & Learning** packages, which include days spent exploring trails with guides coupled with nights at comfortable lodgings throughout the park. Rates range from about $300 to $500 per person per day and include most meals and in-park transportation.

The **Teton Science Schools ★★**, 700 Coyote Canyon Dr., Jackson, WY 83011 (© **307/733-1313;** www.tetonscience.org), is a venerable institution that offers summer and winter programs. Classes review the ecology, geology, and wildlife of the park, and there are photography and tracking workshops as well. Classes cater to different age groups, and the emphasis is on experiential, hands-on learning. College credit is available.

The Teton Science Schools' **Wildlife Expeditions** include trips in open-roof vans, on rafts, in sleighs, and by foot. These tours bring visitors closer to wildlife than they're likely to get on their own. Wildlife Expeditions offers trips ranging from a half-day sunset safari ($139) to weeklong trips through the park, usually with lodging in park hotels (about $500 per day).

Adventure Trips

For a detailed list of outfitters, guides, and equipment rental providers categorized by activity, see the "Other Activities" sections in chapters 4 and 6.

In addition, **AdventureBus,** 375 S. Main St., No. 240, Moab, UT 84532 (© **888/737-5263;** www.adventurebus.com), offers trips on its customized buses with an emphasis on outdoor adventures in Yellowstone and Grand Teton National Parks. The rate is about $1,000 per person for a weeklong trip. **Austin Adventures,** P.O. Box 81025, Billings, MT 59108-1025 (© **800/575-1540;** www.austinadventures.com), offers guided multiday tours that include biking, horseback riding, hiking, and rafting in and around Yellowstone and Grand Teton National Parks. Six-day trips start around $2,700 per person. **Backroads,** 801 Cedar St., Berkeley, CA 94710 (© **800/462-2848** or 510/527-1555; www.backroads.com), offers a variety of guided multiday trips involving horseback riding, hiking, wildlife safaris, and rafting in and around Yellowstone and Grand Teton National Parks. The rate is about $4,000 to $5,800 per person for 6-day trips staying in park lodges. The **World Outdoors,** 2840 Wilderness Place, Ste. D, Boulder, CO 80301 (© **800/488-8483** or 303/413-0946; www.theworld outdoors.com), runs hiking and multisport tours (biking, hiking, rock climbing, and rafting) that incorporate camping and stays in park lodges in both parks as well. Rates start at about $2,200 per person for 6 days. And **Escape Adventures,** 10575 Discovery Dr., Las Vegas, NV 89135 (© **800/596-2953** or 702/596-2953; www.escapeadventures.com), offers 6-day road cycling/mountain biking tours of Grand Teton that also include rock climbing, rafting, and hiking. The rate is about $2,000 per person (camping) to $3,000 per person (park lodgings).

EXPLORING YELLOWSTONE

3

Get used to the idea right now: Yellowstone is a colossal park, and you'd never see everything here if you tried for a lifetime. Just embrace the fact that *anything* you choose to do while you're here will be fascinating, wondrous, and 100-percent worth your time. Whether you go off in search of wolves and bears, tour the geyser basins, hike the trails, or cruise the park roads, Yellowstone is guaranteed to blow your mind.

Grand Loop Road, the 154-mile, figure-eight road looping through the heart of the park, connects most of the major and minor attractions, and you're bound to spend some time cruising it. But stop frequently and get out of the car: Exploring the park's highlights and, even better, getting out into the backcountry on a hiking trail will enrich your trip by leaps and bounds.

You *could* visit Yellowstone for a single day—and if that's your only option, by all means, take it—but you need a minimum of 3 days to really get a feel for the place. A week or more is even better. Hit up the must-sees, such as **Old Faithful, Grand Canyon of the Yellowstone, Mammoth terraces, Lamar Valley,** and **Yellowstone Lake,** but also to check out some of the lesser-known but still incredible destinations. Attend a ranger-led program or sign up for a class with **Yellowstone Forever** for an in-depth experience. Consider spending a night under the stars, either in a drive-in park campground or deep in the backcountry. The farther you go from the road, the more solitude you'll enjoy, and the more Yellowstone's wild heart will be revealed to you.

ESSENTIALS

ACCESS/ENTRY POINTS   Yellowstone has five entrances. The **north entrance,** near Mammoth Hot Springs, is located just south of Gardiner, Montana, and U.S. 89. In the winter, this is the only access to Yellowstone by car.

The **west entrance,** just outside the town of West Yellowstone, Montana, on U.S. 20, is the closest entry to Old Faithful. Inside the park, you can turn south to Old Faithful or north to the Norris Geyser Basin. This entrance is open to wheeled vehicles from late April to early November, depending on snow levels, and to snowmobiles and snowcoaches from mid-December to mid-March.

About 64 miles north of Jackson, Wyoming, the **south entrance,** on U.S. 89/191/287, approaches Yellowstone from Grand Teton National Park. On the way, drivers get panoramic views of the Teton Range. Once in the park, the road skirts the Lewis River to the south end of Yellowstone Lake, at West Thumb and Grant Village. It's open to cars from mid-May to early November and to snowmobiles and snowcoaches from mid-December to March.

The **east entrance,** on U.S. 14/16/20, 53 miles west of Cody, Wyoming, is open to cars from early May to early November and to snowmobiles and snowcoaches from late December to early March. The drive over Sylvan Pass is the most scenically stunning approach to the park, but it might make you nervous if you're not used to mountain driving.

The **northeast entrance,** at Cooke City, Montana, is closest to the Tower-Roosevelt area, 29 miles to the west. This entrance is open to cars year-round, but from early October, when the Beartooth Highway closes, until around Memorial Day, the only route to Cooke City is through Mammoth Hot Springs. When it's open, the drive from Red Lodge to the park is a grand climb among the clouds.

VISITOR CENTERS   There are five major visitor and information centers in the park, and each has something different to offer.

The **Albright Visitor Center** (© **307/344-2263**), at Mammoth Hot Springs, is the largest and is open daily year-round (8am–7pm in summer; 9am–5pm in winter). It houses an info desk, backcountry office, and wildlife exhibits. The

Yellowstone National Park

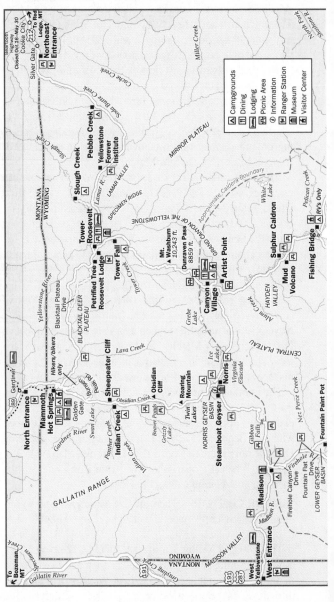

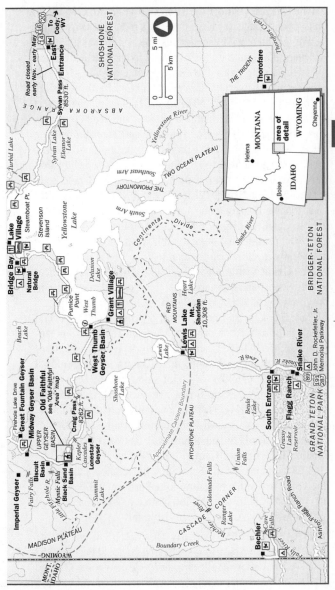

33

building was once the bachelor officers' quarters in the era when the U.S. Army patrolled the park.

The **Canyon Visitor Education Center** (© **307/344-2550**), in Canyon Village, is one of the park's most expansive, inter-active facilities, with excellent exhibits on the park's super-volcano. It's open 8am to 8pm daily in summer and staffed by friendly rangers used to dealing with crowds.

The park's newest visitor center, the **Old Faithful Visitor Education Center** (© **307/344-2751**), has picture-perfect views of Old Faithful, exhibits on how the geothermal fea-tures work, and an engaging Young Scientist area for budding geologists. It also displays projected geyser-eruption times, making it a good first stop for those looking to see Old Faith-ful do its thing. It's open daily in summer from 8am to 8pm.

The **Fishing Bridge Visitor Center** (© **307/344-2450**), near Fishing Bridge on the north shore of Yellowstone Lake, has an excellent display that focuses on the park's bird life. You can get information and publications here as well. It's open daily in summer from 8am to 7pm.

The **Grant Visitor Center** (© **307/344-2650**) has publica-tions, videos, and a fascinating exhibit on the role of fire in Yellowstone. It's open daily in summer from 8am to 7pm.

Park literature and helpful staff are also found at several small information stations: the **Madison Information Sta-tion** (© 307/344-2821; summer daily 9am–6pm), home of the **Junior Ranger Station;** the **Museum of the National Park Ranger** (© 307/344-7353; summer daily 9am–5pm) and the **Norris Geyser Basin Museum and Information Station** (© 307/344-2812; summer daily 9am–6pm), both at Norris; the **West Thumb Information Station** (© 307/344-2876; summer daily 9am–5pm); and the **West Yellowstone Visitor Information Center,** 30 Yellowstone Ave. (© 307/344-2876; summer daily 8am–8pm, limited hours the rest of the year). In Gardiner, **Yellowstone Forever,** 308 E. Park St. (© 406/848-2400; www.yellowstone.org), contains a small gift shop with books and other visitor info.

ENTRANCE FEES A 7-day pass costs $30 per private vehicle; tack on a pass to Grand Teton National Park for $50 total. A 7-day snowmobile or motorcycle pass costs $25, and someone who comes in on bicycle, skis, or foot will pay $15 for 7 days. The National Park Service also offers several free days or weeks every year; for this year's schedule check www.nps.gov/planyourvisit/fee-free-parks.htm.

If you're lucky enough to visit Yellowstone more than once a year, the $60 annual pass is the way to go. Even better, pick up the $80 **Interagency Annual Pass,** which grants entry to all national parks and most other federal fee areas for a year. Other special passes include the **Interagency Senior Pass,** for a one-time fee of $10, for those ages 62 and up; the **Interagency Access Pass,** free for those with permanent disabilities; and the free **Interagency 4th Grader Pass** for American 4th graders and their families. Buy any pass at any entrance to the park.

CAMPING FEES   Fees for camping in Yellowstone range from $15 to $29 per night, depending on the number of amenities the campground offers. RV sites run up to $48 per night. For information on camping, see "Where to Camp in Yellowstone," in chapter 7. It is possible to make reservations at some campgrounds in both parks.

SPECIAL REGULATIONS & WARNINGS   More detailed information about the following rules can be requested from the park rangers, at visitor centers throughout the park, or at **www.nps.gov/yell**.

o **Bicycles:** Bicycles are allowed on the park's roadways and a few gravel roads, but not on trails or boardwalks. Spring (late Mar to early Apr) and fall (Nov) are some of the best times for cycling, as the park opens the roads to bikes before and after cars are allowed, but be prepared for nasty weather. Helmets and bright clothing are recommended because of the narrow, winding park roads and the presence of large RVs with poor visibility.

o **Camping:** A person may camp in the park for no more than 30 days in any given year, and no more than 14 days during the summer season (except at Fishing Bridge RV Park, where neither limit applies). Food, garbage, and food utensils must be stored in a hard-sided vehicle or locked in a campground's bearproof locker when not in use.

o **Defacing park features:** Collecting, removing, or destroying any natural or archaeological objects is prohibited, including picking wildflowers or collecting rocks. Only dead-and-down wood of wrist size or smaller can be collected for backcountry campfires, and only when and where such fires are allowed.

- **Firearms:** As of 2010, firearms are allowed in national parks (shooting them remains illegal). Those in possession of a firearm must have a legal license from their state of residence. Firearms are prohibited in marked facilities.
- **Littering:** Littering in the national parks is strictly prohibited—if you take it in, you take it out. Throwing coins or other objects into thermal features is illegal.
- **Motorcycles:** Motorcycles and motor scooters are allowed only on park roads. No off-road or trail riding is allowed. Drivers' licenses and license plates are required.
- **Pets:** Pets must always be leashed and are prohibited in the backcountry, on trails, on boardwalks, and in thermal areas. If you tie up a pet and leave it, you're breaking the law. Service animals, however, can go on trails and boardwalks in developed areas and, with a permit, the backcountry.
- **Smoking:** No smoking is allowed in thermal areas, on trails, in buildings, or within 25 feet of any building entrance.
- **Snowmobiling:** The park offers limited permits to private snowmobilers via a lottery system; for details see p. 93.
- **Swimming:** Swimming or wading is prohibited in thermal features or in streams whose waters flow from thermal features in Yellowstone. (One exception is Boiling River near Mammoth, where visitors can take a warm soak between dawn and dusk, except during spring runoff.) Swimming elsewhere is discouraged due to the cold water, swift currents, and unpredictable weather.
- **Wildlife:** It is unlawful to approach within 100 yards of a bear or wolf or within 25 yards of other wildlife. Feeding any wildlife is illegal. Wildlife calls, such as elk bugles or other artificial attractants, are forbidden.

THE HIGHLIGHTS

Yellowstone is an enormous park with a staggering number of attractions to see. The park's absolute highlights are accessible via the Grand Loop Road, and you can visit most of them in a few days. Tailor your itinerary to your interests—perhaps wildlife, thermal features, or major scenic hotspots—and hit the road. It takes roughly 30 minutes to drive between major junctions, but traffic and herds of bison crossing the road can significantly lengthen travel time. Be patient.

The Upper Loop

MAMMOTH HOT SPRINGS   The first attraction you'll hit coming in from the north, Mammoth's beautifully sculpted travertine terraces (the **Upper and Lower terraces ★★** are described in "Yellowstone: The Extended Tour," below) are well worth a stroll. History buffs will appreciate the Albright Visitor Center and Fort Yellowstone, a collection of preserved buildings from the 1890s and early 1900s.

NORRIS GEYSER BASIN ★★   Norris is Yellowstone's hottest, most acidic thermal area and a wonderful place to wander two adjoining basins, Back Basin and Porcelain Basin. You'll see examples of geysers, steam vents, and hot springs with colorful bacterial mats, plus the **Norris Museum.**

CANYON VILLAGE AREA   An absolute must-see, the **Grand Canyon of the Yellowstone River ★★★** plunges more than 1,000 feet from rim to river and features two stunning waterfalls. Gaze at the polychromatic rock layers from several lookouts, hike the North or South Rims, or even descend into the canyon on Uncle Tom's Trail. Several fantastic day hikes and overnight trails launch from this area.

TOWER-ROOSEVELT AREA   As the closest road junction to the **Lamar Valley ★★★**, this is ground zero for spotting wolves, bears, bison, elk, and plenty more species. Nearby **Tower Fall ★** is one of the park's most impressive front-country cascades, accessible via a short-paved path.

The Lower Loop

OLD FAITHFUL AREA   Probably the world's most famous geyser, **Old Faithful ★★★** shouldn't be missed—but the rest of the spouters and hot springs in **Upper Geyser Basin ★★★** are equally impressive. Walk the extensive boardwalks for a look at this unique concentration of hydrothermal action (there are more than 150 features within 1 sq. mile). Make sure to explore inside the incredible **Old Faithful Inn** or sit down for a bite at **Old Faithful Snow Lodge.** One of the park's best visitor centers, the historic **Haynes Photo Shop,** and several hiking trails are here, too.

LAKE VILLAGE AREA   Huge, lovely, and very cold, 20-mile-long **Yellowstone Lake ★★** offers plenty adventure: scenic boat tours, paddling opportunities, and shoreline

3

EXPLORING YELLOWSTONE

The Highlights

camping. Stop by the historic **Lake Yellowstone Hotel** to see the park's most elegant lodging, or grab a beer on the front porch of **Lake Lodge.** Nearby **Bridge Bay Marina** offers boat rentals and guided fishing trips. Just north, **Hayden Valley ★★** is another great place to look for bears and bison.

MIDWAY GEYSER BASIN Yellowstone's largest hot spring, **Grand Prismatic Spring ★★**, resembles a portal to another world: a shockingly blue pool ringed by bright yellows, greens, and oranges. A boardwalk swings you right past the steaming spring, or you can get the aerial view on an elevated platform across the street. The **Fairy Falls Trail** also takes off from here.

IF YOU HAVE ONLY 1 OR 2 DAYS

There are two ways to approach a time-crunched visit to Yellowstone, both of which have their merits. One, choose one area to explore in depth, take your time absorbing the sights and get out on a backcountry trail. If that's your cup of tea, skip on to "Yellowstone: The Extended Tour" to choose your destination. But if you'd rather pack as many sights into the day as humanly possible, these itineraries are for you. Keep in mind that it's easy to underestimate the time it will take to travel between highlights; patience and flexibility are key to pulling off this whirlwind.

1 DAY Get an early start: This greatest-hits tour of the lower loop of Grand Loop Road covers 94 to 124 miles and encompasses five major attractions, which doesn't leave much time for dallying. Begin from the west entrance, Yellowstone's most popular entry point, and cruise along the **Madison River,** where you can see the forest recovering from the 1988 fires. You'll also spot ducks and trumpeter swans on the river, and grazing elk and bison. Turn north at Madison Junction and stop at **Norris Geyser Basin** to walk the boardwalks through both larger, geyser-packed Back Basin and the smaller, bleached-white Porcelain Basin. Plan to spend at least an hour here, perhaps a bit more if you want to check out the **Norris Museum.**

Get back in the car and proceed east to the **Canyon Village** area (a good spot for a snack or to stop by the visitor center). Then continue down the road to **South Rim Drive** for a peek at the **Grand Canyon of the Yellowstone,** including the awe-inspiring **Upper Falls** and **Lower Falls.** Hike part of the South Rim Trail for rimside views, or go straight to **Artist Point** for a picture-perfect view of Lower Falls.

Next stop: **Hayden Valley.** Drive south and keep an eye out for bison and bears roaming near the Yellowstone River. Just beyond is the **Lake Village** area, your best bet for lunch. Dine at the Lake Yellowstone Hotel or picnic along the shore. The lake will be your constant companion along the next stretch of road, curving southwest to **West Thumb.** Hop out and walk the boardwalk through this small lakeside geyser basin.

Press west, crossing the Continental Divide Twice, to the **Old Faithful** area. You'll easily catch Old Faithful itself at least twice, as it erupts every 60 to 110 minutes (check at the Old Faithful Inn or the visitor center for the next predicted show). In between eruptions, stroll the boardwalk through **Upper Geyser Basin** to gaze at more than a hundred other thermal features. If you're lucky enough to score at room at Old Faithful Inn, Old Faithful Snow Lodge, or Old Faithful Lodge, this is your stopping point. If you'd rather sleep al fresco, head back north to Madison or Norris campgrounds.

2 DAYS With a second day, you can tack on the sights of the upper loop to your plan (the loop itself is 70 miles long, although visiting the Lamar Valley will add roughly 15–20 more miles out and back). If you spent the night at Old Faithful, make your way north to Norris (stop by **Midway Geyser Basin** to see Grand Prismatic Spring en route). From there, continue north to **Mammoth Hot Springs.** Get out and walk the upper and lower terraces to watch travertine formations being built before your eyes. Stop by **Albright Visitor Center** for background on the history and wildlife of the park, then take the self-guided tour of **Fort Yellowstone.**

Next, the road swings east. Take the one-way **Blacktail Plateau Drive** for even better wildlife-spotting chances than you already have on the road, then press on into the **Lamar Valley.** This wide, rich expanse is home to most of the park's major wildlife species (although dawn and dusk are the best times to look for them, especially wolves).

Backtrack to **Tower-Roosevelt** and make a quick stop to see **Tower Fall** from the overlook. The next stretch is one of the park's most scenic: a winding road that climbs to 8,859-foot

Dunraven Pass, delivering sweeping views the whole way up and down. You'll end up back at Canyon Village.

YELLOWSTONE: THE EXTENDED TOUR

If you have the option, extend your visit to 4 or 5 days (or even longer): You'll see so much more, will have the time to get out and hike a few trails, and will be able to soak in the scenery without feeling quite so rushed.

A stop at any of the park **visitor centers** is an excellent way to kick off your trip. Most have exhibits on Yellowstone's wildlife, geothermal features, volcanic activity, or history, plus brochures and maps. Rangers are on hand to answer questions, provide info on current conditions, and make insider suggestions based on your particular fancy. There are 10 centers and information stations (see "Essentials," earlier in this chapter), but some might be closed if you visit the park off-season. **Albright Visitor Center** at Mammoth is open year-round, and **Canyon Visitor Education Center** and **Old Faithful Visitor Education Center** have winter hours from December to March. Outside the park, the **West Yellowstone Visitor Information Center** is also open year-round.

You can begin a Yellowstone tour from any of the park's five entrances, but this section assumes you'll be starting from the most popular one, the west entrance, and driving clockwise around **Grand Loop Road.** Simply adjust the order of attractions if you jump in at any other point.

West Yellowstone to Norris

Closest entrance: West Yellowstone (west entrance)

Distances: 14 miles from West Yellowstone to Madison; 14 miles from Madison to Norris.

The west entrance road takes you through a lush valley along the **Madison River.** The distant peaks of the Gallatin Range beckon to the northwest, and bison and elk frequently browse in the grasses here. This is also a prime spot to see the lingering effects of the historic 1988 wildfires that burned 36 percent of the park. The **Two Ribbons Trail,** one of the first pullouts you'll reach, offers a .8-mile accessible boardwalk through a forest of blackened trunks, heat-shattered boulders, and fresh new growth. Lodgepole pines have what are called serotinous cones, which are sealed in a sticky resin and depend on the high temperatures of wildfire to melt them and allow them to drop their seeds—and evidence of the success of this adaptation are all around.

Next, keep your eyes peeled for the entrance to **Riverside Drive,** a secluded paved road about 6 miles from the entrance station. The road doubles back west along the Madison and grants access to several ideal fly-fishing spots. This river is known for its top-notch trout waters and remains on the warm side year-round, thanks to upstream hot springs. Riverside Drive also makes for a quiet escape for a picnic.

As you continue toward Madison Junction, you'll see more vivid evidence of the 1988 fires and, odds are, a herd of bison that hang out during summer months. As frightening as the fires were, they had their advantages: There is evidence that the 1988 fires burned hotter here because the old lodgepole pines had been infected by beetles, decimating the trees long before the fires blazed. The good news is that the fire killed the beetles and remineralized the soil. When temperatures exceeded 500°F (260°C), pine seeds were released from serotinous pine cones, quickening the regrowth cycle.

Another lovely pullout on the south side of the road features an interpretive display about the major explorer parties in the region and the 1877 Nez Perce retreat. A band of Nez Perce traveled through this area trying to escape the U.S. Army, which wanted to force them onto a reservation; the Army caught up with them about 40 miles south of the Canadian border. Beyond, the **Mt. Haynes Overlook** has a boardwalk down to the Madison River, where bulbous Mt. Haynes looms just across the water.

Hiking options are limited on this segment, but you can stretch your legs on the 1-mile (round-trip) **Harlequin Lake Trail,** a mellow uphill hike to the lily pad-covered lake. The trailhead is about 1.5 miles west of Madison Junction. There's also the **Purple Mountain Trail,** a more challenging 6-miler (round-trip) that gains 1,500 feet on the way to a gorgeous overlook of the Madison and Gibbon Rivers. Pick this one up a quarter-mile north of Madison Junction.

Madison Junction marks the place where the Firehole and Gibbon Rivers meet, flowing together to form the Madison River. (The Madison meets the Jefferson and Gallatin

Rivers about 183 miles away to form the mighty Missouri River.) These are excellent trout waters. The sprawling **Madison Campground** sits here in a lodgepole forest with river views; it's one of Yellowstone's most popular options. The **Madison Information Station,** just south, has a ranger on hand, kid-friendly animal exhibits, and trail guides.

You're now on Grand Loop Road. The next 14-mile section follows the Gibbon River through a canyon lined with flaky magenta rock. The river was named for Gen. John Gibbon, who explored here in 1872 but whose main, dubious claims to fame were as the cavalry leader who buried Custer's army and who chased Chief Joseph and the Nez Perce Indians from the park as they attempted to escape to Canada.

Make sure to stop at 84-foot **Gibbon Falls,** a lacy fan of water cascading off the edge of the Yellowstone Caldera rim (it's one of the few places in the park where the caldera boundary is in plain sight). Continue past **Beryl Spring** (better thermals await) and hike 2 miles (round-trip) to **Monument Geyser Basin** if you're up for a steep challenge. The trail leads to a mostly extinct thermal area littered with ancient white geyser cones.

The last attraction before Norris, **Artist Paintpots ★** holds a series of milky white and bluish pools alongside gurgling mudpots spitting glop several feet in the air. The 1.2-mile loop trail is refreshingly uncrowded—hike the upper trail option for an aerial view over the colorful basin. Across the road from the trailhead is **Elk Park,** where you have a good chance of seeing a large herd of the majestic ungulates.

Norris Geyser Basin

Closest entrances and distances: 28 miles from West Yellowstone (west) entrance; 26 miles from Gardiner (north) entrance.

Even if you've visited Yellowstone's oldest, hottest, and most acidic basin before, you haven't really seen it: The volatile **Norris Geyser Basin ★★** changes constantly as old features go dormant, new geysers force their way from the earth, mineral-laden hot springs plug up old tunnels, and earthquakes scramble up the underground "pipes." Here, heat-loving microorganisms called thermophiles form intricate mats of yellow, green, red, and black among the superhot features; most of the hot springs and fumaroles (steam vents)

A Deadly Misstep

The signs warning against stepping off the boardwalk are no joke—in thermal areas, the ground might be just a thin crust over a boiling spring, and it's far too easy to blunder into an unsafe zone. In summer 2016, a man died after intentionally venturing off the boardwalk and then (accidentally) falling into a hot spring.

have temperatures above the boiling point (199°F/93°C at this elevation). In fact, the park's hottest geothermal temperature ever recorded, a bit more than 1,000 feet underground here, was a blistering 459°F (237°C).

Norris encompasses two loop trails. The shorter one, a .8-mile figure eight through **Porcelain Basin,** starts with a grand overlook across the baked-white landscape of steaming pools and vents. Highlights include the 20- to 30-foot-high Constant Geyser (despite the name, it's not always erupting); pulsing Whirligig Geyser; and the hot spring Congress Pool, which might be a hissing dry vent or a boiling puddle.

Back Basin Loop contains many more features on its 1.5-mile loop trail. The most exciting one is undoubtedly Steamboat Geyser, the world's tallest at 400 feet. Major eruptions are erratic and rare, but some witnessed it blow its top in 2013 and 2014—so you could get lucky! Echinus Geyser is the biggest known acidic geyser, with a pH approaching vinegar's. Viewing platforms held crowds when it was a more frequent spouter, but lately Echinus's shows have been few and far between. A number of other geysers, springs, and fumaroles fill out the basin.

When you're through pounding the boardwalks, stop by the stone-and-log **Norris Geyser Basin Museum** (© 307/344-2812) for exhibits on Yellowstone's thermal features. The building dates back to 1929–30 and also houses a bookstore. Several free ranger programs and hikes take off from here daily in season; check the park newspaper for details. The **Museum of the National Park Ranger** (© 307/344-7353) is worth a stop to see historic photos and information on the evolution of the ranger job.

Both museums open in mid- to late May, weather permitting, and are open until September; hours vary by season, but you can expect the museums to be open from 9am to 5 or

6pm during the busiest times (roughly Memorial Day to Labor Day, but weather is a factor).

The **Norris Campground,** which is just slightly north of Norris Junction, is another very popular campground. Its best attribute just might be that it lets you walk to the geyser basin and skip the parking problems of high summer.

Norris to Mammoth Hot Springs

Closest entrances: Norris is 28 miles from the West Yellowstone (west) entrance; Mammoth Hot Springs is 5 miles from the Gardiner (north) entrance.

Distance: 21 miles from Norris to Mammoth Hot Springs

Driving north from Norris wends you past grassy meadows on one side and jagged cliffs on the other, with plenty of stands of trees and small lakes providing habitat to bison and elk. Pause at the **Nymph Lake Overlook** for a nice vista over the water and several steaming hot springs. The boggy meadow areas just beyond are popular with moose.

Pull over at **Roaring Mountain,** 4 miles north of Norris, to check out a hillside steaming with fumaroles. As steam vents developed here, the ground became hot and acidic, bleaching and crumbling the rock and taking the undergrowth with it. The hill earned its name in the 1880s, when the vents were loud enough to "roar." Today, the sound is more like a hiss.

A half-mile past Beaver Lake, you'll reach **Obsidian Cliff.** Native Americans began collecting chips of this glassy black volcanic rock for tools as long as 11,000 years ago, and pieces from this very cliff were discovered as far away as western Canada and the Midwest, thanks to ancient trade routes.

Continue on as **Willow Park** opens up to the west, an open meadow where you might see beaver, moose, or coyotes. **Indian Creek Campground,** one of the park's choicest places to pitch a tent, lies on the north end of this area. Just up the road, the **Sheepeater Cliffs** picnic spot is worth the short detour. The peaceful area sits well off the road along a basalt column cliff that cooled into its present columnar shape from lava 500,000 years ago.

Keep going north to cruise through **Swan Lake Flat,** a wide-open expanse with huge views of the Gallatin Range, including Little Quadrant Mountain and Antler Peak to the west, and Bunsen Peak to the north.

At the northernmost edge of the Yellowstone Plateau, you'll begin a descent through **Golden Gate.** This steep, narrow stretch of road was once a stagecoach route constructed of wooden planks anchored to the mountain near a massive rock called the **Pillar of Hercules,** the largest rock in a pile that sits next to the road.

Beyond Hercules are the **Hoodoos,** an ominous-looking jumble of travertine boulders on the north side of the road, which have tumbled off the mountainside above to create a pile of unusual formations.

One of the best hikes in the area is to 8,564-foot **Bunsen Peak.** The 4.6-mile round trip travels through grizzly-frequented meadows to a sweeping view over the Blacktail Plateau and Yellowstone River Valley. And though you can't summit the peak on a bike, the old Bunsen Peak Road circling the mountain is one of the few off-road spots open to bicycles. Access both trailheads 5 miles south of Mammoth.

Once you head north from Mammoth, you're off the Grand Loop and on the North Entrance Road. The biggest highlight on this segment is the **Boiling River ★★**, a spot where a hot spring pouring into the Gardner River forms a soak-friendly pool (no skinny-dipping allowed). Park at the 45th parallel lot and walk the short trail to the best place for a dip; do it early in the morning to escape the crowds or, even better, at dusk to watch the canyon's bats put on a show.

Mammoth Hot Springs

Closest entrance and distance: 5 miles from the Gardiner (north) entrance

The northernmost developed area at Yellowstone revolves around the one-of-a-kind travertine terrace features here—one of the planet's best examples of this type of geologic sculpture. Though they're fueled by the same potent combination of heat, geology, and water that power the rest of the park's thermal features, Mammoth's terraces are unlike anything else you'll see here.

Mammoth's signature feature looks like a series of stair steps frosted with a chalky white trimming. Bright greens, oranges, and yellows cover some of the terraces, and intricate ripples of rock glaze others. Steaming pools rise in some areas, and others resemble dry, bare white fields. In this area, limestone deposited by an ancient sea is common. As in other thermal areas, an underground heat source causes groundwater to rise back to the surface; as it does, the water dissolves the calcium carbonate in the limestone. Once on the surface, the water quickly deposits the mineral to build the terraces at the pace of a ton of limestone every 24 hours. Heat-loving microorganisms called thermophiles create the color swatches in some areas.

This is one of Yellowstone's most dynamic zones. Old hot springs may go dry for days, weeks, or much longer, leaving bare expanses. New springs perpetually seep up in different places, sculpting fresh terraces. Such constant shifting makes Mammoth an especially fascinating stop: Where else can you watch geologic changes practically before your eyes?

A series of interconnected boardwalks, some of which are wheelchair accessible, wind through the active terraces, granting an up-close look. Start with the **Lower Terraces ★★**, where the boardwalk connects you to major features and then climbs 300 feet to an observation deck up top. Walking the whole thing out and back covers about 1.5 miles.

Liberty Cap greets you near the start of the trail: This 37-foot, pointy pillar formed when a high-pressure hot spring steadily deposited minerals over hundreds of years. Next up is **Palette Spring,** a gorgeously furrowed slope painted in broad strokes of orange and brown. **Minerva and Cleopatra Terraces** are just beyond. This area changes frequently from active to dry. **Jupiter and Mound Terraces** are similarly volatile: Mound has cycled through on-and-off periods for decades, and Jupiter flowed so forcefully in the 1980s that it overtopped the boardwalks a few times. Hoof it up the final staircases to the overlook, where you'll get a top-down view of the terraces and several hot springs.

From here, you can connect to **Upper Terrace Drive** to walk the 1.5-mile loop through more terraces (alternatively, hop back in the car and drive it). Though there's a collection of live and dormant terraces and several nice views from up here, particularly around **Canary Spring,** this loop is skippable unless you're a real terrace fiend.

Back in the main Mammoth Hot Springs area, consider taking the short, self-guided **Fort Yellowstone** tour (from the **Albright Visitor Center**). In Yellowstone's early days, before

Mammoth Hot Springs

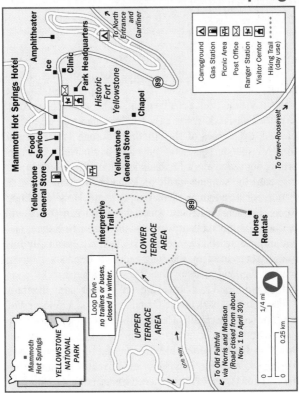

there was a National Park Service, the U.S. Army played the role of protectors of the park's wildlife and resources. Many structures from that era (1886–1916) still stand; check out officers' quarters, a chapel, cavalry barracks, and more (although you can't enter most buildings).

Just steps from the lower terrace is the trailhead for the **Beaver Ponds Loop Trail,** a 5-mile jaunt through fir and spruce, then sagebrush and aspen, along a trail that follows **Clematis Gulch.** The ponds are about 2.5 miles from the trailhead, where the resident toothy engineers are most active in early morning and at night. The area is also a hangout for elk and bears, and can be closed early in the summer season.

Mammoth Hot Springs to Tower Junction

Closest entrance: Mammoth is 5 miles from the Gardiner (north) entrance

Distance: 18 miles from Mammoth to Tower

The first highlight you'll hit heading east out of Mammoth is a lovely pair of waterfalls. The first, triple-tiered **Undine Falls,** is visible from a road pullout, while seeing the second, **Wraith Falls,** requires an easy 1-mile (round-trip) hike. Also of note: the **Forces of the Northern Range Trail,** 8 miles from Mammoth. This flat .5-mile loop augmented with interpretive signs delivers a firsthand lesson on fire ecology.

Escape the summer traffic on **Blacktail Plateau Drive,** a 7-mile, scenic alternate route running parallel to Grand Loop Road. The unpaved route winds through aspen stands and meadows with excellent views of the Northern Range, and you might spot elk, deer, or bears. The drive essentially follows a route used by the long-vanished Bannock Indians; scars in the land made by their travois (luggage racks made of twin poles tied to a horse) are still evident along the trail.

You'll end up back on the Grand Loop Road a mile west of the Petrified Tree turnoff. That **Petrified Tree** is well worth the short detour. Here stand the remains of an ancient redwood that was swiftly buried by volcanic debris and mudflows between 45 and 50 million years ago. Eventually, silica from the eruptions filled in the tree's cells, preserving it to this day.

Tower-Roosevelt

Closest entrances and distances: 23 miles from the Gardiner (north) entrance; 29 miles from the Cooke City (northeast) entrance.

Frontiersy **Tower-Roosevelt** is the most relaxed of the major park junctions—a far cry from the hordes that sometimes descend on Old Faithful or the Canyon area. The 26th president really did camp in the area in 1903, and much of the spirit of Teddy Roosevelt's Old West remains here. **Roosevelt Lodge,** a rustic log building dating back the 1920s, houses a BBQ restaurant and bar, plus a check-in desk for the clutch of simple log cabins scattered nearby (see "Where to Stay and Eat in Yellowstone," in chapter 7, for details). A concessionaire-run corral also offers trail rides, stagecoach rides, and a mighty fun cookout accessed on horseback or wagon.

Just east of the junction, the **Yellowstone River Picnic Area** is worth a quick stop to see if the bighorn sheep that frequent the cliffs in this area are out. Continue along the Northeast Entrance Road 4.5 miles past the Tower junction to reach the unmarked trailhead to **Specimen Ridge.** A short (3 miles round-trip) but very steep hike up this hillside leads to a fossilized forest—the largest concentration of petrified trees in the world, in fact. You can still pick out the rings on many of these 50-million-year-old trees, which were buried and subsequently fossilized by a series of volcanic eruptions.

A Detour: The Beartooth Highway

Closest entrance and distance: 29 miles to the Cooke City (northeast) entrance

The dramatic scenery of the park's Northeast Entrance Road remains something of a secret. It's far enough removed from the Grand Loop Road to shake most of the hordes—all the better for those with the time to cruise the area's wildlife-packed valleys, idyllic creeks, and striking peaks. Just beyond the park boundary and the towns of Silver Gate and Cooke City, the high-mountain Beartooth Highway picks up for one of the prettiest drives in the Rockies.

Driving east from **Tower Junction** on the Northeast Entrance Road, you'll quickly enter the **Lamar Valley ★★★**. This grand expanse is one of the park's best zones for wildlife-watching: You might see elk, deer, badgers, bison, osprey, and bears, but the area's real stars are the wolves. Biologists reintroduced this native predator to Yellowstone in 1995 and 1996. Today, almost 100 wolves in 10 packs inhabit the park. For your best chance of spotting them, head to the Lamar Valley at dawn and look for the park's wolf-watchers set up at pullouts with large spotting scopes. These volunteers often have the most up-to-date intel on where the wolves are and will usually let you take a peek through their scopes.

Continuing east, you'll pass the turnoff to **Slough Creek Campground** (one of the best in the park) and the historic **Lamar Buffalo Ranch,** where a bison-breeding program ran from 1906 to the 1950s to replenish the species' dwindling population. The scenery grows more striking as you press on along Soda Butte Creek, with views of summits like 9,583-foot Druid Peak and 10,404-foot Barronette Peak rising before you. **Pebble Creek Campground,** another choice place to pitch a tent, is in this area, as are several lovely hiking trails.

The northeast gateway towns of **Silver Gate** and **Cooke City** don't offer much in the way of dining and lodging choices, but they're gorgeous, quiet, and make an excellent base for exploring this forgotten end of the park. See chapter 8, "Gateways to Yellowstone and Grand Teton National Parks," for details.

Now, begin your climb into the high country on the spectacular **Beartooth Highway** ★★, a 68-mile stretch of U.S. 212 connecting Cooke City to Red Lodge, Montana. The summer-only route delves into a far-reaching wilderness with views of lakes, flowery alpine meadows, and the Absaroka and Beartooth Mountains, hitting its apex on 10,947-foot Beartooth Pass. I'd go at least this far for the best sampling of the highway's charms; then, you can backtrack to the northeast entrance or swing southeast on the **Chief Joseph Scenic Highway** ★★ (Wyo. 296), which connects to Wyo. 120 into Cody. This highway, also called the Sunlight Basin Road, offers great opportunities for viewing wildlife.

From Tower Junction to the Grand Canyon of the Yellowstone

Closest entrances: 23 miles from the Gardiner (north) entrance; 29 miles from the Cooke City (northeast) entrance

Distance: 19 miles from Tower Junction to Canyon Village

Grand Loop Road veers south here, cruising up and over Dunraven Pass on one of the park's most beautiful drives. The first highlight on the way is the **Calcite Springs Overlook,** a vantage point 500 feet above the Yellowstone River. Just north you'll spot a series of hot springs at the foot of a white- and yellow-splotched slope, colored by white calcite crystals and oil deposits brought to the surface by underground heat. Across the canyon stands a cliff of columnar basalt, left behind by a long-ago lava flow. Bighorn sheep or soaring raptors might also add to the view.

Just beyond is a general store and short trail to an overlook of **Tower Fall,** a powerful, 132-foot plume. Unfortunately, you can no longer hike to the base of the falls, but the aerial view is worth catching. **Tower Fall Campground** is across the road, a secluded and rustic option.

The drive gets even more scenic from here, climbing a winding road with sweeping vistas over the Lamar Valley and the **Washburn Range** (where the 1988 wildfires left a visible scar). Look for bighorns and bears as you scale the side of **Mount Washburn ★★★**—grizzlies are frequently spotted up here. The peak itself makes an excellent destination for a day hike; start your trip either on the northwest side, from Old Chittenden Road (another spot where mountain bikes are kosher), or from the southwest at 8,859-foot **Dunraven Pass.** See chapter 4, "Yellowstone Hikes," for details.

It's all downhill from here. Make sure to pause at the **Washburn Hot Springs Overlook,** from which you can spot the rim of the Grand Canyon of the Yellowstone and miles beyond on a clear day. If you need a break, the **Cascade Lake Picnic Area** is a particularly nice, wooded spot with fire pits.

Canyon Village

Closest entrances and distances: 40 miles from West Yellowstone (west) entrance; 38 miles from Gardiner (north) entrance; 48 miles from the Cooke City (northeast) entrance; 43 miles from the east entrance

The Canyon area should be on the top of any Yellowstone visitor's to-do list for one simple reason: the **Grand Canyon of the Yellowstone ★★★**. Along with Old Faithful, it's one of the park's two marquee destinations. Seen from above, the canyon looks like the earth itself has a loose seam: A 20-mile-long, sheer-sided gorge plunges more than 1,000 feet to the Yellowstone River, widening up to 4,000 feet across in places. Two thundering waterfalls pour over two immense drops in the river's course, and a palette of bright reds, yellows, oranges, whites, and browns swirls across the rocky walls. In short, it's every bit as impressive as that *other* Grand Canyon, if not quite as big.

The Yellowstone River carved this massive chasm over thousands of years. Volcanic activity deposited rhyolite and tuff over the area, and heat from the geyser basins here weakened the rock, making it soft and easily eroded by the rushing river. Upper and Lower Falls owe their existence to bands of harder volcanic rock, which didn't erode as quickly as the softer stuff; these more resistant spots formed dramatic drops that the river plummets over, to grand effect. And those colors? There's plenty of iron in the rhyolite. As different layers of rock are exposed at different times, varying stages of oxidation turn the cliffs their signature hues.

Canyon Village is the base for exploring the canyon, a sprawling development featuring lodging, dining options, a general store, **Canyon Campground,** and the **Canyon Visitor Education Center** (✆ **307/344-2550**). Stop here for a primer on Yellowstone's supervolcano and its effects on the landscape: Exhibits include a floating globe showing the world's volcanic hotspots; a 3D map; video reenactments of the major Yellowstone eruption 640,000 years ago; and blocks of ash illustrating the volcano's destructive power.

Then go see that geology in action. One-way **North Rim Drive** begins 1.2 miles south of the village and cruises past a series of canyon rim overlooks before returning to the village. If you only have time to see the canyon from one side, I'd go for the South Rim—but the north side offers perspectives you can't see across the way, so it's well worth the trip.

First stop: **Brink of Lower Falls Trail,** a .8-mile (round-trip) paved trail that dips 600 feet to a precarious perch above the 308-foot waterfall. It's a steep trip to a gorgeous vantage point and also grants a peek at 109-foot Upper Falls near the top. Next up is **Lookout Point** for a wider perspective on Lower Falls (and an osprey nesting site). If you're feeling energetic, continue down the **Red Rock Trail,** a boardwalk staircase that dives 500 feet deeper into the canyon in .4 mile. The next pullout, **Grand View Overlook,** is unique in that it points not to the waterfalls, but downstream, where you'll see the rich canyon colors and the Yellowstone River below. The final view, **Inspiration Point,** offers another astounding vista of Lower Falls and the canyon downstream.

You can drive between these major viewpoints, but the better option is hoofing it on the **North Rim Trail ★★** connecting Inspiration Point to the Wapiti Lake Trailhead on the South Rim. This 3-mile (one-way) track links all the North Rim Drive highlights, but you won't have to fight for parking spaces, plus you'll drink in extended views along the chasm's edge. The section between Lookout Point and Grand View is wheelchair accessible.

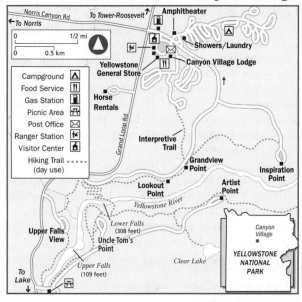

Back out on Grand Loop Road, a short spur south of North Rim Drive leads to the **Brink of Upper Falls** viewing platform. Take the .3-mile trail to an overlook so close to the pounding cascade, you'll get a visceral sense of just how powerful this incredible plume truly is.

The turnoff to **South Rim Drive** shoots east off Grand Loop Road 2.3 miles south of Canyon Village. The first stunner here is the **Upper Falls Viewpoint,** which gives a longer view than the up-close-and-personal one you just saw at Brink of Upper Falls. A bit farther down the canyon you'll find **Uncle Tom's Trail ★★**, the canyon's best view. But it's not for the acrophobic: The "trail" is really a set of 328 open-grate steel steps bolted to the rock, which plummets steeply into the inner canyon. Though the staircase is steep and a bit vertigo-inducing, the perspective of Lower Falls waiting at the bottom platform is nothing short of amazing. Take heart on the climb back up: At least you're not seeing the sights like early-20th-century visitors did, who journeyed down the canyon on a series of ropes and ladders.

Artist Point ★ is the final stop off South Rim Drive. If this encompassing view of Lower Falls, the Yellowstone River, and the polychrome canyon looks familiar, it's probably because this vista is one of the park's most-photographed spots. Well before it earned that distinction, artist Thomas Moran made Artist Point famous with his landscape painting from this very perspective; you've likely seen a reproduction of it in a gallery or art book. Head this way early in the morning for the best light and to avoid midday crowds. Several hikes also take off from here, including the trail to **Lily Pad Lake, Ribbon Lake,** and **Point Sublime.** That last one is especially notable: Hike 3.3 miles (one-way) along the rim to a much more private vista over the canyon.

Just like on the North Rim, hiking all or part of the **South Rim Trail ★★** is the best way to take in the airy views. The 1.8-mile, partially paved path links the Wapiti Lake Trailhead to Artist Point and winds through a high-elevation forest with near-constant peeks into the canyon.

Canyon Village to Fishing Bridge

Closest entrances: 27 miles to the east entrance; 43 miles to the south entrance

Distance: 16 miles from Canyon Village to Fishing Bridge

Heading south from Canyon Village, Grand Loop Road follows the wide Yellowstone River through **Hayden Valley ★,** the park's largest valley. Glacial till, sediments left behind from an ice sheet that once covered the valley, interferes with water soaking into the ground here, resulting in marshy areas and few trees. The valley is an idyllic place where grizzly bears, bison, wolves, moose, elk, and coyotes roam.

About 12 miles south of Canyon you'll run into the unusual **Mud Volcano/Sulphur Caldron** area. Fumaroles (steam vents) and mudpots are the stars here: The area's soil and clay sit over chambers of hydrogen sulfide gas, which forms sulfuric acid as it rises through the ground. That acid dissolves the soil into mud pools, which more rising gases (including steam and carbon dioxide) pass through to delightful effect—roiling, slurping gurgles of mud. If you've ever wondered what boiling mud would look like, well, here's your answer.

The **Mud Volcano** itself was once much more dramatic: In 1870, members of the Washburn Expedition found a looming cone of mud over the feature, and by 1872, a thermal explosion had blasted it away. Today, its burbling mud pools are still fun to watch. A mile-long boardwalk extends through this small thermal zone to more features. At **Dragon's Mouth Spring,** turbulent pulses of water splash out from an underground cavern; tongues of water combined with steady bursts of steam really do call to mind a lurking medieval beast. **Black Dragon's Caldron** emerged from the earth in 1948 in a grand explosion, uprooting nearby trees and spraying the surrounding forest with mud. Since then, seismic activity has moved the feature several hundred feet south.

Just across the street, **Sulphur Caldron**'s yellowish, bubbling waters represent one of the park's most acidic hot springs, with a skin-melting pH similar to battery acid. If you're pressed for time, this is an easy attraction to skip.

A couple of miles beyond you'll hit **LeHardy Rapids,** the geographic point where Yellowstone Lake technically ends and the Yellowstone River resumes. Topographer Paul LeHardy, a member of the 1873 Jones Expedition, gave the spot its name when he capsized his raft attempting to run the rapids. Watch for cutthroat trout leaping over the drops en route to their springtime spawning grounds at Fishing Bridge.

Fishing Bridge itself spans the Yellowstone River as it flows out of Yellowstone Lake, just off Grand Loop Road on the East Entrance Road. Built in 1937, the bridge once attracted mobs of fishermen eager to dip a line directly into the trout spawning area directly below; after trout populations subsequently dropped, the park outlawed fishing here in 1973. But it remains a prime spot for watching the trout swim, as well as the lake's resident pelicans and Canada geese.

Fishing Bridge Visitor Center (© 307/344-2450) is worth a stop to peruse its displays on park bird life. There's also a general store in the area, along with the **Fishing Bridge RV Park** (p. 140). This is the only campground restricted to hard-sided vehicles (because of the area's abundant grizzlies).

You'll find an excellent hiking trail, **Elephant Back Loop Trail ★**, leading off the road between Fishing Village and the Lake Village area. The 2-mile loop leads to an overlook with panoramic views of Yellowstone Lake and its islands, the Absaroka Range, and Pelican Valley to the east. Instead of taking the entire loop around to the overlook, you can shorten the hike a half-mile by taking the left fork approximately

1 mile from the trailhead and doubling back from the overlook.

A Detour: The East Entrance Road

Closest entrance and distance: 27 miles from Fishing Bridge to the east entrance.

The mountainous East Entrance Road is second only to the Beartooth Highway in terms of scenically splendid ways to access the park. If you're bound for Cody, Wyoming, or want to make the gorgeous loop drive from here to the Chief Joseph and Beartooth Highways and back through the northeast entrance, you'll peel off from the Grand Loop Road here.

Begin by tracing the shores of Yellowstone Lake past **Indian Pond** and the **Pelican Valley Trail.** This trail leads into remote and beautiful country, but this is ground zero for grizzlies, and hiking is restricted to daytime hours only. Continue around **Mary Bay,** the hottest part of the lake at 252°F under the lakebed. A hydrothermal explosion formed this bay, and a small thermal area remains today.

Steamboat Point provides a nice vista over the lake, but the **Lake Butte Overlook,** a short spur off the road, is better. Cruise up here for sweeping views over the lakeshore, various thermal zones, and an old wildfire burn. Between them you'll find one of the park's best picnic grounds at **Sedge Bay:** a stony beach right along the shore that doubles as a boat launch.

The road climbs into the high country from here, and 10,000-foot peaks crop up on either side of the pavement. After passing the delicate **Sylvan Lake** and **Eleanor Lake** (both dynamite picnic spots), you'll reach 8,530-foot **Sylvan Pass.** This high point flanked by steep, craggy peaks makes a fine turnaround spot if you're not continuing to Cody.

Yellowstone Lake Area

Closest entrances: Approximately 27 miles from Fishing Bridge to the east entrance; 43 miles from Fishing Bridge to the south entrance

Distances: The lakefront from Fishing Bridge to the West Thumb Geyser Basin is 21 miles.

Clear, deep, and expansive **Yellowstone Lake ★★** dominates the southeastern part of the park. At 132 square miles, with 141 miles of shoreline, it is North America's largest natural freshwater lake above 7,000 feet. It's a magnet for human and animal visitors alike: People cruise and paddle its waters,

Yellowstone Lake: Fishing Bridge to Bridge Bay

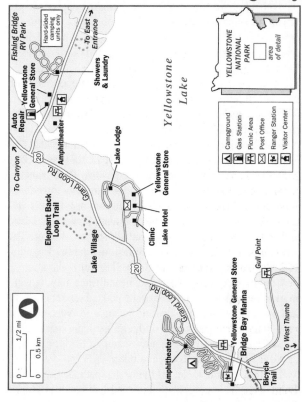

fish for trout, and camp along its rocky shores, while the lake and its beaches provide excellent habitat for grizzly bears, moose, golden and bald eagles, pelicans, and cormorants.

A lake this large can act more like a sea, with frequent winds whipping up treacherous waves. Combine that chop with a water temperature that averages just 41°F even in the height of summer, and swimming becomes inadvisable—and boating or paddling risky endeavors that demand plenty of know-how. Under the surface, Yellowstone Lake is just as turbulent: Researchers have discovered underwater fumaroles, geysers, and hot springs, and canyons plunge to at least 410 feet in depth. In two places, underwater volcanic vents called resurgent domes are rising and falling with an average uplift of an inch a year—lickity-split in geologic time.

The lake, which is roughly shaped like a four-legged octopus, has several distinct zones. Most boating happens in the broad main area, while the West Thumb branch features an active thermal zone. The South and Southeast Arms are much more remote and have more restrictions on motorboats, making them excellent places for kayak or canoe camping.

Lake Village forms the area's primary developed hub, with a couple of lodging and dining options, plus a general store. The canary-yellow **Lake Yellowstone Hotel** is the park's most elegant, while nearby **Lake Lodge** offers rustic cabins and a killer front-porch view. See p. 134 for more details.

Continue south on Grand Loop Road to **Bridge Bay Marina,** the hub for water-based activities. Boat launches grant entry for DIYers, and you can also rent motorboats or rowboats from park concessionaires in summer. There's also a popular, 1-hour scenic cruise around Stevenson Island complete with historic tales from the boat's skipper. The small general store sells food and fishing permits. The adjacent **Bridge Bay Campground** is Yellowstone's largest.

Although the **Natural Bridge,** near Bridge Bay, is well-marked on park maps, it's one of the park's best-kept secrets, and you might end up enjoying the hike by yourself. The mile-long path down to the bridge, a geologic masterpiece consisting of a massive rock arch spanning Bridge Creek, is also one of the few trails open to bikes.

If you're looking to get off the beaten path, one-way **Gull Point Drive** shoots off the main road just south of Bridge Bay and traces the lakeshore past a lovely picnic spot. If not, continue west to West Thumb.

So called because it would be the thumb on Yellowstone Lake's "hand," **West Thumb** represents a caldera within the larger Yellowstone caldera, formed by an eruption 174,000 years ago. The heat from underground hydrothermal features here can melt the ice that covers the rest of the lake surface for much of the year. It's a great spot to look for bears and elk (especially in spring), river otters playing in the warm waters in winter, and bald eagles or osprey year-round. The small **West Thumb Information Station** is open 9am to 5pm summer through early fall and as a warming hut in winter.

The primary attraction here is **West Thumb Geyser Basin** ★, a unique shoreline thermal area where you can see hot springs pouring into the lake, brightly hued pools, brownish-green paint pots, and shoreline geysers. It's less crowded than the bigger basins, but still advisable to stroll the .25-mile inner loop and .5-mile outer loop early or late in the day to avoid tour bus jams. **Fishing Cone** gained fame in the late 1800s, when anglers would catch trout and then cook them, still on the line, in the spring's hot water (a practice that is decidedly not allowed today, for health reasons).

As you depart the West Thumb area, you are presented with two choices: either to head south, toward Grand Teton National Park, or to head west, across the **Continental Divide** at Craig Pass, en route to Old Faithful.

Grant Village to the South Entrance

Closest entrance and distance: 22 miles from Grant Village to the south entrance

The **Grant Village** complex lines the lakeshore on the south side of West Thumb. It's a convenient home base if you're combining your visit with a trip to Grand Teton National Park, and it boasts stunning sunset views, but the lodging and dining choices are more serviceable than they are inspiring. The **Grant Village** lodges provide motel-style accommodations, **Grant Village Campground** lets you sleep under the stars, and **Grant Village Dining Room** serves upscale dishes. Better bet: **Lake House Restaurant,** a casual eatery located right on the water with unbeatable lake views. For more details about dining and accommodations in the area, see chapter 7. **Grant Village Visitor Center** (© **307/242-2650**) has exhibits on the 1988 wildfires and the forest's subsequent recovery, plus animal hides and skulls for kids to touch and a beautiful porch overlooking the lake.

Heading south on the South Entrance Road soon takes you over the **Continental Divide** and on to evergreen-lined **Lewis Lake.** This lake makes for excellent boating, paddling, and fishing. Indeed, one of the park's best paddling trips starts at the boat ramp here: Paddle across Lewis Lake, up the **Lewis River,** and into **Shoshone Lake,** a gorgeous backcountry waterway and the park's second-largest lake. The **Lewis Lake Campground** on the southern shore is one of Yellowstone's quietest, most away-from-it-all camps.

Yellowstone Lake: West Thumb to Grant Village

Just south of here is **Lewis Falls,** a lacy, 29-foot waterfall pouring right over the lip of the Yellowstone caldera. Then follow the river south through the dramatically plunging **Lewis River Canyon;** don't blow past the pullouts here without getting out to gaze across the chasm at least once.

West Thumb to Old Faithful

Closest entrance: 22 miles from West Thumb to the south entrance

Distance: 17 miles from West Thumb Geyser Basin to Old Faithful

The high-altitude road west of West Thumb crosses the **Continental Divide** twice in this section, the second time at 8,262-foot **Craig Pass.** At both points, precipitation falling on the east side of the divide eventually flows to the Atlantic Ocean, and anything falling to the west is Pacific Ocean-bound. An interesting phenomenon takes place at **Isa Lake** atop Craig Pass. Unlike most lakes and streams, it has both eastern and western drainages and ends up in both the Pacific Ocean and the Gulf of Mexico. Amazingly, because of a gyroscopic maneuver, the outlet on the *east* curves *west* and drains to the Pacific, and the outlet on the *west* curves *east* and drains to the gulf.

About 3 miles south of the Old Faithful area, an overlook grants a peek at **Kepler Cascades,** a 150-foot stair-step waterfall on the Firehole River. This is also the trailhead for one of Yellowstone's best easy day hikes, the 4.8-mile (round-trip) hike to **Lone Star Geyser ★★**. The trail winds along the Firehole River to the geyser's cone (bikes are allowed most of the way, and it's also a fun cross-country ski route), where a 30- to 45-foot plume erupts every 3 hours or so (a logbook on site should tell you when the last eruption occurred). Wide meadows and sunny riverside basking rocks make waiting for the next spout more than pleasant.

Old Faithful Area

Closest entrance and distances: 16 miles from Old Faithful to Madison Junction, then 14 miles to West Yellowstone (west) entrance

Interested in seeing a few geysers? Boy, have you come to the right place. The Old Faithful area contains the world's largest concentration of these geothermal spouters, including, of course, the world's most famous example. It's Yellowstone at its best—don't miss it.

The area is also exceedingly popular, and offers the widest variety of services in the park. Choose from three different lodging options—**Old Faithful Lodge, Old Faithful Snow Lodge,** and the magnificent **Old Faithful Inn**—and dining option from casual cafeterias and ice cream stands to the swanky Snow Lodge's **Obsidian Dining Room.** (See chapter 7 for info on lodging and dining here.) There's also a general store, gas station, clinic, backcountry office, and post office.

One must-do stop: the **Old Faithful Visitor Education Center** (✆ **307/344-2751**). It will walk you through the mechanics of all the hydrothermal features waiting outside, and giant picture windows let you see Old Faithful in all its glory, too. If you can stand to wait, head here first for a primer on Yellowstone's grand plumbing system before exploring the basins; rangers post the next predicted eruption times for several major geysers, so you'll know exactly how much time you have to browse. **Haynes Photo Shop** is also worth a stop if you're a photography fan: Check out historic photos and cameras, learn about early photo expeditions, or just stop for a moment to charge your phone at the charging stations.

And now for the main event. Several distinct basins sit in close proximity here: **Upper Geyser Basin, Black Sand Basin,** and **Biscuit Basin.** Upper Geyser Basin is the star, containing the most interesting features, but all are worth a look. **Old Faithful Geyser ★★★**, around which all the area's buildings cluster, is a fine place to start. It's not the park's largest or most frequent eruptor, but it has remained about as predictable as it was when the 1870 Washburn Expedition named it. Eruptions occur about every 90 minutes, spewing 3,700 to 8,400 gallons of boiling water up to 184 feet. No matter how many times you've seen Old Faithful on postcards or videos, there's nothing like the thrill of seeing the real thing.

Views of Old Faithful are excellent from the boardwalk and the second-floor deck of Old Faithful Inn, but an even better vantage point is atop **Observation Point ★★**. The 1.6-mile (round-trip) trail departs from the boardwalk on the way to Geyser Hill, just past the Firehole River Bridge, and climbs 160 feet to an eagle-eye view over the entire basin. Continuing a bit farther along the trail loops you past frequent eruptor **Solitary Geyser** for the 2.2-mile trip back to the boardwalk.

Begin your geyser gazing with the 1.3-mile boardwalk loop around Geyser Hill. You'll likely catch **Anemone Geyser** in action; the 6-footer goes off every 7 to 10 minutes. **Beehive Geyser** is much less predictable but more impressive, shooting a towering column of water up to 200 feet. The four-geyser **Lion Group** comes next. The largest member, Lion Geyser, announces an impending eruption with steam plumes and a guttural roar. Farther down the path, you'll have to be lucky to glimpse **Giantess Geyser:** This powerhouse shoots

---

Top 5 Places to Watch Old Faithful Erupt

1. From above, at Observation Point
2. From Old Faithful Inn's second-floor porch
3. Front and center on the boardwalk
4. Through the picture windows in the Old Faithful Lodge lobby
5. Framed in the viewing window at Old Faithful Visitor Education Center

Old Faithful Area

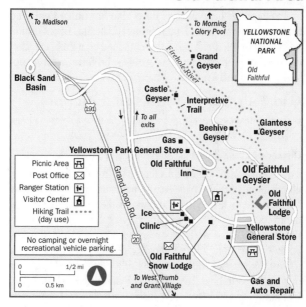

water 200 feet high and shakes the ground with its steam blasts. If it is active (which happens every 2–6 months), eruptions happen as frequently as every 30 minutes.

Plenty more features await along the boardwalk northwest of Geyser Hill. One star, **Castle Geyser ★★**, erupts from a fortresslike sinter cone formed over thousands of years. It's one of six geysers that rangers predict, so check at the visitor center or the hotels for the next show time (about every 14 hr.). **Grand Geyser ★★**, another predicted spouter, lets loose powerful water pulses up to 200 feet high.

Closer to the Firehole River, **Beauty Pool** and adjacent **Chromatic Pool** display brilliant rings of blue, green, yellow, and orange created by thermophile microorganisms. Rangers also predict **Riverside Geyser's ★★** eruptions: Every 6 hours or so, the waterfront feature blows water and steam in an arch over the Firehole. The paved trail ends at **Morning Glory Pool,** a once-vibrant blue hot spring now gone yellow and brown thanks to thoughtless visitors tossing trash and rocks into its underground portal over the years.

Continuing to **Biscuit Basin** (a 5.2-mile round-trip from the visitor center) takes you to a smaller collection of geysers and hot springs headlined by deep-blue **Sapphire Pool.** The final basin in this area, **Black Sand Basin,** lies about a mile northwest of Old Faithful and does indeed contain black sand (a derivative of obsidian) as well as brightly colored hot springs and **Cliff Geyser.**

Old Faithful to Madison Junction

Closest entrances: 30 miles from the Old Faithful area to the West Yellowstone (west) entrance; 39 miles to the south entrance

Distance: 16 miles from the Old Faithful area to Madison

The hydrothermal fireworks continue as you move north along Grand Loop Road. At the next major stop, **Midway Geyser Basin ★★**, you'll see two of the largest features of their type in the world. **Excelsior Geyser** used to erupt mightily in the 1880s—its bursts reached 300 feet, and were as wide as they were tall (perhaps we're lucky it's rather quiet today). The geyser still issues 5.8 million gallons of water per day into the Firehole River. **Grand Prismatic Spring,** at 370 feet across and 125 feet deep, is the second-largest hot spring on the planet. A boardwalk leads you close to the colorful spring, a bright blue pool ringed by striking bands of yellow, green, and orange thermophiles. The park is constructing an aerial viewing platform set to open in 2017 or 2018.

About 8 miles north of Old Faithful, take the turnoff to **Firehole Lake Drive ★**. This 2-mile, one-way detour winds through another remarkable thermal area—and it's much less crowded than Norris or Old Faithful. **Great Fountain Geyser** is one highlight: One of the six geysers that rangers publish predicted eruption times for, this fountain blows water 100 feet in the air, and the pulsing eruptions last up to an hour. **White Dome Geyser** features a giant sinter cone built up over hundreds of years; watch for its frequent 30-foot eruptions. And at **Firehole Lake,** stroll the boardwalk along a massive hot spring circled with travertine deposits.

Firehole Lake Drive will deposit you at the parking lot for **Lower Geyser Basin ★**, home to **Fountain Paint Pot.** A .5-mile boardwalk loops past the highlights, though what you'll see depends on the season: Early in the year, the bubbling mud will be thin with abundant water, but later in

Know Your Bacteria

Even the most casual visitor can do some scientific sleuthing at the **Fountain Paint Pots ★**, learning to identify water temperature by observing the colors in the pots. The colors result from different types of bacteria that survive at specific water temperatures. Some are yellow until temperatures reach 161°F (72°C), above which the yellow bacteria cannot live. As temperatures approach boiling—199°F (93°C) at this elevation—pinks begin to appear.

summer it thickens to a muddy paste. Take care here—the reddish paint pots have been known to toss blobs of mud all the way to the boardwalk. Nearby **Red Spouter** sprang to life after the 1959 Hebgen Lake Earthquake. It, too, changes seasonally, from a hot spring and small, red-colored geyser in the spring to a mudpot in late summer to a steaming fumarole at year's end.

The boardwalk swings west to a small geyser area packed with six spouters in close proximity. Chances are excellent you'll see at least a few go off: **Spasm Geyser** tosses up 20-foot-high spray frequently, and **Clepsydra Geyser**'s burbling is almost constant.

As you continue toward the Madison Junction, consider a detour along **Fountain Flat Drive,** a left turn about 2 miles beyond Fountain Paint Pot. This scenic paved road ends a quarter-mile north of Ojo Caliente, after which it is open only to hikers and bikers. One mile south of the Firehole River Bridge, you'll find the **Imperial Meadows Trailhead.** Park the car and head up the 4-mile trail to the 200-foot **Fairy Falls.**

The last side road you'll hit before Madison Junction is also the best: The 2-mile **Firehole Canyon Drive ★★**. You'll have to backtrack a bit after cruising the one-way, south-only road when coming from this direction, but the payoff is worth it. The road winds through a super-sheer gorge along the Firehole River, abutting 7,500-foot National Park Mountain and passing 800-foot-thick lava deposits. Stop for a peek at the tumbling cascade of 40-foot **Firehole Falls** before reaching the cherry on top: a **swimming hole ★★** near the end of the road. This is one of the only places in the park where it's safe to splash around, and the cool water can't be beat on a sweltering August afternoon.

ORGANIZED TOURS

Yellowstone guide services and commercial bus tours abound, based both inside the park and in the gateway towns. Concessionaire **Xanterra** (© **307/344-7311;** www.yellowstonenationalparklodges.com) operates the in-park tours, many of them in historic yellow tour buses, a throwback to tourism of yesteryear. The most intensive option whirls you to the major highlights on Grand Loop Road, an all-day affair taking off from Old Faithful, Mammoth, and Gardiner ($114–$121 adult). Other trips are shorter and more specialized, focusing on wildlife-watching, geyser basins, photography, and more. These tours range from 2 to 6 hours and cost $28 to $93 for adults. When the snow flies, **snowcoach tours** take over for the buses (p. 92).

Xanterra's tours don't stop at the water's edge, either: You can also hop on a **Yellowstone Lake Scenicruise** for a boat trip around Stevenson Island, complete with historic tales from the boat's skipper. The cruise lasts an hour and costs $18 for adults. Guides will also take you out on chartered fishing and sightseeing rides on a 22-foot powerboat ($94/hour). Chefs at some of the park restaurants will even cook up your fresh-caught lake trout for you.

Several standout tours begin outside the park. **Buffalo Bus Touring Company** (© **877/600-4308;** www.yellowstonevacations.com) is one favorite out of West Yellowstone: Choose from an upper loop or lower loop tour, or combine the two, and visit park hotspots with a certified naturalist. Single-loop trips are $75, and doubles cost $140. **Yellowstone Alpen Guides** (© **406/646-9591;** www.yellowstoneguides.com), also out of West Yellowstone, offers evening wildlife tours

---

DIY Drives

Depending on your driving skills and your tolerance for large numbers of slow-moving cars, RVs, and auto-towed trailers, there is no substitute for a self-driven tour of the park. For $45 a day, gadget fiends can rent dashboard-mounted GPS units with prerecorded audio keyed to locations in both Yellowstone and Grand Teton from **GaperGuide.** You can pick up and drop off units in every Yellowstone gateway town, plus Jackson, Teton Village, and Moran (© **307/733-4626;** www.gaperguide.com).

and private photo tours along with a general lower loop trip; expect most tours to last 8 hours and cost $90 for adults. If you'd rather hand over trip-planning entirely, **Adventure Bus** (✆ **909/633-7225;** www.adventurebus.com) will whisk you from Salt Lake City through Yellowstone, Grand Teton, and Jackson on a 7-day tour, including hiking excursions and camping nights ($995 per person, most food included).

One of the best ways to really get to know Yellowstone is through the park's nonprofit partner, **Yellowstone Forever** ★★★ (✆ **406/848-2400;** www.yellowstone.org), formerly the Yellowstone Association. The group runs a staggering number of day and multiday courses on wildlife, geology, hiking, photography, fishing, and more. **Field Seminars** base you out of the Lamar Buffalo Ranch Field Campus in the Lamar Valley or the Yellowstone Overlook Field Campus in Gardiner, both excellent perks of participating. **Lodging & Learning** programs are even more inclusive, including nights in park hotels and most meals. For more information, see "Academic Trips" (p. 27).

RANGER PROGRAMS

One of the national parks' most valuable services are its highly informative free **ranger programs** ★★★: At practically every park, rangers lead hikes, tell stories around the campfire, help you gaze into the heavens, and school you on the area's natural wonders and human history. Do all you can to catch at least one. Programs run all year, but the most options are found from late May to early September. Check www.nps.gov/yell/planyourvisit/rangerprog.htm or the park newsletter for places and times. Some require reservations. You're also likely to run into a roving ranger happy to answer your questions on geyser basin boardwalks or popular hiking trails. Just keep an eye peeled for the signature wide-brimmed hat bobbing among the crowds.

You can learn enough for an honorary degree in geyserology on one of the many guided walks through the Old Faithful, Norris, Mud Volcano, West Thumb, and Mammoth areas, where rangers will teach you all about the basins' hydrothermal features. Brush up on basic wildlife safety at talks in several locations, or focus on history at Canyon, Fishing Bridge, and Mammoth. Guided hikes are great for anyone concerned about exploring on their own in bear country, and rangers might take you along the Grand Canyon of the Yellowstone's rim, up Mt. Washburn or Avalanche Peak, or out to Shoshone Lake or Lone Star Geyser.

Yellowstone offers several fantastic after-dark talks, too. **Evening campfire programs** at almost every campground or developed area cover topics from biology and geology to human history. And Madison is the place for stargazing during one of several **astronomy programs** held in conjunction with the Museum of the Rockies. Rangers point out constellations, watch for shooting stars, and let visitors peer into the heavens with powerful telescopes. Programs are usually held on select Friday and Saturday nights in June and July.

If you have kids (or remain a kid at heart), you won't want to miss the **Junior Ranger Program.** Pick up a $3 workbook at any visitor center and complete the activities inside—they often include attending a ranger program and going on a hike—then demonstrate your newfound knowledge with a ranger to earn a special patch and sticker. The similar **Young Scientist Program** for kids ages 5 and up guides participants to solve science mysteries through investigating visitor center exhibits and trails. Find a $5, self-guiding booklet at Canyon or Old Faithful Visitor Education Centers.

GETTING OUTDOORS IN YELLOWSTONE

The Great Outdoors: It's why you're here. And Yellowstone's natural wonders are unlike anything you'll see elsewhere on the planet. Roads will show you only a fraction of the immense wilderness here, but more than 1,200 miles of trails can lead you to peaceful lakes, up airy peaks, and through steaming backcountry geyser basins. Make sure to hike at least one trail while you're here—you haven't really visited the park if you don't.

4

With hikes ranging from short, easy strolls to strenuous, multiday endeavors, there's something for everyone at Yellowstone. Even better, the trails offer the best way to escape the inevitable summer crowds: Believe it or not, only a tiny fraction of visitors get out of their cars and explore the trails. Besides hiking, the park is also a terrific place for boating, paddling, biking, and winter sports.

In fact, there's so much to see and do here that it's easy to get overwhelmed with the choices. Here is the crème de la crème: Choose one or more, and you won't be disappointed.

DAY HIKES

Yellowstone's trails range from flat, easy strolls to extended paths that delve deep into the wilderness. And though you'd need months to explore all the hidden corners here, even a single day hike will reveal a whole new side of the park to you. These selected day hikes from every developed area are the best of the best—you won't regret saving time to make tracks on at least one of them. *Note:* The trails through the geyser basins also make for excellent day hikes. See details on those trips in chapter 3.

Keep in mind that hiking in Yellowstone can be hazardous for the unprepared: Bad weather, river crossings, and wildlife all pose real risks. Check in at a visitor center or ranger station for details on the weather forecast and trail conditions for your hike, and make sure to pack the essentials (see p. 83).

West Yellowstone to Madison

Purple Mountain ★　You'll truly earn your views on this challenging trail—reaching the summit of the flat-topped mountain requires hoofing it up 1,500 vertical feet in 3 miles—but the eagle-eye vistas from the top are worth it. Begin hiking through a lodgepole pine forest, then pop out on a plateau with views of the twisty Gibbon and Madison rivers and extending all the way to the Tetons on bluebird days.

6 miles round-trip. Difficult. Access: Trailhead is at a turnout .25 mile north of Madison Junction.

Norris Geyser Basin Area

Artist Paintpots ★　This small loop trail between Madison and Norris provides an uncrowded quick fix for geothermal junkies. Stroll the trail/boardwalk combo through a young lodgepole pine forest to see brightly colored hot springs, hissing steam vents, and mud pots tossing mud several feet in the air. A slight climb to the top of the basin gives you a lovely aerial view over the thermal features and a distant peek at 10,336-foot Mt. Holmes.

1.2-mile loop. Easy. Access: Trailhead is 4.5 miles south of Norris Junction.

Mammoth Hot Springs Area

Beaver Ponds Loop Trail ★　Start at Clematis Gulch and hike through sage-filled meadows and Douglas fir/aspen forest to a series of beaver ponds. Your best chance of seeing the big-tailed beasts is early morning or late afternoon, and you might spot a moose, pronghorn, or elk on the way. There are also some good views, including of Mount Everts.

5 miles round-trip. Moderate. Access: Trailhead is located at Mammoth Hot Springs Terrace.

Bunsen Peak Trail ★★　Climb an 8,564-foot mountain to big views of the Absaroka Range to the northeast and

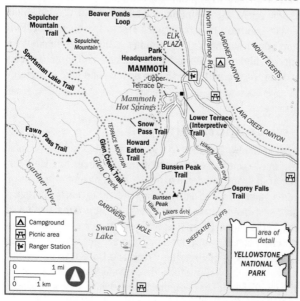

Map legend:
- △ Campground
- ⊞ Picnic area
- ⛨ Ranger Station

0   1 mi
0   1 km

area of detail

YELLOWSTONE NATIONAL PARK

10,969-foot Electric Peak to the north on this moderate outing.
You'll switchback 1,300 feet up the peak's northwest ridge,
gaining better vistas with each step, before reaching the summit. Continue down the other side of the peak toward Sheepeater Cliffs, then loop back to the trailhead on Bunsen Peak
Road. Tack on the 2.4-mile (round-trip) out-and-back spur trail
that picks up near the road junction to see Osprey Falls. Take
the steep, rocky trail into Sheepeater Canyon to see the multi-
tiered waterfall dropping 150 feet into the Gardner River.

4.6 miles round-trip. Moderate. Access: Trailhead is across the road
from the Glen Creek Trailhead, 5 miles south of Mammoth.

Sepulcher Mountain Trail ★★   There are several ways
to approach this broad-sided, 9,652-foot peak just west of
Mammoth Hot Springs, but the top route begins on the Sepulcher Mountain Trail at Mammoth, ascends the summit,
loops back on the Glen Creek Trail, and crosses Snow Pass
to return to the trailhead. Hike west across an old burn area
now strewn with wildflowers in summer, then begin gaining
for a total of 3,400 feet. You'll get views across the

Absaroka-Beartooth Wilderness and Gallatin National Forest, and down into Mammoth and Gardiner. A 360-degree panorama opens at the summit. Switchback your way down the peak's southeast ridge and swing east to approach Snow Pass and your route back to the trailhead. Be on the lookout for moose, bighorn sheep, mountain goats—and grizzlies. This is a favorite habitat for bears, so be loud and hike in a group.

11-mile loop. Moderate to difficult. Access: Sepulcher Mountain Trailhead at Mammoth Hot Springs Terrace.

Tower-Roosevelt Area

Hellroaring Trail ★ An ideal early-season hike because the snow melts here sooner than in other areas, the Hellroaring Trail drops you down to a sage-filled plateau where bison often gather. Traipse across the open field to reach an impressive suspension bridge that spans a steep, roiling section of the Yellowstone River (the bridge also makes a good turnaround point if you're looking for a shorter hike). Continue to the banks of Hellroaring Creek and trace it to its confluence with the Yellowstone (both waterways are great for fishing). The trail goes on much farther into the backcountry, but turn around here for a manageable day hike.

6.2 miles round-trip. Moderate to difficult. Access: Trailhead is 3.5 miles west of Tower Junction.

Specimen Ridge Loop ★★ This shuttle hike packs a whole lotta geologic marvels into a few beautiful miles: petrified trees, basalt columns, and plunging canyon cliffs, to name a few. Start by dropping a car or bike at the Yellowstone River Picnic Area, then proceed to the trailhead for the unnamed but official trail (not to be confused with the Specimen Ridge Trail). From here, you'll climb steeply to excellent views over the Lamar Valley and Absarokas until you reach a rocky outcrop scattered with fossilized, 50-million-year-old sequoias, firs, and other trees. Take care in this area, as it's quite steep, and resist the temptation to take a fossil home—not only does that damage the precious resource, it's also illegal. Continue west across a sage-filled meadow on the Specimen Ridge Trail (it's faint up here) to the east rim of a narrow canyon on the Yellowstone River; trace the rim northwest on the Yellowstone River Picnic Trail, looking out for osprey, peregrine falcons, bighorn sheep, and the distinctive volcanic basalt columns across the river. The trail will take you back down to the picnic area.

6-mile shuttle. Difficult. Access: Trailhead is 4.5 miles east of Tower Junction, in a striped pullout marked "trailhead." Ending trailhead is Yellowstone River Picnic Area, 1.3 miles east of Tower Junction.

Lamar Valley Area

Slough Creek Trail ★★ Anglers and wildlife-watchers, this one's for you. Pretty Slough Creek is revered for its cutthroat trout fishing, and bears, moose, and bison are frequently spotted in the meadows along its banks. For a day-sized chunk, follow the Slough Creek Trail up a short, steep section of Douglas firs, then descend to First Meadow. This grassy expanse features rocky outcroppings, peak views, and easy access to fishing holes. Extending your hike along the creek to Second Meadow adds another 5.2 miles round-trip.

3.4 miles round-trip. Easy to moderate. Access: Trailhead is on the dirt road to Slough Creek Campground; park where the road curves left.

Trout Lake Trail ★ A short, somewhat steep hike through spruce and fir, this trail's destination is the small Trout Lake, which is encircled by a footpath. The lake, nestled between dramatic cliffs and Druid and Barronette peaks, is a favorite fishing hole and one of the best places in the park to witness the fascinating cutthroat spawn. Because of the density of the fish, the lake once served as a major source of food for Cooke City and still attracts otters, beavers, and bears.

1.3 miles round-trip. Easy. Access: 10 miles west of the northeast entrance, at the trailhead 1 mile west of Pebble Creek campground.

Upper Pebble Creek ★★ The lesser-traveled region off the Northeast Entrance Road holds some of the most dramatic scenery in the park, including this gorgeous ramble in a remote valley. Even better, abundant wildflowers decorate the meadows in July. The first mile climbs fairly steeply to views of the cliffs along Soda Butte Creek and the area's imposing stone buttes, then flattens to an easy meadow stroll. Turn around at the first backcountry campsite along Pebble Creek, where you'll spy still more giant summits. Alternately, you can park a shuttle car at the Pebble Creek Trailhead and hike all the way there for a 12-mile day.

4 miles round-trip. Moderate. Access: Warm Springs Trailhead is 8 miles east of Pebble Creek Campground.

Grand Canyon of the Yellowstone River Area

Clear Lake and Ribbon Lake Loop ★   A relatively easy loop hike combines a trio of backcountry lakes with a stroll along the canyon rim. You can start from several spots, but we like beginning at the Clear Lake Trailhead. After less than a mile, turn left to reach tree-ringed Clear Lake. Lily Pad Lake is just beyond, and peaceful Ribbon Lake is about a mile past that. Retrace your steps to Lily Pad Lake, then turn north, then west, to approach the knockout vista of the Lower Falls at Artist Point. The rest of the loop follows the South Rim Trail along the canyon's edge, offering views of thundering waterfalls and brightly colored rock walls.

5.8-mile loop. Easy to moderate. Access: Clear Lake Trailhead, 2.3 miles south of Canyon Junction on South Rim Dr.

Mount Washburn ★★★   This is one of Yellowstone's most popular day hikes for good reason. The climb up to 10,243 feet is challenging but gradual, the peak's slopes are known for a rainbow of wildflowers in summer, and the view from the summit is practically unmatched. You might spot bighorn sheep, black bears, or grizzlies up here—in fact, grizzlies tend to congregate on the slopes in fall to munch on whitebark pine nuts. The top approach begins from Dunraven Pass and follows a wide trail up above the tree line with ever-expanding views. From the top, you'll see the Grand Canyon of the Yellowstone, the Hayden Valley, Specimen Ridge, Slough Creek, and even the Tetons on a clear day. There's also a lookout on the summit, which provides welcome shelter from the often-whipping winds. You can also hike it from the Old Chittenden Road, a slightly shorter (5 miles round-trip) but steeper trail. Much of this hike is exposed to the elements, so don't attempt it if there's a chance of lightning.

6 miles round-trip. Moderate. Access: Trailheads are at Dunraven Pass and the end of Old Chittenden Rd.

North Rim Trail ★   The trail skirting the north rim, which is described more fully under "Canyon Village," in chapter 3, offers better views of the falls and the river than you'll get

Grand Canyon Area Trails

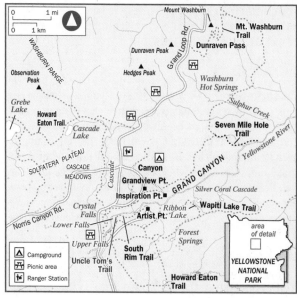

from the parking areas. It's a nice way to see a longer stretch of the canyon.

6 miles round-trip. Easy. Access: Trailheads are at Wapiti Lake Trailhead and Inspiration Point.

Seven Mile Hole ★   The only way to reach the Yellowstone River in the Grand Canyon area, Seven Mile Hole Trail is a doozy: You'll drop more than 1,000 feet in just 2.3 miles going from rim to river. But first, the trail wanders along the north rim, stopping at overlooks with views of 1,200-foot Silver Cord Cascade across the canyon. Soon you'll graduate from gazing at to hiking into the canyon, passing dormant and active hot springs along the way to the wide Yellowstone River. Keep in mind that this exposed hike can be hot, and don't underestimate the challenge of climbing back out of the canyon.

10 miles round-trip. Moderate to difficult. Access: Trailhead is at Glacial Boulder pullout on the road to Inspiration Point.

South Rim Trail ★ As with the North Rim Trail, there are more and better views of the canyon and river here than you can see from a vehicle. It's easy and not long, yet you'll have it mainly to yourself because most folks are in and out of the bus at the parking lots.

7 miles round-trip. Easy. Access: Trailheads are Wapiti Lake Trailhead and Artist Point.

Observation Peak ★★ Climb past a riot of purple and pink wildflowers en route to 360-degree views on this classic summit hike. The trail begins by crossing patches of forest and meadows to Cascade Lake, a great spot for fishing or even swimming on hot days. Then hoof it 1,400 vertical feet in 2.6 miles through a whitebark pine forest to the Observation Peak summit. There's an old wooden fire tower up here, but you'll be more interested in the encompassing views of the Gallatins, Absarokas, and the Grand Canyon of the Yellowstone.

9.6 miles round-trip. Difficult. Access: Cascade Lake Trailhead, 1.3 miles north of Canyon Junction.

Yellowstone Lake Area

Avalanche Peak ★★ Looking for the best bang for your buck? It's tough to beat this peak, which delivers fantastic panoramas of the park's remote corners in just 2.1 miles. Of course, you'll have to work for it—the trail rises a vertiginous 2,100 feet in that distance—but keep your eyes on the prize. The 10,566-foot summit is in view for most of the climb up talus slopes and narrow ridgelines, and once you get there, you'll have unimpeded views over Yellowstone Lake and across to many of the park's craggiest peaks, such as Hoyt Peak, Mount Sheridan, Mount Stevenson, and Top Notch. The window to ascend to these heights is narrow: It's often snow-covered into July, and increased grizzly bear activity makes fall a dicey proposition. Be alert for lightning risks anytime.

4.2 miles round-trip. Difficult. Access: Trailhead is 8 miles west of the East Entrance.

Elephant Back Loop Trail ★ Here's an opportunity to look down (literally!) on the island-dotted expanse of Yellowstone Lake, the Absaroka Range, and the Pelican Valley.

This is a great photo opportunity and a fairly easy hike for a novice.

3.5 miles round-trip. Moderate. Access: From the east, the trailhead is on the right side of the road, just before the turnoff for the Lake Yellowstone Hotel.

Pelican Valley Trail ★   This trip across marshy meadows and alongside a peaceful creek could be either a hiker's dream or nightmare—depending how you feel about grizzly bears. The remote Pelican Valley is some of the best grizzly habitat in the continental U.S., and as such, the park restricts hiking to daytime, and only after July 4. If that excites rather than terrifies you, get a group of at least four and strike out into the wide-open valley. The trail wanders through meadows and traces the meandering Pelican Creek, where you might also see bison, wolves, elk, and eagles. The washed-out bridge across the creek at mile 3.1 makes a good turn-around point, but the trail extends all the way into the Lamar Valley for multiday excursions.

6.2 miles round-trip. Easy. Access: Trailhead is 3 miles east of Fishing Bridge, just past Storm Point/Indian Pond Trail.

Storm Point Loop ★   One of the park's nicest lakeside rambles, this trail begins at Indian Pond and passes through a pine forest before popping out at Storm Point, the rocky western corner hemming in Mary Bay. You'll gaze across the lake to views of Stevenson Island, distant Mount Sheridan, and the Tetons. Bonus: Marmot sightings are practically guaranteed on a stony outcrop near the shore. Grizzlies frequent the area in spring and early summer, so check with rangers to make sure the trail is open to hikers.

2.3 miles round-trip. Easy. Access: Trailhead is 3 miles east of Fishing Bridge, directly across from the Pelican Valley Trailhead (on the lake side of the road).

West Thumb/Grant Village Area

DeLacy Creek Trail ★★   Yellowstone's largest and most impressive backcountry lake, Shoshone Lake, requires a significant haul on foot or kayak to reach—except by this quick, sneaky route. Head south along DeLacy Creek, passing open meadows that make wonderful habitat for moose and sandhill cranes, to Shoshone's northern shores. Bask by the rocky beaches, explore farther down the lakeshore, or brave a dip in the frosty waters.

5.8 miles round-trip. Easy. Access: Trailhead is 8.8 miles west of West Thumb Junction.

Riddle Lake ★   Kick back on a (small) sandy beach with views of the Red Mountains on this mellow stroll to a back-country lake. You'll hike over the Continental Divide, through lodgepole pine forest, and past meadows where elk and grizzly bears often graze. Riddle Lake itself is a pictur-esque lake dotted with lily pads and is sometime home to nesting trumpeter swans. The trail is closed to hiking until July 15 because of bear activity; it's smart to hike in larger groups after that, too.

4.8 miles round-trip. Easy. Access: Trailhead is 3 miles south of Grant Village.

Old Faithful Area

Fairy Falls Trail ★   Feel the spray from a 200-foot water-fall on this flat, family-friendly hike. The trail follows an old roadbed through young forest, approaching the Firehole River. Turn west at the Fairy Falls Trail proper and go another 1.4 miles to a grotto where the plume of Fairy Falls plunges over a cliff. When trail crews finish constructing a viewing platform for Grand Prismatic Spring (scheduled for 2018), you can also access Fairy Falls from a trailhead 1 mile south of Midway Geyser Basin, shortening the round trip to 5 miles. This hike can easily be combined with other trails for a longer loop (see below).

8.8 miles round-trip. Easy. Access: Trailheads are at the end of Foun-tain Flat Dr. and 1 mile south of Midway Geyser Basin (closed until 2018).

Lone Star Geyser ★★   Front-country geysers are spec-tacular, but there's something extra-special about a back-country spouter you have all to yourself (or more likely, to yourself and a few other hikers). Lone Star Geyser is one of the easiest ones to reach, and it's predictable enough (erup-tions happen every 3 hr. or so) to make catching its show likely: The 12-foot-high cone sprays water 45 feet in the air. Getting there means tracing the Firehole River on an old service road, passing intermittent meadows along the way;

Old Faithful Area Trails

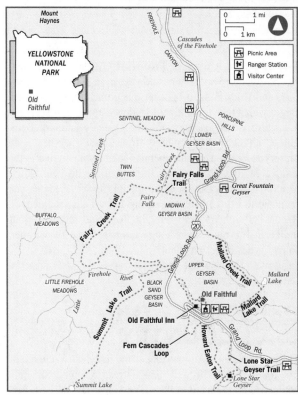

bikes can follow it almost all the way to the geyser. Check the register near the geyser to estimate the next eruption time.

4.8 miles round-trip. Easy. Access: Trailhead is at the parking lot opposite Kepler Cascades.

Observation Point & Solitary Geyser Loop ★★

An alternate look at Old Faithful's famous eruption—with a grander scope, no less—is just a short climb away from the busy Upper Geyser Basin. From the boardwalk, ascend 160 feet in .8 mile up to the natural viewing platform of Observation Point, then enjoy the geyser doing its thing. Backtrack to the trail junction and turn west to hike through thick forest to Solitary Geyser. This frequent spouter steams in the middle of a wide, white circle, and its runoff has created a colorful, mineral-laden slope streaked with thermophile bacteria. Heading south down the hill will link you back up with the boardwalk.

2.2-mile loop. Easy to moderate. Access: Trailhead is at the Old Faithful boardwalk.

Sentinel Meadows & Imperial Geyser Loop ★★
See backcountry hot springs and geysers, a National Historic Site, and Fairy Falls to boot on this attraction-packed loop. Begin with a hike to Sentinel Meadows, a grassy area speckled with thermal features, and the Queen's Laundry Bathhouse, an unfinished building from 1881 that has been preserved by the thermal minerals. Then swing around to the south to follow Fairy Creek through more lush meadows. You'll pass Spray Geyser and Imperial Geyser (the latter can erupt up to 60 ft.) before reaching Fairy Falls (see above). Reconnect with Fountain Freight Road and return to your trailhead. This area can be boggy and buggy in early summer, so pack your insect repellent.

10.5-mile loop. Easy. Access: Trailhead is at the end of Fountain Flat Drive.

EXPLORING THE BACKCOUNTRY

The backcountry of Yellowstone is the real deal: a domain of free-roaming wildlife and natural treasures predominately untouched by the hand of man. The U.S. National Park Service, through its system of permits, designated camping areas, and rules (for more on these, see below), has managed to preserve a true wilderness. Yellowstone has more than 1,200 miles of trails (most of which are in the backcountry) and 300 backcountry campsites.

For information on backpacking and safety, see chapter 10.

INFORMATION BEFORE YOU GO Contact the **Yellowstone Backcountry Office,** P.O. Box 168, Yellowstone National Park, WY 82190 (© **307/344-2160;** www.nps.gov/yell/plan yourvisit/backcountryhiking.htm), with questions about campsites, permits, and reservations. The website above has a link to the useful *Backcountry Trip Planner,* which has a detailed map showing where the campsites are, as well as information on preparation.

BACKCOUNTRY PERMITS Backcountry permits are required for any overnight trips on foot, horseback, or by boat. They cost $3/person/night (maximum group fee $15/night) for backpackers and boaters and $5/person/night for parties on horseback. If you're lucky enough to be spending many nights in the backcountry, an annual backcountry pass costs $25. You can arrange for permits in person at a back-country office no more than 48 hours in advance of your trip, or you can make reservations ahead of time by fax, mail, or in person only. The park accepts permit applications from Jan 1 to Oct 1 of each year, with those received by March 31 processed first, and charges a $25 fee. Camping is allowed only in designated campsites, many of which are equipped with food-storage poles to keep wildlife out of your stores. Some are also equipped with pit toilets.

Pick up your permit in the park within 48 hours of your departure at one of the following stations any day of the week during the summer: Bechler, Bridge Bay, Old Faithful, and South Entrance Ranger Stations; Canyon, Grant Village, Mammoth, and West Yellowstone Visitor Centers; or Tower Backcountry Office.

WHEN TO GO Many of the trails into the park back-country remain covered with snow and become muddy in the first weeks of melt, well into June. At the higher elevations, over 9,000 feet, summer doesn't truly begin until early July, and even then the weather is unpredictable at best. Creeks and streams described as "intermittent" during summer months might be filled with snowmelt that transforms them into impassable, swiftly running rivers that often drench trails and convert them to mud. Generally, mid-July through mid-September brings the best backpacking weather. Look

---

Bear Safety

Grizzly bear attacks in the park are incredibly rare, but possible. Reduce your chances of an encounter by respecting seasonal bear closures, hiking in groups of four or more, not hiking off-trail, and making noise by talking loudly, singing, or clapping your hands. Always carry bear spray, a very effective deterrent to a charging bear, and know how to use it.

in the *Backcountry Trip Planner* for approximate dates for when specific campsites will be accessible and habitable.

MAPS   A good topographic map is essential for backcountry trips. GPS units and smartphone mapping apps can be very useful, but always carry a paper map as backup. Park rangers suggest using maps from the Trails Illustrated Map series, published by National Geographic Maps. There are five Yellowstone maps printed on durable plastic; the maps also show backcountry campsite locations. For more information, contact **National Geographic Maps** (✆ **800/962-1643;** www.natgeomaps.com) or **Yellowstone Forever** (✆ **406/848-2400;** www.yellowstone.org).

OUTFITTERS   An alternative to venturing into the backcountry on your own is to go with an outfitter. Outfitters usually arrange for backcountry permits and provide most equipment, which can offset the cost of their services. And some offer a more catered experience, setting up your tent for you and preparing meals. Check www.nps.gov/yell/planyourvisit/backpkbsn.com for a list of companies with permits to operate inside the park.

The Yellowstone Backcountry

Auto touring is great, and day hiking is grand—but if you *really* want to experience Yellowstone, spending a night or more in the wilderness is the way to go. With its vast and varied terrain, this park has something to satisfy everyone from the novice camper to the backpacking junkie. Trip options range from short, easy overnights to multiday excursions spanning dozens of miles. Peruse the park's *Backcountry Trip Planner,* call the park backcountry office, and check out these top trips to find your ideal escape.

SHOSHONE LAKE

Gorgeous, expansive, and quiet, Shoshone Lake is the largest backcountry lake (that is, you can't drive to it) in the lower 48. There's no motorized boating allowed, making the scenic campsites dotting its shoreline especially peaceful. Add to that good trout fishing and a notable backcountry geyser basin, and it's no wonder Shoshone Lake is such a beloved destination. Camping is best starting in July, when spring flooding has usually eased up.

THE 10 essentials + 1

Though hiking is a very safe activity and most visitors run into no problems while exploring the park, don't forget that you're entering a true wilderness. It's vital to be prepared for changing weather conditions, rugged trails, and wildlife encounters. Experienced backcountry travelers swear by carrying the "Ten Essentials," or a must-pack list of comfort and safety gear to stash in your daypack. Make sure you have the following items with you before any hike, even if you're only going a short distance.

1. **Navigation:** Always carry a map and compass. The map you get at the entrance stations is not detailed enough for true navigation, so pick up a topographic map that shows terrain details. GPS units and smartphone apps are helpful too, but they shouldn't replace a paper map and compass in case you run out of power or they malfunction.
2. **Sun protection:** Everyone in your party should have a hat (wide-brimmed sun hats are best), sunglasses, and sunscreen with an SPF of at least 30.
3. **Extra clothing:** This should include both warm layers (such as fleece or down jackets) and waterproof rain gear.
4. **Light:** Pack a headlamp or flashlight in case you're unexpectedly caught out after dark.
5. **First-aid kit:** You can buy compact, ready-made wilderness kits or assemble your own. Carry pain relievers, bandages, and blister treatments.
6. **Fire-starting materials:** Waterproof matches and/or a lighter, plus tinder, can be the difference between life and death if you're lost in bad weather.
7. **Repair kit:** A knife or multitool plus duct tape can temporarily fix a surprising number of gear malfunctions.
8. **Food:** Trail mix, trail bars, dried fruit, jerky, and peanut butter are all calorically dense, long-lasting foods for extra energy.
9. **Water:** Prevent dehydration by making sure everyone in your group has a sizeable water bottle or hydration bladder.
10. **Emergency shelter:** A space blanket is small and light, but even a large garbage bag can add essential warmth and weather protection.

And, at Yellowstone, there's an 11th Essential:

11. **Bear spray:** Don't be caught without this highly effective deterrent against a charging bear.

The quickest way here is via the **DeLacy Creek Trail** (see "Old Faithful Area," under "Day Hikes," earlier in this chapter), which begins 8 miles east of Old Faithful. A 2.9-mile (one-way) hike takes you to the northern shore, with a couple of campsites just west. For a longer trip, you can either hike southwest along the **North Shoshone Trail** or southeast on DeLacy Creek Trail. The **Shoshone Lake Trail** connects the two, enabling a multiday trip circling the lake. The highlight of any trip in this area is a visit to **Shoshone Geyser Basin ★★**, a backcountry thermal area with hundreds of features. A trail winds through the hot springs, vents, and geysers—stick to it, as no boardwalks protect you from the steaming water just under the thin earth here. If you're heading straight for the basin, the shortest route is the Shoshone Lake Trail starting at Kepler Cascades; you'll pass Lone Star Geyser and cross **Grants Pass** on the way.

For a shorter overnight, make for the southeastern corner of Shoshone Lake on the **Channel Trail** following the Lewis River Channel. You might spy eagles and osprey near the water's edge before reaching the lake. Some of the campsites in this area are for boaters only, so you might need to hike a bit farther to spend the night along **Moose Creek.** Return on the **Dogshead Trail** for a 10.8-mile loop.

This is also the place for one of the park's classic paddling trips. Launch at Lewis Lake and canoe or kayak up the Lewis Channel (be aware that wind can make this a real workout). You'll have to drag your boat the final mile before reaching Shoshone Lake, but then the enormous lake's shoreline will be yours to explore. Many beach sites are reserved for paddlers only.

THE BECHLER REGION

This area in the park's southwest section is often referred to as Cascade Corner because it contains most the park's waterfalls. It escaped the fires of 1988 and offers great opportunities to view thermal features. Backpacking options abound here. Mid- to late summer is the best time to travel here, as early-season runoff makes the creek crossings high and dangerous.

To reach the **Bechler Ranger Station,** a primary jumping-off point for exploring the region, drive in from Ashton, Idaho. Take Cave Falls Road 17 miles, then turn north on Bechler Ranger Station Road and go another 1.5 miles.

The **Bechler River Trail ★★** starts here and leads to one of Yellowstone's coolest spots: the soakable backcountry hot spring called **Mr. Bubbles ★★**. It's one of the only places where getting into a spring is safe (or permitted), and the crowds will be a fraction of what you'll encounter at the front-country Boiling River. Follow the Bechler River 13.5 miles up to the Ferris Fork Campsite; Mr. Bubbles, a large pool deep enough to submerge yourself and splash around, lies a quarter-mile beyond.

The **Bechler Meadows Trail ★★** also departs from the ranger station, but heads into waterfall-rich country northwest of the River Trail. About 6 miles into the journey, the trail fords the river several times as it enters Bechler Canyon, where it passes Colonnade and Iris Falls. Along this trail, you can view the Tetons in the distance and the hot springs that warm the creeks. You can cover a good 30 miles in 3 or 4 days, depending on what turns you take. For a shorter trip, hike 3.5 miles along the Bechler River Trail to the **Boundary Creek Trail,** and then return to the station via the **Bechler Meadows Trails,** a round trip of 7 miles.

Another knockout waterfall hike begins off Grassy Lake Road to the east on the **Cascade Creek Trail.** Link the **Mountain Ash Creek** and **Union Falls Trails,** braving several creek fords along the way, for a 15.6-mile round trip to **Union Falls ★★**. Two creeks merge at the top to form a 260-foot cascade resembling a frothy white volcano, and you'll also find a fine swimming hole off a short spur trail in the area. Choose from several campsites lining the route.

The Bechler River Trail extends all the way to the Old Faithful area for an epic, 32-mile shuttle hike. Beyond Iris Falls and then Ragged Falls, you'll reach a patrol cabin at Three Rivers Junction at the 13-mile mark, a popular camping area. If you continue toward Old Faithful, you'll intersect the **Shoshone Lake Trail** and exit 6.5 miles later.

HEART LAKE AREA

This (somewhat) heart-shaped lake in south-central Yellowstone makes for another popular destination for backcountry travelers: It's relatively easy to get to, cutthroat trout swim its waters, and it offers the chance to summit one of the park's iconic peaks, too. You can do it as an overnight by taking the 7.5-mile (one-way) **Heart Lake Trail ★** out and back; this section of trail overlaps with the 3,100-mile **Continental Divide Trail** that follows the spine of the continent from Mexico to Canada. You'll hike through small thermal areas on the lake's northwestern shore and catch dreamy sunrises on 10,308-foot Mount Sheridan, which looms just to the west. Or make it a 3- or 4-day excursion by continuing around the lake to the **Heart River Trail,** a loop with stretches in an old burn area and involving several challenging river crossings. Don't miss the excellent peak-bagging detour on the **Mount Sheridan Trail,** a steep, 7-mile round trip across alpine tundra to huge views.

THOROFARE AREA

Serious about getting away from it all? This is your trip. The vast meadows, remote peaks, massive plateaus, and abundant wildlife of Yellowstone's southeastern corner—a zone known as the Thorofare—is as off the grid as it gets. You can't get farther from a road anywhere else in the lower 48. Throughout the area, tepee rings and lean-tos are reminders that Native Americans once used this trail as the main route between Jackson Hole and points north. Because it's such a far-flung destination, you're far more likely to see bears, moose, elk, river otters, and loons than you are other backpackers. But if you're experienced enough to handle a week or more in the backcountry, you'll find the Thorofare's relatively flat terrain makes for a thoroughly enjoyable trip. Seasonal bear closures and high water in early summer mean mid-July to early September is prime time in these parts.

The 68-mile point-to-point hike on the **Thorofare Trail ★★** and **South Boundary Trail ★★** takes you deep into the heart of this wild area. Start by tracing the eastern shoreline of Yellowstone Lake (waterfront campsites included) and then the Yellowstone River, traversing grassy meadows in the shadow of 11,000-foot peaks. You'll reach the out-there Thorofare Ranger Station at mile 32, near the horizon-dominating Trident Plateau, then turn west to cross Two Ocean Plateau. The trail briefly dips out of the park and into the Teton Wilderness before following the Snake River en route to the South Entrance Road. Backcountry junkies can also turn the trip into a lollipop loop by connecting to the **Trail Creek Trail** and hiking back to the start for an 80-miler. The **Deer Creek Trail** grants slightly shorter access into the Thorofare from the east, but there's no quick fix for getting here—all part of this wilderness's charm.

BLACK CANYON OF THE YELLOWSTONE

One of the earliest backpacking routes to melt out in the spring, the shuttle hike linking Hellroaring Creek, Yellowstone River, and Blacktail Deer Creek between Mammoth and Tower-Roosevelt travels through some of northern Yellowstone's prettiest river country. The 2- or 3-day trip crosses a pair of suspension bridges, hugs the banks of the mighty Yellowstone, and passes beneath craggy Hellroaring Mountain and through the steep, thickly forested Black Canyon. Wildflowers like golden arrowleaf balsamroot bloom in spring and summer, and there's a good chance of spotting bison, elk, and pronghorn around here. Begin on the **Hellroaring Creek Trail ★** (see Tower-Roosevelt Area day hikes in this chapter) and turn west on the **Yellowstone River Trail ★★**. This stretch features excellent fishing, blufftop views over the waterway, and basalt columns high on the cliffs. Finish by turning south on **Blacktail Creek Trail** and climbing back to the road. Camp along the Yellowstone and/or Hellroaring Creek. Early fall is the best time to hike the canyon, but it's usually passable by mid-May (just watch for high water and ticks). Avoid the dog days of summer, as this area can get hot.

OTHER ACTIVITIES

BIKING   You'd think Yellowstone would be a primo spot for road cycling, what with its hundreds of miles of paved roads through some of the country's most spectacular country. But while bikes are allowed on all public roads, cycling here isn't exactly a Sunday cruise. Roads tend to be narrow and twisty and often lack a shoulder, and traffic is often heavy. Count on dealing with enormous RVs and trailers if you go. Still, well-prepared cyclists can have a great time; make sure to ride cautiously and use reflectors and lights for visibility.

The happy exception to the status quo here is during early spring (typically late Mar and early Apr) and fall (typically Nov), when the park opens roads to cyclists before and after cars are allowed. You'll have the pavement to yourself, but the weather can be brutally cold these times of the year.

Mountain bikers have better luck. Though you can't bike on most backcountry trails, a handful of old dirt or gravel roads are open to cycling. **Blacktail Plateau Drive,** a 6-mile scenic detour near Tower, allows two-way bike traffic, as does the **Old Gardiner Road** near Mammoth. Those with quads of steel can pedal 3 miles uphill to the Mount Washburn summit via **Chittenden Road** or circle Bunsen Peak on the 6-mile **Bunsen Peak Road. Fountain Freight Road** follows Fairy Creek near Midway Geyser Basin for 5.5 miles and makes the trip to Fairy Falls much faster, and cyclists can also zip along the Firehole River most of the way to **Lone Star Geyser.**

Bike rentals are available inside the park at **Old Faithful Snow Lodge** (© **307/344-7311;** www.yellowstonenational parklodges.com) for $35 per day and in the gateway town of West Yellowstone at **Free Heel and Wheel** (© **406/646-7744;** www.freeheelandwheel.com) for $35 to $40 per day.

BOATING   Powerboats are permitted on most of **Yellowstone Lake** (which has the most services and panoramic views) and on **Lewis Lake.** Park concessionaire Xanterra rents motorboats and rowboats out of **Bridge Bay Marina:** A 16-foot rowboat costs $10/hour or $45/day, while an 18-foot motorboat will run you $52.50/hour.

Canoeists and kayaks can paddle on these lakes as well as most other park lakes; the **Lewis Channel** between Lewis and **Shoshone Lakes** is the only river that's open to paddling. Many boat-only campsites along Yellowstone and Shoshone Lakes enable fantastic multiday trips, but be aware that high winds and very cold water can make paddling dangerous. Both motorized and non-motorized boaters need permits, which can be obtained at the South Entrance, Grant Village Backcountry Office, and Bridge Bay Ranger Station ($5/week for nonmotorized and $10/week for motorized).

FISHING   Seven varieties of game fish live in the parks: cutthroat trout, rainbow trout, brown trout, brook trout, lake trout, Arctic grayling, and mountain whitefish. Of the trout, only the cutthroats are native, and they are being pressured in the big lake by the larger lake trout. As a result, you *must* release every cutthroat caught anywhere in Yellowstone, as well as the native Arctic grayling and mountain whitefish. And you *must* keep or kill every single lake trout. In some waterways, you're also required to release some non-native species, too: Check the park's *Fishing Regulations* guide carefully (www.nps.gov/yell/planyourvisit/fishdates.htm).

Other Activities

GETTING OUTDOORS IN YELLOWSTONE

The Yellowstone season opens on the Saturday of Memorial Day weekend and ends on the first Sunday in November. Yellowstone Lake has a slightly shorter season, and the lake's tributaries are closed until July 15 to avoid conflicts between humans and grizzly bears, both of which are attracted to spawning trout.

Many fine anglers come to Yellowstone, and they are well informed about which seasons are best on which stretches of river. In June, try the **Yellowstone River** downstream of Yellowstone Lake, where the cutthroat trout spawn. Fish the **Madison River** near the west entrance in July, and fish again in late fall for rainbow and some brown trout. In late summer, you can try to hook the cutthroats that thin out by September on the **Lamar River,** in the park's beautiful northeast corner.

Fishing on **Yellowstone Lake** was popular until recent years, when regulations designed to bring back the waning population of cutthroat trout began to send some of the trolling powerboats elsewhere. Certain areas of the lake, such as the southeast arm, are closed to motorized boats; this makes the Yellowstone River inlet a lovely area to canoe, camp, and fish.

You can fish the **Yellowstone River** below the Grand Canyon by hiking down into **Seven Mile Hole,** a great place to cast (not much vegetation to snag on) for cutthroat trout from July to September. You'll have the best luck around Sulphur Creek. Other good fishing stretches include the **Gibbon and Firehole Rivers,** which merge to form the Madison River on the park's west side, and the 3-mile **Lewis River Channel** between Shoshone and Lewis lakes during the fall spawning run of brown trout.

There is access on the **Madison River** for anglers with disabilities, 3.5 miles west of Madison Junction at the Haynes Overlook, where you'll find an accessible fishing platform over the river's edge along 70 feet of the bank.

Permits   Park permits are required for Yellowstone anglers ages 16 and older; the permit costs $18 for 3 days, $25 for 7 days, and $40 for the season. Children 15 and under don't need a permit if they are fishing with an adult who has one, but need to pick up a free permit if they're fishing without supervision. Permits are available at any ranger station or visitor center, Yellowstone General Store, and most fishing shops in the gateways.

Supplies & Fishing Guides   If you need supplies or a guide in Gardiner, stop at **Parks' Fly Shop,** 202 Second St. South (℡ **406/848-7314;** www.parksflyshop.com). In West Yellowstone, check **Jacklin's Fly Shop,** 105 Yellowstone Ave. (℡ **406/646-7336;** www.jacklinsflyshop.com). Full-day trips typically cost about $500 for two people in high summer.

Several Jackson, Wyoming–based fishing guides also lead trips into Yellowstone. See "Fishing," in the "Other Activities" section of chapter 6, and the "Getting Outside" section, in chapter 8.

HORSEBACK RIDING   You can BYO horse (or llama, or mule) to the park for day rides or horse-packing trips; all overnight outings require a backcountry permit. If you're more in the market for a catered day ride, concessionaire **Xanterra** (℡ 307/344-7311; www.yellowstonenationalpark-lodges.com) offers mellow, 1- and 2-hour horseback trips out of Canyon Village and Tower-Roosevelt on well-mannered horses ($49 or $72 for riders 8 and up).

Many outfitters have permits to run horse-packing trips to a variety of destinations inside the park (go to www.nps.gov/yell/planyourvisit/stockbusn.htm for a full list). Saddling up with one of them typically means horses, gear, meals, camping equipment, and permits are all included. Prices vary widely according to trip length and number of people, so contact individual outfitters for your options.

WINTER SPORTS & ACTIVITIES

Nope, the park doesn't shut down in the winter. Instead, an entirely new Yellowstone emerges when the snow—all 150 annual inches of it, or 300 inches in the high country—starts flying. Why is a winter trip a great idea? Let us count the ways. One, the crowds melt away, leaving visitors who do venture out into the cold with a shockingly quiet, solitude-filled landscape. Two, snow makes park wildlife easier to spot and track. Winter is an especially great time to look for wolves, which hunt bison slowed down by deep drifts (the bears, however, will be hibernating—which could be a plus, depending on your perspective). Three, snow and ice create a whole new feel: Waterfalls freeze into ripply ice sculptures, geysers and hot springs spew and steam over whitewashed basins, frozen thermal vapors transform trees into "snow ghosts," and thick ice blankets Yellowstone Lake. And four, winter opens up a slew of new outdoor activities, from skiing and snowshoeing to zipping along in a snowmobile.

Naturally, you'll want to be ready for Yellowstone's winter conditions. Daytime highs might be anywhere from 0°F (-18°C) to the 30s (negative teens Celsius), and nighttime lows can reach -20°F (-29°C). The coldest temperature ever recorded here was a frostbite-inducing -66°F (-54°C)! Dress in warm layers and make sure to both eat and drink frequently to stay energized and hydrated.

Only two park hotels open for a December-to-March winter season after a brief shutdown in the fall: **Mammoth Hot Springs Hotel** (p. 132) and the **Old Faithful Snow Lodge** (p. 137). (Mammoth is undergoing renovations and will be closed until the winter of 2018–19.) And the Northeast Entrance Road between Mammoth and Cooke City is the only one that's cleared for cars in winter; traveling anywhere else requires a snowcoach or snowmobile.

Park concessionaire **Xanterra** handles all of the in-park amenities, including lodging, dining, ski shops, ski shuttles, and snowcoach tours. Several other outfitters and gear shops in the gateway towns can also set you up for winter fun. And if you're looking to combine recreation with education, **Yellowstone Forever's** (✆ **406/848-2400;** www.yellowstone. org) winter courses can't be beat. Depending on the season's lineup, you might be able to sign up for wolf-watching expeditions, field-journaling classes, cross-country ski lessons, or winter photography workshops.

CROSS-COUNTRY SKIING   Yellowstone is an amazing place to be on skinny skis. The park grooms ski trails at Mammoth, Old Faithful, and Tower; many other ungroomed, marked ski trails are available in those places too, as well as in the park's northeast corner and at Canyon. Skiers also have free reign over any unplowed road or trail, though you'll want heavy-duty skis to break trail in powder.

Gliding among the geysers is one of Yellowstone's most unique winter activities, making Old Faithful a top spot to explore. You can ski 2.5 miles (one-way) on the groomed **Lone Star Geyser Trail** for a backcountry water show (return via the **Howard Eaton Trail** for a more challenging loop) or circle past geysers and hot springs on the **Biscuit Basin** and **Black Sand Basin Trails.** At Mammoth, the groomed **Upper Terrace Loop** tours around steaming travertine terraces, and the untracked **Bighorn Loop** traces Indian Creek up to expansive views over the Gallatin Range.

The **Bear Den Ski Shops** at Mammoth and Old Faithful rent skis ($16/half day, $25/day) and offer both group and private ski lessons ($35 or $40/hour). Xanterra's ski shuttles will drop you off at Indian Creek, several stops along the Divide Route, and several stops along the Fairy Falls route; either ski back to the hotels or catch the return shuttle after exploring each area. You can also hop on guided ski tours of places like Canyon ($264) or Lone Star Geyser ($57), which include transportation to the trailheads and lunch.

ICE SKATING   **Old Faithful Snow Lodge** maintains an ice rink with free skate rentals, weather permitting. **Mammoth Hot Springs Hotel** has one too, set to reopen in winter 2018-19.

SNOWCOACH TOURS   What, exactly, is a snowcoach? Picture a midsize van or bus with heavy-duty tank treads instead of tires, plus big windows and a toasty heating system, and you get the idea. These lumbering vehicles are one of the primary ways that travelers access Yellowstone when snow blankets the landscape, and they're a lot of fun. If you're bound for Old Faithful Snow Lodge, this is probably how you'll get there. Xanterra's shuttle from Mammoth costs $117 for adults and $58.50 for children each way, and you're allowed two pieces of luggage; you can also find private outfitters out of West Yellowstone or Jackson.

Snowcoaches do more than shuttle you from place to place: You can also sign up to tour the park in one. It's a much warmer way to see the winter sights than a snowmobile, though you'll want to bundle up for the many stops along the way. Xanterra's options range from half-day or full-day scenic routes to tours focused on wildlife-watching or photography, and cost about $50 to $265 for adults. Private outfitters also run a variety of group and custom tours.

For info on Xanterra's tours, call ✆ **307/344-7311** or go to www.yellowstonenationalparklodges.com. **Yellowstone Vacations** (✆ **877/600-4308;** www.yellowstonevacations.com),

Winter Sports & Activities

GETTING OUTDOORS IN YELLOWSTONE

winter **ROAD CONDITIONS**

Due to the high elevation and the abundance of snow, most roads in Yellowstone are closed to all wheeled vehicles in winter. The only major park area that is accessible by car is Mammoth Hot Springs; cars are allowed to drive in the village there. Signs will alert you as to how far south into the park you can go (usually to Tower Junction, 18 miles away). From Tower Junction, it's another 29 miles to the northeast entrance. This entrance is open but not accessible from Red Lodge, Montana, and points east (because the Beartooth Hwy. is closed in winter). You can go only as far as Cooke City, Montana, and the roads are only kept open so that the folks in Cooke City aren't stranded during the long winters. **Snowmobiles, snowcoaches,** and **cross-country skiers,** however, use park roads regularly throughout the winter season. For up-to-the-minute information on weather and road conditions, call ✆ **307/344-2117.**

Basing yourself in **West Yellowstone** is another winter option. From the West Yellowstone entrance, it's only 14 miles to Madison Junction, which presents opportunities to head south to Old Faithful or north to the Grand Canyon and Mammoth Hot Springs. Because this is the most popular way to access the park, plan on making reservations early.

out of West Yellowstone, offers tours to Old Faithful and Canyon. On the south side, Jackson's **Scenic Safaris** (✆ **888/734-8898;** www.scenic-safaris.com) can get you to Old Faithful.

SNOWMOBILING For a faster and more thrilling way to see the park, a snowmobile is the way to go. Suit up (mind that wind chill) and take off over the park's oversnow routes, connecting top destinations and scoping for wildlife along the way. **Warming huts** at West Thumb, Old Faithful, Madison, Indian Creek, Mammoth, Canyon, and Fishing Bridge provide welcome respite from the bitter cold en route.

Winter access rules designed to protect Yellowstone's resources from both noise and emissions pollution make it challenging to plan private snowmobiling trips. Hopefuls can apply for a permit to the **Non-Commercially Guided Snowmobile Access Program** through a lottery open September 1 through 30 for the following winter; four snowmobiling "events" (groups with up to five snowmobiles) are allowed to enter the park at each entrance station per day. Permittees must also complete an online snowmobile education course, and their vehicles must meet certain standards for noise and emissions. For details, go to www.nps.gov/yell/learn/management/ngsap.htm.

If you haven't planned ahead or didn't get lucky in the lottery, guided snowmobile trips can get you cruising in the park without the paperwork. Several outfitters operate in the gateway towns, with West Yellowstone boasting the most options. **Backcountry Adventures** (*C* **406/646-9317;** www.backcountry-adventures.com) runs several daily tours to different park highlights for $209 per snowmobile. **Two Top Snowmobile Rental** (*C* **406/646-7802;** www.twotopsnowmobile.com) is also popular for its tours to Old Faithful and Canyon ($90/snowmobile), as well as private options. The only option near the East Entrance, **Gary Fales Outfitting** (*C* **307/587-3970;** www.garyfalesoutfitting.com) trips take you over Sylvan Pass on an all-day circle tour for $375 per double snowmobile.

SNOWSHOEING   The winter travel method with the lowest learning curve—just strap on the snowshoes and walk—is another excellent way to soak in the snowy landscape. Explore along any of the park's marked ski trails (just don't step in the ski track) or unplowed roads; at Old Faithful, the loop up to Observation Point and Solitary Geyser is snowshoe-only. Park rangers lead free snowshoe walks at Mammoth and West Yellowstone several times a week, and Xanterra runs guided trips to Lone Star Geyser, Canyon, and the Firehole River ($30–$264 for adults). The **Bear Den Ski Shops** at Mammoth and Old Faithful Snow Lodge rent snowshoes for $12.50/half day and $21.75/full day.

EXPLORING GRAND TETON

G rand Teton is a bit like Yellowstone's kid brother—a much smaller slice of a similar ecosystem populated by similar wildlife. But it's also a premier national park in its own right: Few, if any, other parks can claim such a stunning mountain skyline, and the Tetons' backcountry is the stuff of legend for hikers and river rafters. You could blaze through the park roads in a day, but you'd merely be scratching the surface of this fascinating combination of geologic artistry and ecological diversity.

One more bonus Grand Teton has on its northern neighbor: The park's proximity to Jackson, Wyoming, means you can easily combine the alpine wilderness with an A-list travel destination. Where else can you hike in the shadow of 13,000-plus-foot peaks by day, then sit down to a perfectly prepared steak and dance the two-step by night?

ESSENTIALS

ACCESS/ENTRY POINTS Grand Teton National Park runs along a north-south axis, bordered on the west by the Teton Range. **Teton Park Road** skirts along the lakes at the mountains' base. From the **north,** you can enter the park from Yellowstone National Park, which is linked to Grand Teton by an 8-mile stretch of highway (U.S. 89/191/287) running through the **John D. Rockefeller Jr. Memorial Parkway,** along which you might see some bare and blackened trees from the 1988 and 2016 fires. If you enter this way, you will already have paid your entrance fee to both parks,

Grand Teton National Park

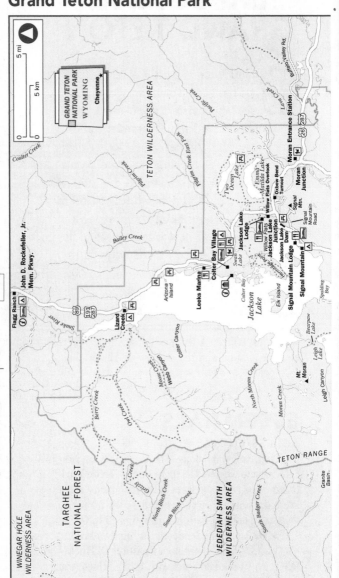

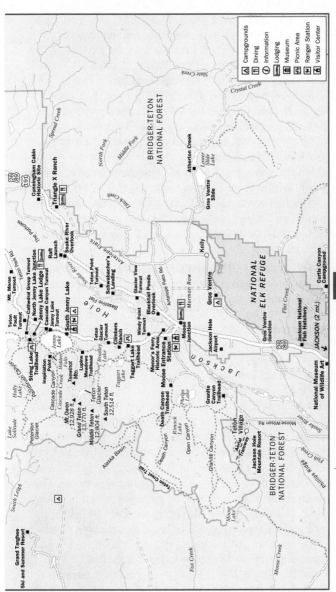

Legend

- ▲ Campgrounds
- ⊞ Dining
- ⓘ Information
- ⌂ Lodging
- ⊞ Museum
- ⊞ Picnic Area
- ⊞ Ranger Station
- ◉ Visitor Center

State Creek

Crystal Creek

Spread Creek

BRIDGER-TETON
NATIONAL FOREST

North Fork

Middle Fork

Ditch Creek

Cunningham Cabin
Historic Site

Triangle X Ranch

Mt. Moran Turnout

The Potholes

Teton Park Rd.

Cathedral Group Turnout
North Jenny Lake Junction
Jenny Lake Lodge
Cascade Canyon Turnout
Jenny Lake

Raft Launch

Snake River Overlook

Atherton Creek

Gros Ventre Slide

Lower Slide Lake

Teton Fault Turnout

String Lake Trailhead

Inspiration Point

Holly Lake

Lake Solitude

South Leigh

Hidden Falls

Cascade Canyon
Cascade Creek

Teewinot Mtn.

Lupine Meadows Trailhead

Mt. Owen
12,928 ft.

Grand Teton
13,770 ft.

Middle Teton
12,804 ft.

South Teton
12,514 ft.

Peterson Glacier

Teton Glacier

Bradley Lake

Taggart Lake

Taggart Lake Trailhead

Climbers Ranch

Teton Glacier Turnout

Menor's Ferry Historic Area
Moose Entrance Station

Windy Point Turnout

Glacier View Turnout

Blacktail Ponds Overlook

Schwabacher's Landing

Teton Point Turnout

Antelope Flats

Baseline Flat

South Jenny Lake

Jenny Lake Turnout

JACKSON HOLE

Moose Junction

Mormon Row

Kelly

Gros Ventre

NATIONAL ELK REFUGE

Gros Ventre Junction

Flat Creek

Curtis Canyon Campground

Jackson National Fish Hatchery

JACKSON (2 mi.)

26 89

National Museum of Wildlife Art

Jackson Hole Airport

Moose-Wilson Rd.

Snake River

Death Canyon Trailhead

Granite Canyon Trailhead

Phelps Lake

Rimrock Lake

Open Canyon

Death Canyon

Granite Canyon

Teton Village

Jackson Hole Aerial Tramway

Jackson Hole Mountain Resort

Alaska Basin

Teton Crest Trail

Fish Creek

Phillips Ridge

Moose Lake

Fox Creek

Moose Creek

BRIDGER-TETON
NATIONAL FOREST

Grand Targhee Ski and Summer Resort

but you can stop at the park information center at Flagg Ranch, just outside Yellowstone, to get Grand Teton information. From mid-December to mid-March, Yellowstone's south entrance is open only to snowmobiles and snowcoaches.

You can also approach the park from the **east,** via U.S. 26/287. This route comes from Dubois, 55 miles east on the other side of the Absaroka and Wind River ranges, and crosses **Togwotee Pass,** where you'll get your first views of the Tetons towering over the valley. Travelers who come this way can continue south on U.S. 26/89/191 to Jackson without paying an entrance fee, and enjoy spectacular mountain and Snake River views.

Finally, you can enter Grand Teton from Jackson in the **south,** driving about 12 miles north on U.S. 26/89/191 to the Moose Junction turnoff and the park's south entrance. Here you'll find the park headquarters and the Craig Thomas Discovery and Visitor Center, plus a small developed area that includes restaurants and shops.

VISITOR CENTERS & INFORMATION There are three visitor centers in Grand Teton National Park, plus a couple of smaller information centers. The **Craig Thomas Discovery and Visitor Center** (© 307/739-3399) is a half-mile west of Moose Junction and jam-packed with info and exhibits about the park's natural and human history. Here you'll find displays on glaciation and park ecosystems, old wagons, Native American artifacts, and a wall on the history of mountaineering in the area. In summer, it's open 8am to 7pm; hours change to 8am to 5pm in May and mid-September to late October and 9am to 5pm in March and April. **Colter Bay Visitor Center** (© 307/739-3594), the northernmost option, features an Indian Arts Gallery and a big porch with Jackson Lake views; it's open 8am to 7pm in summer and 8am to 5pm in May, September, and the first half of October. The **Jenny Lake Visitor Center,** at the southern end of Jenny Lake, is getting an upgrade during summer 2017. Rangers will staff a temporary visitor center in the area until the new center opens in 2018. It's open 8am to 7pm in summer and 8am to 5pm in late May/early June and September.

On the Moose-Wilson Road, you'll find the **Laurance S. Rockefeller Preserve Center** (© 307/739-3654), open 9am to 5pm daily in summer. Finally, there is an information station at the **Flagg Ranch** complex (© **307/543-2372**), which is located approximately 5 miles north of the park's northern boundary, open daily 9am to 4pm from early June through early September, although it may be closed for lunch.

FEES There are no park gates on U.S. 26/89/191, so you can get a free ride through the park on that route; to get off the highway and explore, you'll pay $30 per automobile for a 7-day pass ($50 for both Yellowstone and Grand Teton). If you expect to visit the parks more than once in a year, buy an annual pass for $60. And if you visit parks and national monuments around the country, purchase an **Interagency Annual Pass** for $80 (good for 365 days from the date of purchase at nearly all federal preserves). Anyone ages 62 and older can get an **Interagency Senior Pass** for a one-time fee of $10, and people who are blind or who have a permanent disability can obtain an **Interagency Access Pass,** which is free. All passes are available at any entrance point to the parks. Most of the money from entrance fees goes back into the park where it was collected, so consider it a contribution worth making.

Fees for **tent camping** are between $24 and $37 at all six park campgrounds. For recorded information on campgrounds, call © **307/739-3603.** For more information on camping, see "Where to Camp in Grand Teton," in chapter 7. All tent campgrounds are first-come, first-serve.

SPECIAL REGULATIONS & WARNINGS See chapter 3 for a summary of the major park regulations, which are nearly identical in both parks.

THE HIGHLIGHTS

There's no missing the centerpiece of Grand Teton's natural wonders: The stunning, craggy peaks lining the western skyline of the park dominate pretty much every view. But tear your eyes away from them and you'll find gorgeous lakes, wildflower-lined trails, and a mighty river, too.

THE PEAKS Each of the park's signature peaks has its own personality. The **Cathedral Group** ★★★ encompasses a series of the tallest peaks in the Teton Range, all clustered between Death Canyon to the south and Cascade Canyon to the north. The big daddy is 13,770-foot **Grand Teton,** one of the mountaineering world's prized summits, but **Mount Owen** (12,928 ft.) and **Teewinot** (12,325 ft.) are equally impressive. Nearby peaks like **Middle Teton** (12,804 ft.), **South Teton** (12,514 ft.), and **Mount Moran** (12,605 ft.) make for spectacular bookends. The Teton Range was uplifted along the Teton fault starting 10 million years ago, and the magic of wind, water, and ice has been carving the peaks into their jagged shapes ever since. The Teton peaks tower about 7,000 feet higher than the surrounding valley, making them some of North America's most dramatic mountain vistas.

JACKSON LAKE ★   Grand Teton's largest lake is a natural one, even if it was raised 39 feet by the addition of a dam. Its expansive shoreline holds several visitor facilities, marinas, boat launches, hiking trails, and campgrounds (including **Lizard Creek, Colter Bay,** and **Signal Mountain Campgrounds**). **Colter Bay Village** forms the northernmost visitor hub, complete with a visitor center, swimming beach, restaurants, lodging, and a general store. A bit farther south, the swanky **Jackson Lake Lodge** sits alongside primo moose habitat, and the **Willow Flats Overlook** grants views across a marshland and over to Mount Moran. **Chapel of the Sacred Heart,** a beautiful old Catholic church, is just beyond that. The Signal Mountain area is the southernmost development on Jackson Lake and includes **Signal Mountain Lodge** and the winding **Signal Mountain Road** leading to a summit with amazing Teton Range views.

JENNY LAKE ★★   Much smaller than Jackson Lake but charming in its own right, glacially carved Jenny Lake is a favorite place to soak in the views or set out on a trail. The south end of the lake, where you'll find popular **Jenny Lake Campground,** the visitor center, and trailheads to **Jenny Lake Overlook** and **Hidden Falls/Inspiration Point ★★**, tends to get crowded in the summer. You can swim or boat here, or hop on the **Jenny Lake Boating shuttle** to the **Cascade Canyon Trail ★★★**. Don't miss the one-way scenic drive from North Jenny Lake Junction, which passes several excellent vistas and passes the luxe **Jenny Lake Lodge.**

MOOSE   The first developed area you'll hit if you're coming in from Jackson, the Moose District features a snazzy visitor center and dining, lodging, and shopping options in the tiny **Dornan's** complex. **Menors Ferry Historic District**

preserves a late 19th-century homestead and general store, and the peaceful, 1925-era **Chapel of the Transfiguration** is a lovely spot for contemplation. Excellent hiking trails lead to **Taggart Lake, Bradley Lake,** and **Death Canyon,** and you can pitch a tent at **Gros Ventre Campground.**

SNAKE RIVER ★★   The mighty Snake flows out of Jackson Lake and south through the park, providing fantastic opportunities for floating, rafting, fishing, and scoping for wildlife. One of the prettiest river views awaits at **Oxbow Bend,** a riverbend pullout with expansive views of Mount Moran and frequent moose and trumpeter swan sightings; reach it on U.S. 89/191 just east of Jackson Lake Junction.

IF YOU HAVE ONLY 1 DAY

Unlike Yellowstone, Grand Teton is small enough to make touring it in a single day reasonable. You'll be able to hit most of its main attractions, and a loop road means you won't have to retrace all your steps. This itinerary assumes you'll be coming in from Yellowstone to the north, but you can just as easily follow it starting in Jackson.

From Yellowstone's south entrance, take U.S. 26/89/191 south 8 miles through the **John D. Rockefeller, Jr. Memorial Parkway,** passing **Flagg Ranch**'s information center and lodging/dining. Once inside Grand Teton National Park, the road quickly sticks to **Jackson Lake**'s eastern shore, giving you windshield-wide views of **Mount Moran** and the **Cathedral Group.** Skip **Leeks Marina** and continue south.

First stop: **Colter Bay Village.** Take a spin around the visitor center here and check out the **Indian Arts Gallery** inside. This is also a great spot for a quick swim or paddling trip; you can launch your own boat or rent a kayak or canoe from **Colter Bay Village Marina.** If you'd rather go hiking, keep driving south for the park's best quick-fix trails.

Continue about 5 miles down to the road to **Jackson Lake Lodge** and hop out to see the commanding peak view from the hotel's impressive lobby. A stone's throw farther, **Willow Flats Overlook** is also worth a stop for its vantage point on the Teton Range (and to look for moose). At **Jackson Lake Junction,** turn right to follow **Teton Park Road,** the park's inner route that keeps the peaks front and center in your view.

Turn left to follow **Signal Mountain Road** to its 7,727-foot summit. From here, you'll get a spin-around view of the Cathedral Group, Mount Moran, Jackson Lake, and Jackson Hole. Come back down and press on to **North Jenny Lake Junction,** then turn right to drive the one-way loop to Jenny Lake's northern end. Must-stop pullout: **Cathedral Group Turnout.** You can also access a couple of short day hikes here, like the 3.7-mile loop around **String Lake** or the lakeshore **Jenny Lake Trail.** Exploring the north end of Jenny Lake also means you'll avoid some of the hordes that congregate at the south end.

Rejoin Teton Park Road and continue south (you'll pass one more excellent hike, the 3.9-mile **Taggart Lake Loop**). Take a break at **Menors Ferry Historic District** and peek into a preserved late-1800s homestead, smokehouse, icehouse, and general store, then visit perhaps the most scenically blessed church in the country, **Chapel of the Transfiguration.** Get back in the car for the short jaunt over to **Craig Thomas Discovery and Visitor Center** to learn more about the geology and ecology behind the sights you've been seeing.

From **Moose Junction,** take the park's outer road, U.S. 26/89/191, north. You'll be treated to constant wide-angle views of the Teton peaks with several strategically placed pullouts. Turn left at **Moran Junction** and swing over to **Oxbow Bend** for the chance to see waterfowl or moose. Then either head back up to Yellowstone, grab a Grand Teton campsite (if this is your plan, reserve a site as early in the day as possible), or head south to the lights of Jackson.

TOURING GRAND TETON

It's true, Grand Teton is much more amenable to auto touring than Yellowstone: Park roads connect many attractions, and it's a much more manageable size. But as jaw-dropping as the views of the Teton peaks are from the roads, the park's most stunning scenery is in its backcountry. Sticking purely to the car would mean missing out on that unique Teton magic. You need at least 2 days, and preferably 3, to do this park up right. Save 1 day for a longer hike or paddling trip, 1 for lounging and exploring at Jenny Lake, and 1 for checking out Jackson Lake or hitting up off-the-beaten-path historic sites and viewpoints.

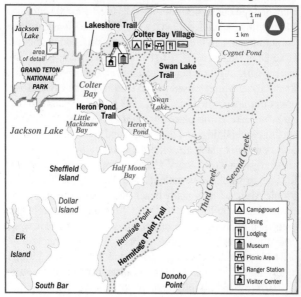

Jackson Lake: Colter Bay Area

Map legend:

- Campground
- Dining
- Lodging
- Museum
- Picnic Area
- Ranger Station
- Visitor Center

Map labels: Jackson Lake · area of detail · GRAND TETON NATIONAL PARK · Lakeshore Trail · Colter Bay Village · Colter Bay · Swan Lake Trail · Heron Pond Trail · Swan Lake · Cygnet Pond · Little Mackinaw Bay · Heron Pond · Jackson Lake · Sheffield Island · Half Moon Bay · Dollar Island · Hermitage Point · Hermitage Point Trail · Third Creek · Second Creek · Elk Island · Donoho Point · South Bar · 1 mi · 1 km

This section kicks off at the northern end of the park, but you could just as easily start exploring from the southern end near Jackson. From Jackson, it's about 13 miles to the Moose Entrance Station, then another 8 miles to the Jenny Lake Visitor Center, another 12 miles to the Jackson Lake Junction, and 5 more miles to Colter Bay.

Jackson Lake & the North End of the Park

Technically, Yellowstone and Grand Teton don't border each other; they're separated by a sliver of federal land called the **John D. Rockefeller Jr. Memorial Parkway.** As you head south from Yellowstone, you'll cover 8 miles of this forested preserve—watch for blackened trunks from the Berry Fire, which forced the evacuation of **Flagg Ranch** in 2016 but thankfully didn't damage the structures. The Flagg Ranch hub has lodging, dining, camping, gas, and a general store. The other important feature here is **Grassy Lake Road,** a remote road granting access to some of the Tetons' wildest, least crowded canyons and free primitive campsites.

The road crosses into Grand Teton National Park and quickly hugs the eastern shoreline of **Jackson Lake ★**. Glaciers gouged out its 400-foot-deep lakebed 10,000 years ago, and melting glacial ice filled it to form the park's largest lake. Though it is a natural waterway, the construction of Jackson Lake Dam (finished in 1916, before Grand Teton was a protected park) to provide irrigation for farmers in Idaho's Snake River Valley raised the lake 39 feet. The Snake River pours into its northern tip, then exits east of the dam. Today, Jackson Lake is the place for sailing, powerboating, windsurfing, waterskiing, and paddling—and swimming, if you're brave enough to face the, er, brisk water.

After passing the **Lizard Creek Campground** (a good bet for late arrivals), a few pullouts, and picnic areas (**Lakeview Picnic Area,** with its sandy beach and aspen groves, is especially nice), you'll come to **Leeks Marina.** You can launch your own boats here, but no rentals are available. There's a casual pizza and ice cream joint open in the summer.

The busiest outpost on the north side, **Colter Bay Village,** is just south. Get oriented at the **Colter Bay Visitor Center** (© **307/739-3594**), most notable for its free **Indian Arts Gallery ★**. Visiting Native American artists display and sell their handiwork during the summer. You'll also find an auditorium showing park programs, an info desk, and a bookstore. Water lovers will appreciate the swimming beach and marina here; rent a kayak, canoe, or powerboat or sign up for a boat cruise or guided fishing outing. A general store stocks groceries. On the hiking front, **Hermitage Point** trail connects Colter Bay to a network of trails through sagebrush meadows and lodgepole forests near the lakeshore. Looking to stay the night? Your options include cabins, an RV park, and **Colter Bay Campground** (see chapter 7 for details).

Continuing south, the next major attraction is the stately **Jackson Lake Lodge,** a National Historic Landmark with a picture-perfect view of Jackson Lake and the Teton peaks. Even if you're not staying here, swing by to check it out. The upscale lobby, with its 60-foot windows framing Mount Moran and the Cathedral Group and cozy fireplaces, makes a wonderful spot for coffee or a cocktail. Several restaurants line the lobby, including the fancy **Mural Room** with its historic namesake paintings, and boutiques round out the offerings. This area is also the jumping-off point for some excellent, lesser-traveled trails in the park's northeast region. Circle **Christian Pond** on an easy, 3.3-mile loop, or connect to the longer trails around **Emma Matilda** and **Two Ocean Lakes.** You can also hike (or drive) to the **Willow Flats Overlook,** a beautiful spot to scope for moose—especially in the fall, when the abundant willow bushes turn gold.

Just beyond, you'll hit **Jackson Lake Junction.** Turning east brings you to the Moran entrance and an alternate access point to Emma Matilda and Two Ocean Lakes. Going south from there traces the Snake River along U.S. 26/89/191 on the eastern edge of the park. But doing so would skip far too many inner-park sights, so turn right to follow **Teton Park Road.** You'll cross **Jackson Lake Dam** and soon reach the resplendent log church, **Chapel of the Sacred Heart ★**. If you're religious, the 1930s-era Catholic chapel holds services from June to September; if not, the church's rustic architecture is worth a look, and it's a peaceful place for a lakeside picnic.

Press on south to reach the hub of Jackson Lake's south side, **Signal Mountain.** The lake side of this junction holds a lodge, a couple of restaurants, a gas station, a general store with surprisingly healthy snack options, and the **Signal Mountain Campground.** Park concessionaire Forever Resorts also runs guided fishing trips and rents boats (powerboats, canoes, and kayaks) from the marina here. Across the street, **Signal Mountain Road** winds up the side of 7,727-foot **Signal Mountain ★**. Don't miss this short detour to drink in views of the lake and the shockingly vertical Tetons to the distant Absarokas, Gros Ventre, and Yellowstone Plateau, all the way across Jackson Hole. About 3 miles from the base of the hill, before you reach the summit, a paved path leads to **Jackson Point Overlook,** the spot where photographer William Henry Jackson shot his famous landscapes of Jackson Lake and the Tetons in the 1870s.

Looking for a hideaway? On the right (west) side of the road between Signal Mountain and North Jenny Lake Junction, approximately 2 miles south of the Mount Moran turnout, is an unmarked, unpaved road leading to **Spalding Bay.** It's a sheltered little backcountry camping area and boat launch area with a primitive restroom. It's a great place to be alone with spectacular views of the lake and mountains. If you decide to camp, a first-come, first-served backcountry

Jackson Lake: Signal Mountain Area

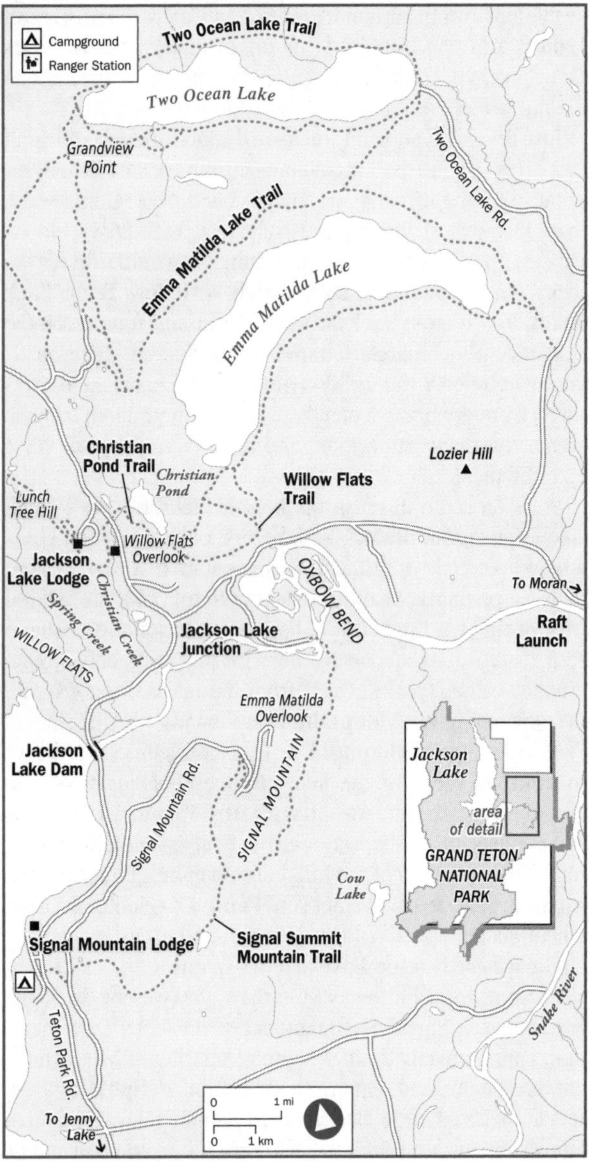

Campground
Ranger Station
Two Ocean Lake Trail
Two Ocean Lake
Grandview Point
Two Ocean Lake Rd.
Emma Matilda Lake Trail
Emma Matilda Lake
Christian Pond Trail
Christian Pond
Lozier Hill
Willow Flats Trail
Lunch Tree Hill
Willow Flats Overlook
Jackson Lake Lodge
Spring Creek
Christian Creek
WILLOW FLATS
OXBOW BEND
To Moran
Raft Launch
Jackson Lake Junction
Emma Matilda Overlook
Jackson Lake Dam
Signal Mountain Rd.
SIGNAL MOUNTAIN
Jackson Lake
area of detail
GRAND TETON NATIONAL PARK
Cow Lake
Signal Mountain Lodge
Signal Summit Mountain Trail
Teton Park Rd.
Snake River
To Jenny Lake
0
1 mi
0
1 km

permit is required (even though it's accessible by road). An automobile or SUV will have no problem with this road, but speed had better not be of the essence to you. Passing through brush and forest, you might just spot a moose.

Jenny Lake & the South End of the Park

Driving in the Tetons is like starring in your own car commercial—all winding roads looping beneath super-scenic peaks—and nowhere is that more true than the Jenny Lake area. At **North Jenny Lake Junction,** turn right to access a one-way drive skirting the trailheads for **Leigh** and **String Lakes,** two mountain-ringed lakes that make top-notch day hikes. Continue past **Jenny Lake Lodge** to trace the northeast shore of **Jenny Lake ★★**. Named for a Shoshone woman married to a prominent 1870s mountain guide, this bucolic lake tucked between Teewinot and Rockchuck Peak has been a favorite travelers' destination since the early 1900s.

The scenic drive pops you back out on Teton Park Road just north of the bustling **South Jenny Lake Junction.** Here you'll find the newly remodeled **Jenny Lake Visitor Center** (slated to open in 2018), a general store, a backcountry office—and very limited parking, so arrive early if you don't want to circle the lots. The park's best campground, **Jenny Lake Campground,** is also here; show up first thing in the morning for the best chance at a site. This is a spot for (somewhat polar-bear) swimming, boating, fishing, and hiking. The flat, 6.8-mile **Jenny Lake Trail** circles the lake, or you can hike it partway to reach **Hidden Falls** and **Inspiration Point.** Or take the **Jenny Lake Boating** (✆ **307/734-9227;** www.jennylakeboating.com) shuttle straight across the lake to the **Cascade Canyon** trailhead; round trips cost $15 for adults and $8 for children.

Farther south, the **Teton Glacier Turnout** gives you a peek at one of the few park glaciers visible from the road. Teton Glacier grew for several hundred years until, pressured by the increasing summer temperatures of the past century, it reversed course and began retreating. Just beyond that is the turnoff to **Climber's Ranch,** a dorm-style lodge run by the **American Alpine Club** (✆ **307/733-7271;** www.american alpineclub.org/grand-teton-climbers-ranch). It caters to climbers staging attempts on the Teton's most prized peaks,

Jenny Lake Area & Trails

Map legend:
- Picnic Area
- Primitive Campsite
- Ranger Station
- Visitor Center

Labels on map:
Trapper Lake
Bearpaw Lake
Mystic Isle
Leigh Lake
Paintbrush Canyon Trail
PAINTBRUSH CANYON
Boulder Island
Leigh Lake Trail
North Jenny Lake Junction
To Jackson Lake
String Lake Trail
String Lake
String Lake Trail
Rockchuck Peak
Leigh and String Lake Trailheads
Cathedral Group Scenic Turnout
Jenny Lake Lodge
Mount St. John
Laurel Lake
one way
Lake of the Crags
Ramshead Lake
Arrowhead Pool
HANGING CANYON
Ribbon Cascade
Symmetry Spire
Ice Point
Storm Point
Cascade Canyon Trail
Inspiration Point
Jenny Lake Loop Trail
Hidden Falls
South Jenny Lake Junction
Hidden Falls Trail
Jenny Lake
Jenny Lake Loop Trail
Jenny Lake
GRAND TETON NATIONAL PARK
area of detail
Moose Ponds
Jenny Lake Trailhead
Broken Falls
Moose Ponds Trail
LUPINE MEADOWS
Teton Park Rd.
Delta Lake
Lupine Meadows Trailhead
Glacier Falls
To Moose

but anyone can bunk here for $25 night ($16 club members); it's one of the best lodging deals for miles around. Another stone's throw beyond that, the **Taggart Lake Trail** leads to a beautiful tarn at the foot of Avalanche Canyon.

If you're curious about what life was like in Jackson Hole before it became the recreation mecca/glitterati hotspot it is today, stop at the next attraction down the road: **Menors Ferry Historic District ★**. Homesteader Bill Menor operated a simple ferry across the Snake River and a general store here in the 1890s and early 1900s, and today you can see reconstructed versions of both. The general store is half historic exhibit, half actual store selling local honey and jam; there's also a smokehouse, icehouse, and 1917 cabin furnished in pioneer style. Nearby, the 1925 log **Chapel of the Transfiguration ★** is a sought-after wedding venue; Episcopal services are still held on summer Sundays.

By now you've reached **Moose,** the southernmost entrance to the park. The **Craig Thomas Discovery and Visitor Center** offers a treasure trove of info on the area's human history, ecology, wildlife, and geology: Check out historic wagons and Native American arrows, watch the park movie, and peruse the wall dedicated to the development of modern mountaineering, or just pick up maps and chat with rangers. Just across the road you'll find **Dornan's,** a complex with lodging, restaurants, a grocery store, gift shop, wine shop, and places to buy fishing and climbing gear or rent kayaks.

The East Side of the Park

The 18-mile outer park road, U.S. 26/89/191, is usually a faster trip through the park, and it grants panoramic views of the Tetons from its more removed vantage point. But if you're coming up to the park from Jackson, consider turning east at **Gros Ventre Junction,** just south of the airport, instead of beelining north. The less-busy **Gros Ventre Campground**'s sites line the river of the same name, just north of that is **Mormon Row ★**. Mormon settlers from Utah homesteaded here in the 1890s, and a couple of quaint old barns still stand imposingly in front of the Teton tableau.

For an interesting side trip, continue east on Gros Ventre Road past the tiny town of **Kelly** into the **Bridger-Teton National Forest.** In 1925, a mile-wide slab of Sheep Mountain broke free and poured into the canyon, blocking the Gros

Ventre River with 50 million cubic yards of rock and debris. The landslide dammed the river and formed Lower Slide Lake, but the dam failed in spring rains 2 years later and flooded Kelly almost into nonexistence. Interpretive signs at the site point out remnants of these geologic events.

Otherwise, **Antelope Flats Road** will take you back to the highway. Less than a mile down U.S. 26/89/191, on the left, **Blacktail Ponds Overlook** offers an opportunity to see how beavers build dams and the effect these hard-working creatures have on the flow of the streams. Two miles farther along U.S. 26/89/191, you'll reach the **Glacier View Turnout,** which offers views of an area that 140,000 to 160,000 years ago was filled with a 4,000-foot-thick glacier. Then **Schwabacher Road** gives you your first access to the Snake River: Drive the 1-mile dirt road to **Lower Schwabacher Landing** to launch a raft, try your hand at fly-fishing, or just enjoy the view of the peaks reflected in the Snake. Keep your eyes peeled for bald eagles, osprey, moose, beavers, and river otters.

The **Snake River Overlook ★**, approximately 4 miles down the road beyond the Glacier View Turnout, is the most famous view of the Teton Range and the Snake River, immortalized by Ansel Adams. From this overlook, you'll also see at least 3 separate, distinctive 200-foot-high plateaus that roll from the riverbed to the valley floor, a vivid portrayal of the power of the glaciers and ice floes that sculpted this area. In the early 1800s, this was a prime hunting ground for John Jacob Astor's Pacific Fur Company and a certain David E. Jackson, for whom the lake and valley are named. But by 1840, the popularity of silk hats had put an end to fur trapping, and the hunters disappeared. Good thing—by the time they departed, the beaver population was almost decimated.

A half-mile north of the Snake River Overlook is the paved but steep road (a 19 percent grade) to **Deadman's Bar,** a peaceful clearing on the river. Back in 1886, the unsolved murders of three gold miners gave this spot its morbid name.

History lovers will also appreciate **Cunningham Cabin Historic Site** just up the road. The 1888 cabin built by ranchers John and Margaret Cunningham is fairly nondescript, but it's one of the few remaining buildings left from the homesteading era, and the .8-mile (one-way) hike across sage flats to reach it gives excellent Teton peak views and a great shot at seeing bison.

Touring Grand Teton

EXPLORING GRAND TETON

Once you hit **Moran Junction,** turn west to rejoin the inner park road. You'll pass **Pacific Creek Road,** an alternate access point to trails to Emma Matilda and Two Ocean lakes, and the **Oxbow Bend Turnout ★**, a gorgeous, marshy site along the Snake River where moose and waterfowl roam.

ORGANIZED TOURS

If you'd rather hand over the wheel to someone else and concentrate on the scenery, park concessionaire **Grand Teton Lodge Company** (*© 307/543-2811;* www.gtlc.com) offers 4-hour bus tours of the park, with an emphasis on ecology and wildlife-watching. Adult tickets cost $70 and kids' tickets (ages 3–11) are $32; tours run late May to early October. The company also runs Yellowstone tours, and you'll get a discount for signing up for both. There are also several aquatic tours on offer on Jackson Lake, including a scenic cruise; a kids' cruise; a geology-focused tour; and breakfast, lunch, and dinner tours with al fresco meals on Elk Island. Tickets range from $32 to $67 for adults and $14 to $38 for kids.

Several companies out of Jackson also offer small-group tours of the park. **Brushbuck Tours** (*© 307/699-2999;* www.brushbucktours.com) is one of the best: Sign up for half-day, full-day, or multiday tours built around wildlife-watching and photography. Prices start at $450 for a half day and $700 for a full day for one or two people in summer. The more affordable **Jackson Hole Wildlife Safaris** (*© 307/690-6402;* www.jacksonholewildlifesafaris.com) is also popular for its wildlife-centered tours in Grand Teton and Yellowstone, ranging from a half day to 5 days in length. Tours cost $145 to $275 per person for single-day summer trips. Both outfitters also offer winter tours.

The excellent **Teton Science Schools ★★**, 700 Coyote Canyon Road, Jackson, WY 83001 (*© 307/733-1313;* www.tetonscience.org), runs several immersive all-ages programs on five campuses. Besides summer camps and student-focused options, travelers can sign up for a variety of adult and family programs. Especially popular: biologist-led **Wildlife Expeditions,** from half-day sojourns to multiday trips, designed to be crash courses on the park's wildlife. Some programs add hiking, floating, and sleigh rides to boot.

RANGER PROGRAMS

Like Yellowstone, Grand Teton also offers a wide variety of top-notch free **ranger programs** ★★★ out of Colter Bay, Jenny Lake, Moose, and the Laurance S. Rockefeller Preserve. They run all year, but the widest variety will be found June through early September. Check the park newspaper for details, or visit www.nps.gov/grte/planyourvisit/ranger-programs.htm.

Rangers lead walks on trails such as Taggart Lake, Inspiration Point, or Swan Lake. If history is your thing, look for programs that explore Menors Ferry Historic District or demonstrate how Native Americans constructed their tipis. You'll find science-based programs on park ecology, bear safety, geology, and wildlife at several different stations in the park. Evening programs at Gros Ventre and Colter Bay Campgrounds cover a slew of park topics after the sun goes down, and in winter, rangers will take you on snowshoe hikes around Taggart Lake (reservations required).

And, just like at Yellowstone, Grand Teton offers the **Junior Ranger Program** for kids (and adults, for that matter). Grab a copy of The Grand Adventure workbook at any visitor center and complete the educational activities therein—including attending a ranger program and going on a hike—to earn an official Junior Ranger badge.

GETTING OUTDOORS IN GRAND TETON

Grand Teton may be a smaller park than Yellowstone, but its hiking is every bit as stellar. Backcountry trails skirt placid lakes, delve into wildflower-filled canyons, and even scurry straight up the tallest peaks. With some of the most dramatic wilderness scenery in the country just a hike away, the Tetons are bound to amaze anyone who steps off the beaten track.

If you have limited time to explore, choose your hiking destinations based on your favorite ecosystems. Looking for a lakefront hike? Try the shoreline trails at Jackson or Jenny Lakes. Challenging climbs with great views? Head up one of the canyons. Trying to get away from it all? Hit the Teton Crest Trail. This selection of top trails will help you decide.

DAY HIKES

The park's many trails vary greatly in length and level of difficulty, so you'll want to consult with rangers before tackling them. The rangers can suggest hikes suited to your ability and update you on everything from bear activity to trail conditions to weather concerns. They also conduct guided walks. *Remember:* If you are planning to hike for more than 30 minutes, carry a supply of water and some rain gear.

Colter Bay Area

For a **map** showing the trails in this area, see chapter 5.

Lakeshore Trail ★ Trace both sides of a Jackson Lake peninsula on this figure-eight loop (one circle is .9 mile, the other 1.1 miles) with slap-in-the-face views of Mount Moran, Grand Teton, Teewinot, and the other marquee Teton peaks. You'll follow a wide, tree-lined footpath to pebbly beaches with vistas across the lake to the peaks beyond. This easy hike has a big payoff, making it a good choice for families.

2 miles round-trip. Easy. Access: Trailhead is at the Marina entrance.

TRAILS FROM THE HERMITAGE POINT TRAILHEAD

The **Hermitage Point Trailhead,** near the marina, leads to a series of connecting loops that lead past tranquil ponds, head out on a scenic peninsula, and extend all the way to **Jackson Lake Lodge.** Make sure you have a good map when planning your hike in this area—options abound, and it can be easy to take a wrong turn if you don't know where you want to go.

Hermitage Point Loop ★ This long loop out to Hermitage Point and back crosses through forest, rolling meadows, and wetlands out to the shore of Jackson Lake, making it an excellent opportunity to spot a variety of wildlife, such as bears, moose, elk, beavers, osprey, and herons. Stay close to the lakeshore on your way out, passing ponds and tracing Half Moon Bay before hiking out to the end of Hermitage Point, where the Teton peaks loom large across the lake. Follow Third Creek on your way back to the trailhead.

10 miles round-trip. Moderate. Access: Trailhead is just south of the Colter Bay Ranger Station.

Heron Pond/Swan Lake Loop ★ For a shorter route through the Hermitage Point area, this easy loop cruises past

---

A Blooming Photo Op

Not far from the trail head, the **Hermitage Point Loop** ★ opens to a broad, sagebrush-carpeted meadow. In the summer, the area blooms with wildflowers, offering one of the most spectacular views of colossal **Mount Moran,** which is as impressive in its own way as the Grand Teton. To avoid retracing your steps past Heron Pond, bear right at the third creek intersection and continue straight ahead to the corrals at Colter Bay—this route adds no distance to the hike.

Heron Pond and Swan Lake. You'll still explore a variety of habitats, so keep your eyes peeled for wildlife and summer wildflowers. From the Hermitage Point Trailhead, trace Jackson Lake's shoreline to Heron Pond, a small, lily pad-speckled lake that grants views of the big peaks. This is an excellent spot to scope for moose or beavers. Follow the eastern shore, then turn left at the next junction to head toward Swan Lake. And yes, you might spot trumpeter swans—North America's largest native waterfowl—nesting on this grassy lake. From here, it's a short walk back to the trailhead.

3 miles round-trip. Easy. Access: Trailhead is at Hermitage Point Trailhead, Colter Bay.

Willow Flats Trail ★   What's better than the lovely view from Willow Flats Overlook? This hike, which takes you right into the middle of that idyllic scene. From Colter Bay, head east to Cygnet Lake, then cross Pilgrim Creek to access the marshy, willow-filled wetlands. The mountain views are expansive, and you might spot moose grazing on the abundant greenery. The trail leads to Jackson Lake Lodge, a nice excuse to treat yourself to lunch. Retrace your steps for a longer trip, or drop a car here ahead of time to cut the hike in half.

10.6 miles round-trip. Easy. Access: Horse corrals at Colter Bay.

Jackson Lake Lodge Area

For a map showing the trails in this area, see chapter 5.

Christian Pond to Grand View Point ★   This easy-access hike from Jackson Lake Lodge circles a pleasant pond before climbing to standout views of the Teton Range at 7,286-foot Grand View Point. Head east from the lodge to reach pint-size Christian Pond in just .2 mile. Follow its western shore to a hilltop vista on its southern side, then circle northeast, then north through sagebrush flats where elk, pronghorn, or coyotes might be roaming. After the junction leading to Grand View Point, continue north for the moderate climb to the point. Soak in views of the Grand Teton, Mount Moran, and all the rest, plus Two Ocean and Emma Matilda lakes. Backtrack, then go west to return to the lodge.

6.8 miles round-trip. Easy to moderate. Access: Trailhead is near Jackson Lake Lodge corrals.

A wide-open meadow near the summit of Signal Mountain presents an excellent opportunity to look to the west for photos of both **Mount Moran** and the **Teton Range.** The best time to take those photos is before 11am, when the sun will be mostly at your back, or in the early evening, when the sun will be lower in the sky to the west.

Signal Mountain Trail ★★ Why drive up a mountain when you can hike it? Hoofing it up the peak offers a chance to spot wildlife like bears and mule deer and wander among summer wildflowers—plus bragging rights over everyone who merely motored up. Hike through evergreen forest to a junction at one end of a loop: Take the southern leg on the way up to pass ponds and good wildlife habitat. Press on to Jackson Point Overlook (the trail stops short of the summit) for picture-perfect views of Mountain Moran and the rest of the Tetons, Jackson Lake, and the Snake River. Hike the northern leg of the loop on the way back for views along this wide-open ridge.

6.8 miles round-trip. Moderate. Access: Trailhead is near the entrance to the Signal Mountain Lodge.

Two Ocean & Emma Matilda Lake Trails

You can arrive at these lakes from the east or west: From the west, you begin at the Grand View Point Trailhead, 1 mile north of Jackson Lake Lodge, or at the Christian Pond Trailhead, just east of Jackson Lake Lodge. From the east, you go up Pacific Creek Road, 4 miles east of Jackson Lake Junction on the road to the Moran entrance. There is a pullout for Emma Matilda Lake 2 miles up this road, or you can go a half-mile farther, take a left on Two Ocean Lake Road, and go to the Two Ocean Lake Trailhead parking lot, from which trails lead to both lakes.

Emma Matilda Lake ★ The larger of the two lakes tucked into this northeastern corner of the park, Emma Matilda Lake offers excellent wildlife habitat, rolling terrain, and a splendid backcountry waterfront. We like starting from the trailhead on Pacific Creek Road. Head for the north shore first to hike it counterclockwise, looking out for ripe thimble-berries in high summer—but be aware that bears love them too, so practice good bear safety. Hike through aspen groves and up a steep ridgeline with birds-eye views over the lake, then swing south through sagebrush meadows. The southern shore is primarily a thick spruce/fir forest, save for the sweeping vantage point of Lookout Rock. You can also combine this loop with a circumnavigation of Two Ocean Lake for a much longer trip.

9.9-mile loop. Easy to moderate. Access: Emma Matilda Lake Trailhead on Pacific Creek Rd.

Two Ocean Lake ★★ The hike around this lake is shorter and easier than Emma Matilda's trail, but you still get the same wildlife-scoping, wildflowers, and lake views—plus a chance to ascend to awe-inspiring views at Grand View Point. From the Two Ocean Trailhead, hike counterclockwise through meadows and aspen groves with peekaboo views of Two Ocean Lake and the Teton summits. Look out for water-fowl such as ducks, trumpeter swans, grebes, and loons. Once you start curving around the western edge of the lake, you can add on the 1-mile (one-way) spur up Grand View Point (see the Christian Pond to Grand View Point hike, p. 115) for the best vistas of the day. Huckleberries and thimbleberries are plentiful along the southern shore, so you can enjoy a foraged snack—just be very mindful of bears. This trail links up with Emma Matilda Lake Trail for a longer trip.

6.4-mile loop, or 8.6 miles round-trip with the Grand View Point side trek. Easy to moderate. Access: Two Ocean Lake Trailhead on Two Ocean Lake Rd.

Jenny Lake Area

A **map** showing the trails in this area is in chapter 5.

Amphitheater Lake ★★★ Beeline from the valley floor to the park's stunning subalpine zone in 1 day on this exceptional (if quite steep—elevation gain is nearly 3,000 ft.) hike. Your views of the Grand Teton, Mount Owen, and Jackson get better with every step, and soon you'll ascend to vistas over Bradley and Taggart Lake, too. You know you're almost there when you reach Surprise Lake; press on to the stony cirque cradling Amphitheater Lake, topped off by Disappointment Peak lording over the water to the west. Not

GRAND TETON FOR kids

Children of all ages visiting the park are encouraged to explore and experience Grand Teton as members of the **Junior Ranger** program. To participate, pick up a copy of the Junior Ranger activity brochure at any visitor center, and then complete the projects outlined in the booklet during your stay. When you present a completed project to a ranger at the Moose, Jenny Lake, or Colter Bay visitor centers, you'll be awarded a Young Naturalist patch.

Two trails within Grand Teton are especially kid-friendly. At 7 miles round-trip, the entire Jenny Lake Loop Trail is a bit long for kids, but take the boat shuttle across Jenny Lake to the **Inspiration Point Trail ★★** portion, which is less than a mile long. The **Christian Pond Trail**, a level, 1-mile round-trip from the corrals at Jackson Lake Lodge, is also a nice diversion, offering great views and a chance to see myriad waterfowl.

only is the trail blessed with views, glacial moraine features, and wildflower meadows, but you might see black or grizzly bears, moose, or grouse—making it one of the finest day hikes in the entire park. As an additional or alternate destination, spire-riddled Garnet Canyon awaits just south on a spur branching off the main trail at mile 3.

10 miles round-trip. Difficult. Access: Lupine Meadows Trailhead.

Forks of Cascade Canyon ★★★ One of the park's absolute stunners, Cascade Canyon is a U-shaped glacial valley surrounded by skyscraping peaks. Up here, incredibly jagged mountains fill the horizon, marmots and pikas scamper among boulders, and black and grizzly bears feast on abundant trailside berries. Cascade Canyon is a popular entry point for backpackers seeking to explore the Teton's remote wilderness, but this stretch is doable in a day for fit hikers. Catch the shuttle across Jenny Lake to shave a few miles off the trip, then start with a short, steep grunt up to Inspiration Point (see "Hidden Falls & Inspiration Point," below). Most people turn around here, but press on to climb up this narrowing valley, where Mount Owen dominates the view. You'll also skirt under Table Mountain and The Wigwams, two peaks straddling the western border of the canyon. Turn around at the Forks, the point where the canyon (and trail) split in two: North will take you to Lake Solitude and south heads for Hurricane Pass, both top-shelf backpacking trips.

9.6 miles round-trip via the Jenny Lake shuttle; 14.4 miles round-trip from Jenny Lake Trailhead. Moderate to difficult. Access: Inspiration Point.

Hidden Falls & Inspiration Point Trail ★★   It's easy to see why this short, beautiful hike is one of the park's most popular: You can get a taste of the wildlife, views, and water features that make the Teton so special. The shortest route to **Hidden Falls** starts from the boat dock after taking the Jenny Lake shuttle; from there, you'll cross Cascade Creek and hike through huckleberry patches to the dramatic, 200-foot cascade (via a short spur trail). But don't stop here: The .5-mile (one-way) climb up to **Inspiration Point** is worth it. Tiptoe along a rocky trail cut into a cliff face to reach this, well, inspirational view across Jenny Lake to Jackson and the Gros Ventre Wilderness. For a longer trip, skip the boat and hike the long way around Jenny Lake on the Lakeshore Trail, a move that extends the out-and-back hike to 5 miles.

2.2 miles round-trip from boat dock; 5 miles round-trip from Jenny Lake Trailhead. Moderate. Access: Trailheads are at the east or west shore boat docks of Jenny Lake (if you take the boat shuttle).

Jenny Lake Loop ★★   Circling the park's second-largest lake makes for a mellow, view-packed trip. You can hike it in either direction, but hugging the eastern shore earlier in the day means you'll escape more of the road noise from the Jenny Lake scenic drive. From the east side, the park's biggest peaks rise directly across the lake—the biggies like Grand Teton as well as Rockchuck or Baxter Pinnacle. On the west, wildfire-burned areas alternate with thimbleberry bushes and forest; from here, you can also tack on the out-and-back to Hidden Falls and Inspiration Point. A trail to **Moose Ponds** heads south around the southern tip of Jenny Lake (stop here to look for the namesake beasts) then circles back to the start.

7.1 miles round-trip. Easy to moderate. Access: Trailhead is at the east shore boat dock.

Leigh Lake ★★   Mount Moran looms large in this hike along a large lake just north of Jenny Lake, especially at the start—but you'll also earn a front-row view of Teewinot,

Rockchuck, and Mount Woodring, and probably shake many of the Jenny Lake crowds. The trail starts on the northern end of String Lake, then traces the eastern shore of Leigh Lake through woods with frequent openings to gaze at the peaks. The beaches you'll pass provide the best uninterrupted views. Once you've hit the northern tip of Leigh, you can also continue another .9 mile to **Bearpaw** and **Trapper Lakes,** two smaller, picturesque lakes with even more solitude.

7.4 miles round-trip; 9.2 miles round-trip to Trapper Lake). Easy to moderate. Access: Trailhead is at the end of a spur road off the Jenny Lake scenic drive, .5 mile past the String Lake Trailhead.

String Lake Loop ★   Easy hiking with excellent views are what you get with this pleasant trip circumnavigating String Lake. The trail clings to the eastern shore, with views of Mount Moran and the Cathedral Group. Cross the Leigh Lake outlet and head into the forest, then traverse an open slope that provides a nice look back at String Lake. Ambitious hikers can combine this loop with the Leigh Lake hike, above.

3.7 miles round-trip. Easy. Access: String Lake Trailhead.

Paintbrush Canyon to Holly Lake ★★★   Gorgeous Paintbrush Canyon is a popular backpacking destination, but strong hikers can get a taste of the magic on this trip up to Holly Lake. You'll climb to views over Leigh Lake and wander through a colorful canyon blanketed with paintbrush, gentian, and columbine blossoms, not to mention dip a toe in glacial Holly Lake, a high-country tarn at the base of 11,590-foot Mount Woodring. The trail starts on the String Lake Loop, then ascends through the rocky, rough terrain of Paintbrush Canyon to your turnaround point at the lake.

13 miles round-trip. Difficult. Access: Leigh Lake Trailhead.

Taggart and Bradley Lakes ★★   The effort-to-reward ratio is stacked in your favor on this loop to a pair of super-scenic backcountry lakes: Views of major peaks like Grand Teton, Middle Teton, Teewinot, and Mount Owen await almost from the start, and the peaks look even more impressive rising behind the green-blue lake waters. Head straight for Bradley Lake, passing through a conifer-aspen forest on the way. Turn southwest on the Valley Trail to drop down to Taggart Lake. Both are fine places to unpack a picnic and stay awhile. Finish by hiking another 1.5 miles back on the Taggart Lake Trail.

5-mile loop. Moderate. Access: Trailhead is west of Teton Park Rd., approximately 6 miles south of Jenny Lake.

Laurance S. Rockefeller Preserve

Phelps Lake Loop ★★ The Laurance S. Rockefeller Preserve sits in the southern part of the park, encapsulating beautiful and lesser-traveled backcountry. For a quick taste of the area's trails, loop around peak-ringed Phelps Lake: You'll get views of the mouth of Death Canyon, 10,551-foot Albright Peak, and 11,241-foot Prospectors Mountain, plus a bounty of summer wildflowers and a chance to see bears and moose. Hike around the eastern shore first for the best mountain-lake vistas, passing a few sandy beach rest stops, then swing around to the western shore to stroll through blooming fireweed, asters, and coneflower. The trail also connects to the ominously named Death Canyon, another lovely chasm leading into the Teton high country.

6.9-miles loop. Moderate. Access: Laurance S. Rockefeller Preserve Center, 3.6 miles southwest of Moose Junction off Moose-Wilson Rd.

EXPLORING THE BACKCOUNTRY

The Tetons are impressive enough from the roads—so just imagine how magnificent the park is once you hike into the deep wilderness. As in Yellowstone, a permit is required for camping in the backcountry; some can be reserved, but the majority are set aside for walk-in campers. You can request a permit for a designated campsite or a camping "zone," where you'll have a choice of sites within the zone boundaries.

For general information on backpacking and safety, see chapter 10, plus p. 83 for a list of essential backpacking gear.

INFORMATION BEFORE YOU GO For background information, check out the *Grand Teton Backcountry Camping* guide at www.nps.gov/grte/planyourvisit/back.htm. For recorded information, call ✆ **307/739-3602.**

BACKCOUNTRY PERMITS All backcountry campers need a permit. To reserve one in advance, request a permit via www.recreation.gov. The reservation period runs from the first Wednesday in January through May 15 for the following summer, and reservations cost $35 per party. You can also try for a walk-in permit the day before you intend to set out. They cost $25 at visitor centers or the Jenny Lake Ranger Station.

Note: The reservation is just that, a reservation; upon your arrival at the park, you'll need to secure the permit. Permits are issued at the Craig Thomas and Colter Bay Visitor Centers and at the Jenny Lake Ranger station.

WHEN TO GO   Remember that this region has a short summer and virtually no spring. While the valley floor is usually clear in May, some of the high-country trails might not be free of snow or high water until early July. Check with rangers to find out when specific campsites are usually open.

MAPS   Topographic maps of Grand Teton are available from the U.S. Geological Survey and National Geographic's *Trails Illustrated* Maps series (© 800/962-1643; www.natgeomaps.com). You can buy the latter, as well as maps for nearby national forests, from the **Grand Teton Association** (© 307/739-3406; www.grandtetonpark.org).

The Backcountry in Grand Teton

Just like at Yellowstone, backpacking in the Tetons is the premier way to experience the park. But here you have another option you don't have in Yellowstone: **mountaineering** in the area's classic peaks. For more details on trips and outfitters, see "Climbing," in the "Other Activities" section below.

The most coveted overnight backpacking trip in the park is the 19-mile **Cascade Canyon-Paintbrush Canyon Loop ★★★**. This route takes you through two of the park's most scenically blessed canyons, rife with multicolored wildflowers, jewel-like alpine lakes, incredible mountain views, and a chance to spot moose, bears, and harlequin ducks. Starting from the **Cascade Canyon Trail** west of Jenny Lake, climb to expanding views en route to the North Fork of Cascade Canyon. You can camp here, or continue past Lake Solitude and the Paintbrush Divide to Holly Lake, another lovely tent spot in the cirque rounding Mount Woodring. Finish by descending on the **Paintbrush Canyon Trail** back down to Jenny Lake. Considering its strenuous elevation gain, loose scree, and the possibility of snow lingering in the high country well into the summer, this trip is best for backpackers with some mountain experience.

This route also links up with the all-star **Teton Crest Trail,** a high-altitude route that runs roughly north-south through the Teton peaks. If you have more time, you can expand your loop by hiking out through one of the park's southern canyons. Some of the best views in the Tetons—and truly, in the entire continental U.S.—await on this stunning trail. If you swing south from the top of Cascade Canyon, you'll skirt behind Mount Owen, the Grand Teton, and the Middle Teton to reach **Schoolroom Glacier,** a remnant ice field beside a bright blue tarn, and then 10,400-foot **Hurricane Pass.** Pressing on takes you into the **Caribou-Targhee National Forest's Jedediah Smith Wilderness** and **Alaska Basin,** a wide-open, high-altitude zone dotted with lakes and wildflowers.

Another stellar (and less crowded) trip circles through the southern Tetons via the **Death Canyon Loop ★★★**. This 27-miler takes you to the renowned **Death Canyon Shelf,** a narrow plateau with cliffside campsites and phenomenal mountain vistas. To get there, hike up **Death Canyon** and camp in the shadow of vertiginous granite rock walls. From here you'll cross 9,600-foot **Fox Creek Pass** and reach the shelf, night two's destination. Wrap up the trip by crossing 9,725-foot **Mount Meek Pass,** skirting the southern edge of Alaska Basin, chugging up 10,790-foot **Static Peak Divide,** and looping back to the start.

The park's proximity to Jackson Hole Mountain Resort has a hidden perk for backpackers: You can take the aerial tram up **Rendezvous Mountain ★**, which gives you a fast track into the high country. The tram enables quicker trips north toward **Marion Lake** or south to **Moose Lake** (in the Jedediah Smith Wilderness) or connects to loops through **Granite Canyon ★★** or **Open Canyon ★**.

OTHER ACTIVITIES

In addition to the activities listed here, check out some of the other options in the Jackson area, listed in chapter 8.

BIKING Cycling is allowed on all paved and unpaved roads that also permit cars (but not trails), but you'll want to be choosy about your destinations—in some spots, the park roads are narrow, winding, and choked with traffic, which makes for less-than-satisfying cycling. Fortunately, an off-road, paved multiuse path extending from Jackson all the way to Jenny Lake makes bike trips much safer and more enjoyable. Road cyclists can also link the Teton Park Road with the one-way **Jenny Lake Scenic Loop** for a 7-mile ride that's partially on a multiuse path. Another option: Ride the path to **Antelope Flats Road** and south along (unpaved) **Mormon Row** to see pioneer-era homesteads and big views of the Gros Ventre. Iron-lunged road riders might also try the steep climb up **Signal Mountain Road** to the 7,727-foot summit (best in the early morning, before traffic picks up).

For mountain bikers, **Two Ocean Lake Road** is a 6-mile out-and-back over a rolling landscape, or cruise the 15-mile **River Road** along the Snake River. For a bike-packing trip, 52-mile **Grassy Lake Road** crosses the John D. Rockefeller, Jr. Memorial Parkway past backcountry campsites and serene lakes between Flagg Ranch and Ashton, Idaho.

Look for maps and brochures with bike routes at visitor centers. **Adventure Sports** at Dornan's (© **307/733-2415;** www.dornans.com), inside the park boundaries at Moose Junction, rents adult and child bikes (complete with helmets and repair kits) as well as bike trailers.

BOATING & PADDLING   Watersports aficionados have plenty of opportunities for fun at Grand Teton, in large part thanks to Jackson Lake. There, you can cruise around in a motorboat, waterski, windsurf, sail, or paddle your own kayak, canoe, or stand-up paddleboard (SUP). Jenny Lake is also open to powerboats (maximum 10 horsepower) as well as human-powered watercraft. Paddlers alone have access to most other park lakes: Phelps, Emma Matilda, Two Ocean, Taggart, Bradley, String, Leigh, and Bearpaw Lakes all allow canoes, kayaks, and SUPs.

You'll need a permit to launch your own watercraft, which costs $40 for motorized boats and $10 for nonmotorized craft; pick one up at the Craig Thomas, Jenny Lake, or Colter Bay Visitor Centers. You can rent motorboats from the **Grand Teton Lodge Company** at **Colter Bay Village Marina** (© **307/543-3100;** www.gtlc.com) for $44 per hour or $181 for the day; **Signal Mountain Lodge** (© **307/543-2831;** www. signalmountainlodge.com) also rents deck cruisers, pontoons, runabout boats, and fishing boats for $42 to $129 per hour or $185 to $675 per day, depending on boat type.

Both those outfitters rent kayaks and canoes ($20–$23 per hour at Colter Bay Village, $19–$25 per hour at Signal Mountain Lodge), as does **Jenny Lake Boating** (✆ 307/734-9227; www.jennylakeboating.com) for $20 per hour. And if you want someone else to handle all the logistics, outfitter **O.A.R.S** (✆ 800/346-6277; www.oars.com) offers highly recommended 2-night kayak-camping trips for $549 to $599 for adults ($449–$499 for kids).

Scenic cruises ★ are another popular way to get out on the water. **Grand Teton Lodge Company** (✆ 307/543-2811; www.gtlc.com) runs several options, including an overview trip, a kid-focused ride, a geology-based cruise, and cruises that include cowboy-style fare served on Elk Island. Prices range from $32 ($14 for kids 3–11) to $67 ($38 for kids). **Jenny Lake Boating** (✆ 307/734-9227; www.jennylakeboating.com) offers hour-long cruises on Jenny Lake for $19 ($11 for kids 2–11).

CLIMBING & MOUNTAINEERING   The Tetons loom large in the American climbing community—few other destinations offer the combination of so many classic climbing routes, superlative peaks, a long history of mountaineering, and easy access—here, you can bag an iconic summit in just a day or two. But don't let those so-close-you-can-almost-touch-'em peaks fool you: Mountaineering here is a serious endeavor demanding skill and experience. The park's rock, ice, and mixed routes are very strenuous and can be dangerous, even for the pros, thanks to unpredictable mountain weather. If you decide to tackle them on your own, make sure you know how to use an ice axe and crampons, and travel with experienced partners. Skills not so sharp, but still want to make a go of it? Sign up for lessons or a guided trip with the well-regarded climbing outfitters below.

You don't need a special climbing permit to take to the slopes, but you will need a backcountry camping permit if you'll be out overnight (see "Backcountry Permits," p. 121). **Jenny Lake Ranger Station** (✆ 307/739-3343) is the base for the park's climbing rangers and the best place to get info on current conditions. Climbers often launch their trips from the American Alpine Club's iconic **Grand Teton Climbers'**

Ranch (② **307/733-7271;** www.americanalpineclub.org). You don't have to be a climber to reserve one of the $16 bunks ($25 for non–club members), but the rustic accommodations cater to those with summit hopes.

If you're looking for guidance, two renowned outfitters offer both guided climbs and lessons: **Exum Mountain Guides** (② **307/733-2297;** www.exumguides.com) and **Jackson Hole Mountain Guides** (② **307/733-4979;** www.jhmg. com). Climbing classes will run you about $170 to $190, while an attempt on the Grand Teton costs $600 to $750 for a group trip. Both can also take you up plenty of other Teton summits, such as Mount Moran, Mount Owen, Middle Teton, South Teton, Teewinot, and Buck Mountain.

FISHING   Plentiful fish and beautiful scenery make Grand Teton beloved among anglers. You can cast or troll the lakes and crystal-clear streams for brook, brown, lake, and cutthroat trout, plus whitefish; Jackson Lake, Jenny Lake, and the Snake River are all popular destinations, but most waterways in the park are open for fishing. Many anglers prefer fishing from a boat in Jackson and Jenny Lakes, but you can also stake out spots along the shorelines of both. The Snake River is a biggie for fly-fishing, particularly the first few miles below the Jackson Lake Dam. Blacktail Ponds and Schwabacher's Landing also draw in hopeful anglers.

You'll need a Wyoming fishing license to ply the waters here, which costs $14 per day and $92 per year for nonresidents, plus a $12.50 Conservation Stamp for all but 1-day passes (residents get discounted rates). Nonresidents under age 14 can fish for free with a licensed adult. Pick up a license at Snake River Angler at Dornan's, Signal Mountain Lodge, Colter Bay Marina, or Headwaters Lodge at Flagg Ranch. Also make sure to pick up a copy of the park's fishing brochure to learn rules and regulations, such as seasonal closures. Jackson Lake, for example, closes to fishing in the month of October, and in the Snake River, you must release all cutthroat trout between November 1 and March 31.

Several outfitters based inside the park and in Jackson run guided fishing trips. In the park, **Grand Teton Lodge Company** (② **307/543-3100;** www.gtlc.com) will take you out on a private boat in Jackson Lake or along the Snake River; lake trip rates are $98 per hour, and fly-fishing the Snake is $465 for a half-day and $555 for a full day. **Signal Mountain Lodge**'s (℗ **307/543-2831;** www.signalmountainlodge.com) Jackson Lake boat trips will run you $109 per hour or $295 for a half-day. For a list of other fishing concessionaires, go to www.nps.gov/grte/planyourvisit/fish.htm.

FLOATING & RAFTING   Getting the duck's-eye view of the park from the Snake River is alternately thrilling and idyllic, depending where you are in the 27 miles that wind through the Tetons. Some sections are tranquil, with lots of time to scope for moose, bald eagles, and other animals that frequently visit the river's edge; others are turbulent and challenging, for experienced rafters only. Obstacles such as swift current, confusing braided channels, shifting logjams, and strong upstream winds make paddling difficult. Proceed with caution if you'd like to float on your own, and check with rangers for up-to-date information on flow and conditions. The easiest stretch of the Snake is the 5-mile segment from Jackson Lake Dam to Pacific Creek. North of Jackson Lake and south of Pacific Creek, swifter water and route-finding challenges make rafting a skilled boater's game.

If you're not an advanced boater, never fear: Quite a few outfitters will guide you. **Grand Teton Lodge Company** (℗ **307/543-2811;** www.gtlc.com) runs 10-mile floats on two sections of the Snake River ($75 adults, $48 kids 6–11) and offers meal trips with burgers and hot dogs at lunch or steak and trout at dinner ($78–$88 adults, $55–$60 kids). **Signal Mountain Lodge**'s (℗ **307/543-2831;** www.signalmountain lodge.com) 10-mile floats cost $76 for adults and $47 for kids 6 to 12. Check www.nps.gov/grte/planyourvisit/boat.htm for a list of the other rafting concessionaires who operate trips in the park. Many of these outfitters also offer whitewater trips south of the park (see "Jackson, Wyoming," in chapter 8).

HORSEBACK RIDING   Horses are allowed on some park trails; some backcountry camping zones also allow stock. The most popular trailheads for BYO horse rides are String and Leigh Lakes, Poker Flats, and Taggart Lake. A few outfitters also offer guided horseback rides in the park: **Grand Teton Lodge Company** (℗ **307/543-2811;** www.gtlc.com) has 1- and 2-hour rides out of Jackson Lake Lodge, Colter Bay Village, and Headwaters Lodge at Flagg Ranch ($43–$80). Guests at the nearby **Lost Creek Ranch & Spa**

(© **307/733-3435;** www.lostcreekcom) and **Jenny Lake Lodge** (© **307/543-3100;** www.gtlc.com) also enjoy horseback riding options. For the names of several other companies that organize horseback trips in Jackson Hole, see "Jackson, Wyoming," in chapter 8.

WINTER SPORTS & ACTIVITIES

Park facilities pretty much shut down during the winter, except for a ranger posted at the Jackson Hole and Greater Yellowstone Visitor Center in Jackson, and the park shows no signs of becoming a winter magnet, à la Yellowstone. That may be just as well—you can enjoy some quiet, fun times in the park without the crowds.

WINTER ROAD CONDITIONS The park's primary roads, U.S. 26/89/191 and U.S. 26/287, remain open and plowed all winter from Jackson to Flagg Ranch. **Teton Park Road** and **Moose-Wilson Road** close to cars between November 1 and April 30. The 14-mile section of Teton Park Road between Taggart Lake Trailhead and Signal Mountain Lodge is open and groomed for cross-country skiing and snowshoeing, though.

SPORTING GOODS & EQUIPMENT RENTALS Jackson has enough sporting equipment places to keep all of Wyoming outfitted. **Skinny Skis,** 65 W. Deloney Ave. (© **307/733-6094;** www.skinnyskis.com), is an outdoors shop with a focus on Nordic skiing and touring skis, skate skis, alpine touring skis, and snowshoes for rent. **Teton Mountaineering,** 170 N. Cache St. (© **307/733-3595;** www.tetonmtn.com), also rents all the gear for backcountry ski touring, cross-country skiing, skate skiing, and snowshoeing. And **Teton Backcountry Rentals,** at 565 N. Cache St. (© **307/828-1885;** www.tetonbcrentals.com), offers everything from splitboards to avalanche safety gear to ice axes, plus, they'll deliver to your hotel.

BACKCOUNTRY SKIING Adventurous and experienced skiers flock to the park to earn their turns, preferring the wilderness slopes to the in-bounds skiing at the nearby resorts. There's excellent skiing to be had in these peaks, but fierce weather and significant avalanche risk makes this suitable for advanced-level skiers only. For a safe introduction to backcountry skiing, go guided with **Exum Mountain Guides** or **Jackson Hole Mountain Guides** (see "Climbing & Mountaineering," above).

CROSS-COUNTRY SKIING   Kicking and gliding under the snowcapped Teton Range makes for an unforgettable day in the snow, and there are plenty of options for Nordic skiers in the park. The park grooms 14 miles of the closed **Teton Park Road** (between Taggart Lake Trailhead and Signal Mountain Lodge) for classic and skate skiing. Other winter routes are ungroomed and unmarked, so plan to use burlier touring skis. For an easier day, try the 8-mile, mostly flat loop that takes off from the Taggart Lake Trailhead and follows **Jenny Lake Trail** along Cottonwood Creek, then returns on Teton Park Road. The 3-mile **Swan Lake/Heron Pond Loop** from Colter Bay is just as lovely in winter as it is in summer, and the 4.2-mile **South Flagg Canyon Trail** from Flagg Ranch is another easy outing. For something more challenging, ski up the **Signal Mountain Summit Road,** a 12-mile round-trip with a fun downhill return.

SNOWMOBILING   Snowmobiling is a popular winter option in the area. Snowmobiling is allowed on the frozen surface of Jackson Lake for ice fishing only, on Grassy Lake Road, and in the nearby Bridger-Teton National Forest, immediately east of the park.

SNOWSHOEING   You can snowshoe pretty much anywhere you can cross-country ski in the park. Plus, rangers lead snowshoe trips from the Taggart Lake Trailhead several times a week, late December to mid-March. Call ⓒ **307/739-3399** to make reservations. The Grand Teton Association provides rental snowshoes for a suggested donation of $5.

WHERE TO STAY & EAT IN THE PARKS

Do all you can to stay inside park borders at least 1 night. It's not that the gateway towns around the parks don't have excellent lodging options: They do. But there's something absolutely magical about bunking right where the action is. You'll be treated to a quieter, wilder park after the daytrippers depart, and without the light pollution from civilization, a dazzling night sky awaits. You'll also be inside the park during the prime wildlife-watching times of dawn and dusk; it's quite something to be able to roll out of bed and spy elk, bison, and even bears and wolves steps from your room. What's more, you'll skip the sometimes-lengthy drive into the heart of the parks from the gateway towns, maximizing your time.

Carefully consider your lodging choices before you book. Yellowstone is a vast park, and you might spend several hours driving between its top attractions even when you start inside—so where you sleep can have a big impact on what and how much you'll be able to see in a day. Grand Teton is a bit more manageable, but staying at the southern versus northern ends can determine whether you can venture into Yellowstone the same day, too. If you're most interested in geysers, shoot for a room at Old Faithful; grab a cabin at Roosevelt Lodge or a campsite in the Lamar Valley if you want to join the dawn wolf-watching patrol; go for Lake Yellowstone Hotel, Colter Bay Village, or Jackson Lake Lodge if you're into water activities. That said, though, take advantage of any park lodging you can. Hotels and campsites are in high demand, and every one offers its own incredible experience.

WHERE TO STAY IN YELLOWSTONE

Yellowstone hosts more than 4 million visitors each year—so in-park rooms are at an absolute premium. That's doubly true for summer, but demand is also high in spring and fall. Solution: Book your rooms *early.* A year or even more in advance is not too soon. Make reservations directly with **Yellowstone National Park Lodges,** run by concessionaire Xanterra Parks & Resorts (✆ **307/344-7311;** www.yellowstonenationalparklodges. com). But don't despair if you're late to the party: Cancelations mean that scattered rooms open up almost every day, even in high summer. To snag one, call several times a day to check for new openings, and be ready to snap up anything that opens up.

WHAT YOU'LL REALLY pay

The prices quoted here are rack rates, the maximum that the hotels charge; it is likely that you'll end up paying these rates in Yellowstone and Grand Teton unless you arrive in spring or fall. The concessionaires do not offer a great deal of discounts, thanks to the short summer season in both parks and the fact that occupancy is near 100% all summer long. During slow times, however, it's possible to obtain a room at an expensive property for the same rate as at a more moderate one.

In both parks, April and October are the bargain months, but the sheer number of visitors the rest of the year overwhelms the capacity. If you're looking for a bargain, your best bets are the gateway cities of Cooke City and Gardiner, Montana (see chapter 8). In Cody, Wyoming, you'll be lucky to get a room for less than $100 per night in peak season; in Jackson, Wyoming, $200 is a more realistic baseline for in-town lodgings. You'll want to shop online for deals, but I tend to look hard in Teton Village in summer: You still have easy access to Jackson (and better access to Grand Teton National Park), but the rooms here are intended for the winter ski crowd, and summer vacancies are the norm. In winter, save money by staying in Jackson and taking the free shuttle to the slopes at Jackson Hole Mountain Resort.

Note: Quoted discount rates almost never include breakfast, hotel tax, or any other fees.

Most of Yellowstone's lodges are open from early May to early October, with a few opening their doors in early June. Mammoth Hot Springs Hotel and Cabins and Old Faithful Snow Lodge are the only options that remain open in winter for the cross-country skiing and snowmobile/snowcoach crowd. Both reopen in mid-December and shut down again in mid-March, though Mammoth is scheduled to be closed for renovations in the winter of 2017–18. All park lodges are typically fully booked for most of the summer/fall season, but it's easier to land a room in the first few weeks of May. While visitation used to slow down after Labor Day, in the past few years things have remained humming until the last lodges close, so don't count on an easy autumn getaway.

The park lodges have been lovingly maintained in the historic style in which most of them were built—meaning you won't find in-room TVs or Wi-Fi, pools, or continental breakfasts. Rooms have heat (sometimes from a woodstove, as at Roosevelt Lodge) but no air conditioning, which is usually not a problem in Yellowstone's cool climate. It's all part of the away-from-it-all charm of a Yellowstone vacation, but if you must have cable TV and Wi-Fi, stay in one of the more modern hotels in a gateway town (see chapter 8).

Mammoth Hot Springs Area

5 miles from the Gardiner (north) entrance to Yellowstone.

If you're traveling to the park from points north, Mammoth Hot Springs is the first hub you'll hit—and it's a fine base of operations for history buffs, wildlife-watchers, and geology fans. Besides the historic Mammoth Hotel, the complex also features Fort Yellowstone, where rangers from the U.S. Army lived from the 1890s to 1918. Elk frequently graze on the lawn outside the hotel, and the area's top attraction—the sculpted travertine terraces—should be on everyone's to-do list.

Mammoth Hot Springs Hotel and Cabins ★★ A stone's throw from the steaming stair-step Mammoth terrace formations, this complex's historic buildings (the oldest date back to 1911) and jaunty striped buntings take you back to the era when cars were new inside the park. Historic touches—think clawfoot tubs in some rooms and the lounge's elaborate wooden U.S. map—extend inside the hotel as well, but rooms are generally updated and streamlined, with simple wooden furniture and accents. Cottage-style cabins with small patios cluster behind the hotel; four of them come with private outdoor hot tubs. Some cabins and a few hotel rooms have shared baths, but all hotel rooms have their own bathrooms. On the uniqueness scale, the hotel sits somewhere between the show-stopping appeal of Old Faithful Inn and Lake Yellowstone Hotel and the no-nonsense lodging at Grant Village, but its proximity to attractions, trailheads, and guided tours make it a worthwhile base for a night or two. Plus, it's one of two park properties open in the winter (at least, it will be after renovations are complete; the reopening date hadn't yet been scheduled at press time).

At Mammoth Hot Springs. ✆ **307/344-7311.** www.yellowstone nationalparklodges.com. 215 units. $93–$155 double; $99–$192 cabin; $270 hot tub cabin; $514 suite. Late Apr to Oct and mid-Dec to late Feb. **Amenities:** 2 restaurants; lounge; Wi-Fi in lounge only, starting at $5/hr.

Canyon Village Area

40 miles from the West Yellowstone (west) entrance; 38 miles from the Gardiner (north) entrance.

The Grand Canyon of the Yellowstone, with its two astonishing waterfalls, is one of the park's superstar attractions. Canyon Village serves as its bustling jumping-off point, where hordes of travelers come for food, souvenir shopping, or a stop at one of the park's most impressive visitor centers. Ranger programs and activities give you plenty to do when you're done oohing and aahing at the gorge itself.

Canyon Lodge and Cabins ★ Canyon Lodge's five new buildings opened in 2015 and 2016 (two additional lodges date back to the 1990s). The latest lodges were constructed with the eco-friendly LEED process. They have the feel of a contemporary resort, complete with thoughtful touches like subway-tiled bathrooms and sleek black wooden headboards. The cabins, on the other hand, are a bit dated—but I find their log cabin-style furnishings rather inviting, and they're much more spacious. Don't expect canyon views: The lodging complex actually sits a half-mile from the rest of the village in a nondescript lodgepole pine forest, and you'll have to drive to the canyon itself. And the sheer number of rooms and the super-busy village area mean Canyon isn't the place for a quiet, off-the-grid vibe.

In Canyon Village. ✆ **307/344-7311.** www.yellowstonenational parklodges.com. 600 units. $144–$273 double; $210 cabin; $514 suite. Early June to late Sept. **Amenities:** 2 restaurants; lounge; deli; Wi-Fi in main dining building only; $5/hr.

Tower-Roosevelt Area

23 miles from the Gardiner (north) entrance; 29 miles from the northeast entrance.

This small development in north-central Yellowstone takes half its name from the fact that Teddy Roosevelt once camped in the area (the other half comes from nearby Tower Fall). Our 26th president had a good eye for location: The junction sits at the doorstep of the wildlife-packed Lamar Valley, making early-morning wolf- and bear-spotting expeditions easy. And it's far enough off the beaten path to feel like a throwback to a simpler time; you won't have to jostle with thousands of other travelers like you will at Old Faithful and Canyon.

Roosevelt Lodge Cabins ★★ Yellowstone's simplest lodging is also one of its coolest—a collection of tiny, ultra-rustic cabins, most of which are heated by woodstove (city slickers should request one of the few with electric heat). What the cabins lack in elbowroom and modern hotel amenities they make up for in pioneer ambiance, and you're at Yellowstone—you'll be playing outside all day, anyway. Frontier cabins have bathrooms, while Roughrider cabins share communal facilities with showers. Guests gather in the log-and-wicker rocking chairs on the main lodge's front porch for sunrise and sunset views over the Lamar Valley. "Rosie" is a great spot for families, thanks to its easy access to horseback riding and stagecoach rides at the adjacent corral, and kiddos love the Old West Cookout ride (on horseback or wagon) to an al fresco cowboy-style dinner.

At Tower Junction. ☏ **307/344-7311.** www.yellowstonenationalpark lodges.com. 80 cabins, 12 with private bathroom. $91–$145 cabin with shared bathroom. Early June to early Sept. **Amenities:** Restaurant; lounge; no Wi-Fi.

Lake Village Area

27 miles from the east entrance; 56 miles from the West Yellowstone (west) entrance; 43 miles from the south entrance.

This complex on the northern shore of enormous Yellowstone Lake is *the* spot for an old-fashioned waterfront getaway. Hiking trails, scenic lake cruises, guided fishing trips, and boat rentals are all on offer in the area, but no one would blame you if you simply whiled away the hours staring at the lake, either. You'll also find several dining options, gift shops, and a nearby visitor center at Fishing Bridge.

Lake Lodge Cabins ★ These cabins along Yellowstone Lake are the *I Love Lucy* of park lodging: a bit outdated, perhaps, but still charming. And they're the way to go if you're looking for lakefront lodging without breaking the bank. The cabins are basic, with log furniture and fishing-themed quilts, plus private bathrooms (some with tubs, some just showers). The main lodge offers a much nicer place to hang out: Curl up by the giant stone fireplace or nab one of the rocking chairs on the wide front porch for an unforgettable sunset. The food at the cafeteria is lackluster: Stroll over to the Lake Yellowstone Hotel dining room instead.

On Yellowstone Lake. ℂ **307/344-7311.** www.yellowstonenational parklodges.com. 186 cabins, $90–$209. Early June to late Sept. **Amenities:** Restaurant; lounge; Wi-Fi in lounge and cafeteria only, starting at $5/hr.

Lake Yellowstone Hotel and Cabins ★★★ The most upscale lodging in the park, the creamy-yellow Lake Yellowstone Hotel channels the *Downton Abbey* spirit: From the elegant sunroom with picture windows of the lake to the fancy cocktails to the live piano music tinkling through the lounge most evenings, you could almost believe you've gone back in time to a more genteel era. First built in 1891 and fully renovated in 2014, the hotel has hung on to its Colonial Revival charm. Rooms are beautifully furnished, with large tile bathrooms; some have a lake view (although you'll pay more for it). You'll find older, more standard amenities in the standalone Sandpiper Lodge and cabins, but their proximity to the hotel's glamorous common spaces make them a worthy way to save cash without missing out on the scene.

Yellowstone Lake. ℂ **307/344-7311.** www.yellowstonenationalpark lodges.com. 300 units. $244–$438 double; $162 cabin; $590–$711 suite. Mid-May to early Oct. **Amenities:** 2 restaurants; lounge; business center; wired internet in rooms, starting at $5/hr.

Grant Village Area

22 miles from the south entrance; 47 miles from the West Yellowstone (west) entrance.

Grant is the first developed area you'll hit coming up from the park's south entrance, a sprawling collection of lodge rooms, restaurants, a giant campground, visitor center, and general store. Though the area in general is undistinguished, it still has some excellent lake views and one hidden gem of a restaurant, plus great wildlife-watching opportunities.

Grant Village ★ The rooms in these six lodge buildings, all dating back to the early 1980s and renovated in 2016, are nothing to write home about—most large tours base themselves out of Grant, which perhaps explains the one-size-fits-all feel. But the motel-style accommodations have much nicer furnishings than your standard roadside stop, you're only a short stroll from Yellowstone Lake, and West Thumb Geyser Basin is a 5-minute drive away. There's no grand lobby here, but all buildings have common rooms with couches and tables. Some rooms have lake views.

On the West Thumb of Yellowstone Lake. © **307/344-7311.** www.yellowstonenationalparklodges.com. 300 units. $237 double. Mid-May to early Oct. **Amenities:** 2 restaurants; lounge; Wi-Fi in check-in building only, starting at $5/hr.

Old Faithful Area

30 miles from the West Yellowstone (west) entrance; 39 miles from the south entrance.

If there's a single can't-miss spot in this gigantic park, it's the Old Faithful area. Upper Geyser Basin, home to the world's densest concentration of geysers, is the centerpiece of this hub, but you'll find plenty of manmade attractions, too: three lodging options, five restaurants, a top-notch visitor center, and a general store. And Old Faithful Snow Lodge is one of two hotels open in winter, and the only one open until the winter of 2018-19 (when Mammoth Hot Springs Hotel renovations will be completed).

Old Faithful Inn ★★★ The circa 1903-04 Old Faithful Inn is Yellowstone's most-requested hotel—and it deserves every bit of attention it gets. From its steep, wooden-shingled roof to its 76-foot-tall, log-walled lobby to its towering stone fireplace, you've never seen anything like it—in a national park or anywhere else. Stay in the old house if you can: Although these rooms are rustic, with log or wood-paneled walls and shared bathrooms, they offer the best, most historic vibe (and the bathrooms are quite nice). The crème de la crème rooms are the dormers on the front-center side of the building, with three queen beds and views over Upper Geyser Basin. The East and West Wing rooms are larger but more basic, though they have private bathrooms. Suites come with fridges, couches, and a snack basket. If you can tear yourself away from gazing at the stunning architecture, activities abound: Photo safaris, historic bus tours, and a fascinating guided hotel tour all jump off from here.

At Old Faithful. © **307/344-7311.** www.yellowstonenationalpark lodges.com. 329 units. $118–$191 old house room; $227–$294 old house 2-room unit; $236–$276 double; $519–$590 suite. Early May to early Oct. **Amenities:** 2 restaurants; lounge; no Wi-Fi.

Old Faithful Lodge Cabins ★★

The cluster of cabins east of the geyser basin are typical Yellowstone fare: basic furniture accentuated with pine cones, plaid blankets, tiny bathrooms or shared bathhouse space. But the location elevates these bargain cabins to the next level. They're tucked away in a young lodgepole pine forest and offer a surprisingly peaceful escape from the madness around Old Faithful, just steps away. Some even have views of the famous spouter, but my money is on the cabins that border a back meadow with a stream and several small, unnamed thermal features, where guests often spot bears passing through. The main lodge houses a cafeteria, bakery/ice cream shop, and gift shop, plus a cozy lobby with a huge window framing Old Faithful.

At Old Faithful. © **307/344-7311.** www.yellowstonenationalpark lodges.com. 97 units, with another 67 to be added in 2017. $91 cabin with shared bathroom; $151 cabin with private bathroom. Mid-May to early Oct. **Amenities:** Restaurants; snack bar; no Wi-Fi.

Old Faithful Snow Lodge and Cabins ★★

Yellowstone's newest full-service hotel (finished in 1999) would feel right at home at a modern ski resort. The place is done up in contemporary style featuring exposed beams, wrought iron accents and lots of blond wood, and the lobby fireplace and enclosed sitting porch offer plenty of spaces to curl up with a hot toddy. The high-end feel extends to the spacious lodge rooms, which have beds with high wooden headboards, wood shutters, and evergreen-shaped lamps, plus cozy window seats in some rooms; all have private baths with tubs. The cabins out back are more affordable and less flashy: Western cabins have run-of-the-mill furnishings and closet-sized private bathrooms, while Frontier cabins are much smaller, with wood-panel walls and shower-only bathrooms.

At Old Faithful. ☎ **307/344-7311.** www.yellowstonenationalpark lodges.com. 134 units. $272–$315 double; $117–$195 cabin. Late Apr to mid-Oct and mid-Dec to late Feb. **Amenities:** 2 restaurants; lounge; Wi-Fi starting at $5/hr.

WHERE TO CAMP IN YELLOWSTONE

As wonderful as Yellowstone's hotels and cabins are, nothing compares to a night under the park's stars. If you're remotely interested in camping, this is a phenomenal place to try it—and an excellent way to stay inside the park without maxing out your vacation budget. You have two options: staying in one of the 12 developed, drive-in campgrounds, or backpacking into the wilderness. If the latter is more up your alley, check out rules, regulations, and info about getting a permit at nps.gov/yell/planyourvisit/backcountryhiking.htm or call the **Backcountry Office** at ☎ **307/344-2160.**

GETTING A CAMPSITE Of the developed campgrounds, the park operates seven as first-come, first-serve sites; most of them are on the primitive side. **Xanterra** runs the other five, which can all be reserved ahead of time and have more amenities.

Camping is hugely popular in the park, and campgrounds often fill up every night in summer and early fall. Make reservations for Xanterra sites well ahead of time. If you're gunning for a first-come, first-serve site, get up early and make a beeline for your campground of choice—many fill before 8am. *Tip:* Lewis Lake and Indian Creek tend to book up last, and they're two of the park's nicest campgrounds.

THE CAMPGROUNDS Yellowstone's campgrounds range from enormous tent-and-RV villages with hundreds of sites to intimate, back-of-beyond outposts. The larger, more developed options have showers, laundry, flush toilets, and RV dump stations, while the more rustic ones have pit toilets and more limited spaces for RVs. Most campgrounds have picnic tables, campfire rings, and running water. For details on prices, opening dates, and specific amenities for each campground, see the chart on p. 140.

NORTH

Mammoth ★   The first campground you'll hit coming in from the north entrance, Mammoth is the only year-round camping facility. Sites are clumped among the sagebrush, with a few trees for shade. A short trail connects to the Mammoth Hot Springs attractions, and rangers present seasonal programs in an amphitheater. This is a good option for larger RVs.

Tower Fall ★★   Set off a bit from Grand Loop Road in an evergreen forest, Tower Fall is a small, quiet campground at the west end of the Lamar Valley. A general store and the overlook to the Tower Fall waterfall are a stroll away.

Slough Creek ★★★   Located creekside in the Lamar Valley, this 23-site, generator-free campground is a popular base for anglers and wildlife-watchers (and my favorite in the park, thanks to its out-there feel, small size, and lovely setting).

Pebble Creek ★★★   The park's most out-there option, Pebble Creek is a small, primitive campground deep in the Lamar Valley and another great spot for spotting wildlife and fishing.

Indian Creek ★★   This primitive campground just west of Sheepeater Cliff between Mammoth and Norris sits in an evergreen forest at 7,300 feet, close to the Gallatin Mountains. Its mountain views, fishing ops, and remote feel make it one of the park's best camps.

CENTRAL

Norris ★   This midsize campground on a hill features shady sites (a few near the Gibbon River), the Museum of the National Park Ranger, and frequent bison visits. But the best reason to pitch a tent here? Its proximity to Norris Geyser Basin, so you can walk right over and skip the parking hassles.

Madison ★   A sprawling camp (nearly 300 sites) near where the Firehole and Gibbon Rivers join to form the Madison, Madison Campground is about halfway between Old Faithful and West Yellowstone. It's a good bet for bison- and elk-watching and fly-fishing, and rangers hold evening programs at the amphitheater.

Canyon ★   Big and busy, 7,900-foot Canyon Campground sits in a lodgepole pine forest a short walk from the restaurants and other facilities at Canyon Village. Here you'll find laundry, showers, and evening ranger programs.

Fishing Bridge RV Park ★ This huge campground on the north side of Yellowstone Lake is essentially a large parking lot for RVs—as this is the heart of grizzly country, tents aren't allowed. Though it's a bit short on charm, the RV park has an amphitheater with ranger programs, the Fishing Bridge Museum and Visitor Center, and a general store, and it's the only one with full RV hookups.

Bridge Bay ★ The park's largest campground with 432 sites, Bridge Bay is the best option if you're looking to get out on the water. It's very close to the Yellowstone Lake shoreline and walking distance from Bridge Bay Marina. There's also a general store, as well as evening ranger programs.

SOUTH

Grant Village ★ This mega-campground on Yellowstone Lake's West Thumb is fully loaded with laundry, showers, dump stations, and a boat launch, and it's very close to the restaurants, general stores, and visitor center at Grant Village. You also get evening ranger programs.

Lewis Lake ★★ Shaded and remote, the sites at the midsize Lewis Lake Campground are very private and all a short stroll from the lakeshore and its boat ramp. This

Amenities for Each Campground:
Yellowstone National Park

CAMPGROUND	TOTAL SITES	RV HOOKUPS
Inside the Park		
Bridge Bay*	432	No
Canyon*	273	No
Fishing Bridge RV Park*	325	Yes
Grant Village*	430	No
Indian Creek	70	No
Lewis Lake	85	No
Madison*	278	No
Mammoth	85	No
Norris	111	No
Pebble Creek	27	No
Slough Creek	23	No
Tower Fall	31	No

*Reserve through Xanterra Parks & Resorts; Fishing Bridge RV Park accepts only hard-sided vehicle

generator-free camp, 8 miles north of the south entrance, is also a great spot to scope for moose.

WHERE TO CAMP NEAR YELLOWSTONE

The Gallatin and Shoshone National Forests run several wonderful primitive campgrounds near the north, northeast, east, and west entrances to the park. You won't find space for hundreds of campers, full RV hookups, or flush toilets, but you will enjoy amenities like trout streams, lakeside sites, and quiet nights around the campfire. Most campgrounds are first-come, first-serve and some fill up quickly in the summer. Sites cost $10 or less per night unless otherwise noted.

Three developed campgrounds cluster just north of Gardiner, near the north entrance. **Eagle Creek** is the closest, just 2 miles northeast of town on the Yellowstone River; next come **Timber Camp** and **Bear Creek** (both free).

You'll find four nearby developed campgrounds on the Beartooth Highway outside Cooke City, starting with **Soda Butte** and **Colter;** both are for hard-sided campers only. **Chief Joseph** lies just east of Colter Pass, 4 miles from

DUMP STATION	FLUSH TOILETS	DRINKING WATER	SHOWERS	FIRE PITS/ GRILLS	LAUNDRY	ACCEPTS RESERVATIONS	FEES	OPEN
Yes	Yes	Yes	No	Yes	No	Yes	$24	Late May to mid-Sept
Yes	Yes	Yes	Yes	Yes	Yes	Yes	$29	Late May to late Sept
Yes	Yes	Yes	Yes	Yes	Yes	Yes	$48	Early May to mid-Sept
Yes	Yes	Yes	Yes	Yes	Yes	Yes	$29	Early June to mid-Sept
No	No	Yes	No	Yes	No	No	$15	Early June to early Sept
No	Yes	No	No	Yes	No	No	$15	Mid-June to early Nov
Yes	Yes	Yes	No	Yes	No	Yes	$24	Late April to mid-Oct
No	Yes	Yes	No	Yes	No	No	$20	Year-round
No	Yes	Yes	No	Yes	No	No	$20	Mid-May to late Sept
No	No	Yes	No	Yes	No	No	$15	Mid-June to late Sept
No	No	Yes	No	Yes	No	No	$15	Mid-June to early Oct
No	No	Yes	No	Yes	No	No	$15	Late May to late Sept

Cooke City; continue down the road to reach **Fox Creek** ($20; electric hookups available), a remodeled campground in Wyoming's Shoshone National Forest.

Two popular campgrounds just past the east entrance offer riverside camping along the North Fork of the Shoshone River for hard-sided campers only (due to frequent bear activity in the area). **Threemile** ($15) is 3 miles east of the park entrance and can be reserved ahead of time at recreation.gov. Continue east another 5 miles to reach **Eagle Creek** ($15).

The national forest lands west of West Yellowstone offer a slew of options, and the closest ones to the park boundary are especially desirable for anglers. **Baker's Hole,** 3 miles northwest of town, lies on the Madison River; **Rainbow Point** is 5 miles from West Yellowstone on Hebgen Lake (reservations accepted; www.recreation.gov or www.hebgenbasin campgrounds.com). Both have some electric hookups and cost $16. Among private options in the area, **Madison Arm Resort** stands out for its lakefront campsites, free showers, full RV hookups, and marina with boat rentals ($35 tent site, $48 full hookup site; www.madisonarmresort.com).

WHERE TO EAT IN YELLOWSTONE

Given the park's size and the distances between its developed hubs and the gateway towns, you're something of a captive audience when it comes to dining at Yellowstone: You'll likely find yourself lining up for a seat at the concessionaire-run restaurants at least a few times (it's that or stick only to your camp stove). Generally, prices are high and the food ranges from adequate to pretty good—these outfits serve millions of people a year, and it shows. Still, the higher-end restaurants can offer up a memorable experience, and many menus prioritize local, sustainable and/or organic ingredients.

Mammoth Hot Springs

You have three options for grub near the Mammoth terraces—deli sandwiches and ice cream at the general store, quick cafeteria food at **Terrace Grill,** and sit-down meals at the Mammoth Hotel Dining Room.

Mammoth Hotel Dining Room ★ SEAFOOD/STEAKS

For a meal that pairs an Art Deco-inspired space with relatively casual food, head over to Mammoth's flagship restaurant. The chefs emphasize sustainable options with a distinctively Montana flavor, such as bison sirloin and pistachio-parmesan trout. There's a typical array of burgers, sandwiches, and salads, though starters/small plates get a bit more creative. The dining room's expansive mirrors once hung in the 1883 National Hotel, the first lodging on this site soon after Yellowstone became a national park.

Mammoth Hot Springs Hotel. ✆ **307/344-7311.** www.yellowstone nationalparklodges.com. Reservations required in winter. Main courses $4–$14 (breakfast); $10–$16 (lunch); $15–$31 (dinner). Late Apr to early Oct daily 6:30–10am, 11:30am–2:30pm, and 5–10pm; late Dec to early Mar daily 6:30–10am, 11:30am–2:30pm, and 5:30–8pm. Closed early Oct to late Dec and early Mar to late Apr.

Canyon Village Area

All four options in this bustling area are designed for quick meals. There's the 50's-style **Canyon Soda Fountain** in the general store, where you can grab a cheeseburger and malt; **Canyon Lodge Deli** for hot dogs and sandwiches; and **Canyon Lodge Cafeteria.** Xanterra plans to completely revamp the **Canyon Lodge** food service into a full-service dining room and a fast/fresh/healthy restaurant debuting in summer 2017, but it wasn't open for sampling at press time.

Tower-Roosevelt Area

Roosevelt Lodge Dining Room ★ BBQ The park's most rustic lodge pairs its rough-log decor with a cowboy menu: burgers, steak, fried chicken, and applewood-smoked ribs (this is not the place for inspired vegetarian dishes). It's fairly standard fare, but portions are hearty and there are a few surprises (such as bison tamales). For a more memorable meal, sign up for the Old West Dinner Cookout: You'll hop on horseback (or jump in a wagon) for an al fresco supper of steak, baked beans, watermelon, and cobbler. The price sounds steep at first—$60 to $88 for adults, $49 to $81 for kids—but considering you get a full meal for roughly $10 more than a regular horseback ride, it's actually a pretty good deal.

At Tower Junction. ✆ **307/344-7311.** www.yellowstonenational parklodges.com. Reservations not accepted for the dining room; required for Old West cookouts. Main courses $4–$12 (breakfast);

$11–$27 (lunch and dinner). Mid-June to early Sept daily 7–10am, 11:30am–4:30pm, and 4:30–9:30pm.

Yellowstone Lake

Here, it's best to pick either low or high ends of the dining spectrum: The mid-price meals at **Lake Lodge Cafeteria** are decent at best, so you're better off upgrading to the Lake Hotel's dining room for anything more than deli grub. On the casual side, you can get basic sandwiches, salads, and soups at the general stores (one near Lake Lodge and one at Fishing Bridge) or **Lake Yellowstone Hotel Deli.**

Lake Yellowstone Hotel Dining Room ★★

AMERICAN   This upscale restaurant in the park's fanciest hotel delivers the most refined dining experience at Yellowstone. And though the food is quite good—think bison tenderloin, trout, and grilled quail, all prepared with an eye toward sustainable and organic ingredients—it's only half the appeal. The chance to spend an hour or two sipping wine in the sophisticated dining room, gazing out at front-row views of Yellowstone Lake, is in itself worth the bill. Make reservations for the restaurant well ahead of time, or at least a day or two beforehand.

Yellowstone Lake. ☎ **307/344-7311.** www.yellowstonenationalpark-lodges.com. Dinner reservations required. Main courses $4–$15 (breakfast); $10–$16 (lunch); $15–$42 (dinner). Mid-May to early Oct daily 6:30–10am, 11:30am–2:30pm, and 5–10pm.

Grant Village

Like many of the park's developed areas, Grant Village features a few casual establishments and one higher-end dining room. But unlike the others, one of Grant's quick-service restaurants comes with a truly killer view and fantastic wildlife-watching. At **Lake House Restaurant,** dine on noodle bowls, pho, and banh mi sandwiches with a vista that's as lakefront as you can get—the building extends out over the water on a pier. Early risers will find the best sunrise breakfast around, and wildlife fans may spot pelicans and grizzly bears on the adjacent sandbars, especially in springtime. **Grant General Store** also offers fast-food burgers and sandwiches.

Grant Village Dining Room ★ AMERICAN   Like the
nearby Lake House Restaurant, Grant's dining room offers a lovely lakefront view (if not quite the same on-the-water feel). But the dishes are a step up: Look for prime rib au jus,

sautéed trout, wild game meatloaf, and several pastas, many of which are sustainably sourced. Lunch options range from a smoked bison sandwich to fish and chips, or burgers and entrée salads.

At Grant Village. ℂ **307/344-7311**. www.yellowstonenationalpark lodges.com. Dinner reservations required. Main courses $4–$14 (breakfast); $10–$16 (lunch); $13–$31 (dinner). Late May to early Sept daily 6:30–10am, 11:30am–2:30pm, and 5–10pm.

Old Faithful Area

The bustling Old Faithful zone boasts more dining options than anywhere else in the park, including two upscale dining rooms and an array of casual joints. Grab sandwiches and local Montana ice cream at the Inn's **Bear Paw Deli;** for a hot lunch or dinner, the Snow Lodge's **Geyser Grill** slings burgers, hot dogs, and sandwiches. The **Old Faithful Lodge Cafeteria** offers quick-service entrees: Think teriyaki bowls, pulled pork sandwiches, and roast turkey. You'll also find sandwiches and salads at the adjacent **Bake Shop,** plus soft-serve ice cream. The **general store** and **Old Faithful Basin Store** serve pizzas, chili, burgers, and other quick choices.

Old Faithful Inn Dining Room ★★ SEAFOOD/STEAKS
Along with the Lake Yellowstone Hotel Dining Room, this is one of the quintessential dining experiences in the park. Just like the rest of the storied inn, the atmosphere can't be beat: Giant log beams, chandeliers, and a huge stone fireplace dominate the room. The nightly dinner buffet featuring prime rib, trout, veggie sides, and dessert highlights the menu, but the creative a la carte options are tasty, too—including bison bratwurst, pheasant, grilled quail, and pork *osso buco.*

At the Old Faithful Inn. ℂ **307/344-7311**. www.yellowstonenational parklodges.com. Dinner reservations required. Main courses $4–$14 (breakfast); $10–$16 (lunch); $13–$30 (dinner). Early May to early Oct daily 6:30–10am, 11:30am–2:30pm, and 4:30–10pm.

Old Faithful Snow Lodge Obsidian Dining Room ★
SEAFOOD/WILD GAME   Wild boar, bison, and elk, oh my! Wild game plays a starring role on this menu, showing up in dishes such as bison short ribs, wild boar tenderloin, and wild game Bolognese pasta. More traditional fare—salmon, trout, roast chicken—round out the choices, and there are typically a couple of tasty vegetarian or vegan meals, too.

The dining room is sleek and cozy, with wrought iron mountain scenes on the lamps and bear prints gracing the chairs.

At the Old Faithful Snow Lodge. ℭ **307/344-7311.** www.yellowstone nationalparklodges.com. Reservations not accepted in summer but required in winter. Main courses $4–$14 (breakfast); $9–$16 (lunch [winter only]), $13–$30 dinner. Early May to mid-Oct daily 6:30–10:30am and 5–10:30pm; mid-Dec to late Feb daily 6:30–10am, 11:30am–3pm, and 5–9:30pm.

WHERE TO STAY IN GRAND TETON

Several different concessionaires operate the lodges within the park (including Headwaters Lodge at Flagg Ranch, which is technically inside the adjacent John D. Rockefeller Jr. Memorial Pkwy.). **Forever Resorts** runs the Signal Mountain Lodge (ℭ **307/543-2831;** www.signalmountain lodge.com). **Grand Teton Lodge Company** handles Headwaters at Flagg Ranch, Colter Bay Village, Jackson Lake Lodge, and Jenny Lake Lodge (ℭ **307/543-2861** for Flagg Ranch, 307/543-3100 for the others; www.gtlc.com). In the Moose Junction area, Dornan's runs the **Spur Ranch Cabins** (ℭ **307/733-2522;** www.dornans.com) and a private owner operates **Moulton Ranch Cabins** (ℭ **307/733-3749;** www. moultonranchcabins.com).

Most park lodges open between early May and early June and close in early or mid-October (except for the Spur Ranch Cabins, open most of the year). As at Yellowstone, lodging books quickly and demand stays high throughout the season, so make reservations months in advance (or a full year ahead of time). Lodges are kept intentionally unplugged: You won't find TVs or air conditioning in the rooms, but there is a pool at Jackson Lake Lodge.

Flagg Ranch Village Area

2 miles from the south entrance to Yellowstone; 5 miles from the northern boundary of Grand Teton.

This sleepy outpost on the John D. Rockefeller, Jr. Memorial Parkway had plenty of excitement in 2016, when the fast-moving Berry Fire forced an evacuation of the lodge and closed the road. Luckily, all lodge properties escaped unburned, but scorched trunks now dominate in some patches of surrounding forest. Still, the complex just off the Snake River remains an inviting getaway—or a convenient place to grab a snack and fill your gas tank in between the two parks.

Headwaters Lodge and Cabins at Flagg Ranch ★ Located within striking distance of both Grand Teton and Yellowstone, Headwaters is a convenient lodging if you're planning to explore both parks. Properties are all cabins, most of them with private bathrooms, log-cabin furnishings, and patios. Budget-minded travelers can snag a bare-bones camper cabin—a sparse room with bunk beds but no linens, electricity, or private bathrooms—but I'd opt for a site in the campground instead (you'll rough it only slightly more and save 40 bucks; RV sites available, too; see p. 151). A few short hiking trails take off from the property, as do guided horseback rides. The main lodge features a restaurant, saloon, convenience store, gift shop, and coffee shop.

At Flagg Ranch. ℂ **307/543-2861.** www.gtlc.com. 92 cabins, 171 campsites. $75 camper cabin; $221–$310 cabin double; $73 RV site; $38 tent site. Early June to early Oct. **Amenities:** Restaurant; lounge; no Wi-Fi.

Colter Bay Village Area

11 miles from the park's northern boundary; 10 miles from the Moran (east) entrance.

This complex of lodging, dining, shopping, and activities on Jackson Lake is one of the most happening spots in the park. Looking to launch your kayak, pick up groceries, take a swim, sign up for a guided activity, or chat with a ranger? Colter Bay Village has you covered. There's even a bit of culture in the form of the visitor center's small Indian Arts Gallery.

Colter Bay Village ★ One thing's for sure: You won't get bored by basing yourself out of this bustling resort. You can sign up for a wide range of activities on site, including paddling, fishing excursions, horseback riding, rafting, and wagon rides; a swimming beach and marina also grant access to DIY water recreationists. Lodging is cabin-style: rustic buildings (renovated for 2017) complete with gingham curtains and log wall interiors. There are also sparse tent cabins consisting of pull-down bunks and thin mattress in canvas shelters; as with Flagg Ranch, you're probably better off camping at the adjacent campground and saving 45 bucks (see p. 151). An RV park rounds out the offerings.

At Colter Bay. © **307/543-2861.** www.gtlc.com. 166 cabins, 112 RV sites, 350 tent sites. $189–$250 cabin; $70 tent cabin. Late May to early Oct. **Amenities:** 2 restaurants; free Wi-Fi in public buildings.

Jackson Lake Lodge ★★ Things take a decidedly upscale turn just 5 miles down the road at Jackson Lake Lodge, one of the two fanciest options in the park (Jenny Lake Lodge is even more luxurious). The lodge's upper lobby delivers the biggest wow factor: cozy stone fireplaces in the corners, a stuffed grizzly, and most impressively, 60-foot-wide picture windows facing the Tetons and Mt. Moran. You'll also find several boutiques carrying Western wear and jewelry, plus an activities desk that can hook you up with rafting trips, horseback rides, and guided park tours. And though it's quite chic, a playground and the only pool in park lodging make Jackson Lake Lodge family-friendly, too. Lodge rooms are well-appointed and have double beds; even nicer are the cottages tucked into the woods around the lodge, which have patios. In both cases, you'll pay more for a mountain view.

5 miles south of Colter Bay Village on US 89. © **307/543-3100.** www.gtlc.com. 385 units. $320–$430 double cottage or lodge room; $730–$810 suite. Mid-May to early Oct. **Amenities:** 2 restaurants; lounge; pool; free Wi-Fi.

Signal Mountain Area

15 miles from the north entrance; 9 miles from the Moran (east) entrance.

Shoring up the southeastern corner of Jackson Lake, the Signal Mountain complex offers a campground, marina, guided activities, and a general store. The scenic drive up 7,727-foot Signal Mountain takes off a bit to the south.

Signal Mountain Lodge ★ This mix of rooms and cabins on Jackson Lake has a laid-back, summer-camp vibe, from the board game room in the lodge to the lake-facing porches with Adirondack chairs. Accommodations range from simple motel-style rooms featuring knotty wood furniture to lakefront apartments with balconies and kitchenettes, with the frontier-style log cabins falling in between. Most units were remodeled between 2014 and 2016. The lodge can also arrange for guided fishing tours, boat rentals (motorboats as well as canoes and kayaks), and Snake River float trips.

4.6 miles southwest of Jackson Lake Lodge on US 89. © **307/543-2831.** www.signalmountainlodge.com. 79 units. $200–$255 log cabin; $243–$394 lodge/bungalow room; $353–$394 lakefront; $429 triple cabin. Early May to mid-Oct. **Amenities:** 3 restaurants; lounge; free Wi-Fi.

Jenny Lake Area

28 miles from the northern boundary; 17 miles from the Moran (east) entrance; 16 miles from the south entrance.

The south end of lovely Jenny Lake hosts a visitor center, grocery store, and the launching point for the shuttle boat to Inspiration Point. Jenny Lake Lodge, the area's only hotel, is tucked away just north of the lake.

Jenny Lake Lodge ★★★   The finest accommodations in the Tetons—and indeed, one of the best lodges in any national park—are nestled in the evergreens north of Jenny Lake. Land a room at this intimate resort and you'll get a taste of the A-list life, including champagne welcome receptions, yoga on the lawn, free cruiser bikes, and dining at the lodge's fantastic restaurant. All rooms are in luxurious log cabins featuring slate bathroom floors, quilts, and patios; suite add woodstoves, Jacuzzis, and sitting areas. The main lodge has a mountain-view porch for sipping coffee and a cozy lounge, perfect for curling up with a book by the fire. You can also stroll out your door and connect with several excellent hiking trails to destinations like String Lake, Leigh Lake, and Paintbrush Canyon. Rooms are available on their own for select dates, or you can book a Signature Stay that includes breakfast, a five-course dinner, and horseback rides.

N. Jenny Lake Rd. © **307/543-3100.** www.gtlc.com. 37 units. $737 double Signature Stay ($500 room-only double); $921–$1,021 suite. Extra person $172/night. Signature Stay includes breakfast and dinner, horseback riding, and use of bicycles. Early June to early Oct. **Amenities:** Restaurant; lounge; free Wi-Fi.

Moose Area

36 miles south of the northern boundary; 18 miles from the Moran (east) entrance; 8 miles south of Jenny Lake.

The Dornan's area just west of Moose Junction serves as a mini-village: Here, you'll find a couple of restaurants; shops specializing in fly-fishing, mountaineering and paddling gear;

a whitewater rafting outfitter; groceries; and a wine shop. Just east, on Mormon Row, several ranch buildings dating back to the early twentieth century still squat where early Mormon settlers established a small community.

Moulton Ranch Cabins ★ Technically located on an island of private land surrounded by the park, this cute, historic ranch property near the oft-photographed Moulton Barn homestead is a nice break from the tourist bustle. The five cabins all have decks or patios and private bathrooms, and some offer views of the Teton peaks to boot. The larger cabins sleep up to six, and some have kitchenettes and lofts.

Mormon Row. ✆ **307/733-3749.** www.moultonranchcabins.com. 5 units. $109–$289 double. Late May to late Sept. **Amenities:** Free Wi-Fi.

Spur Ranch Cabins ★ This family-owned clutch of cabins near the Snake River, just east of park headquarters, offers comfortable quarters for a decent price. The log cabins have one- and two-bedrooms, plus fully equipped kitchens, living rooms, and patios with charcoal grills. Picnic tables and Adirondack chairs allow for riverside lounging.

At Moose Junction. ✆ **307/733-2522.** www.dornans.com. 12 units. $225–$250 double; $325–$350 two-bedroom. Lower rates fall–spring. Closed Nov and Apr. **Amenities:** 2 restaurants; lounge; free Wi-Fi.

WHERE TO CAMP IN GRAND TETON

Just like in Yellowstone, the campgrounds in Grand Teton National Park provide a top-notch experience for a bargain price—and few developed campgrounds *anywhere* boast better views than the mountain vistas waiting outside your tent flap in many spots in this park. Concessionaires run all six developed options: The Grand Teton Lodge Company handles Headwaters Campground at Flagg Ranch, Colter Bay, Gros Ventre, and Jenny Lake, while Forever Resorts runs Lizard Creek and Signal Mountain. Grand Teton also boasts some of the best backcountry camping in the country; find details about permits and regulations at nps.gov/grte/planyourvisit/back.htm or call the Backcountry Office at ✆ **307/739-3309.**

GETTING A CAMPSITE All six of the Grand Teton (and John D. Rockefeller Jr. Memorial Pkwy., in the case of Headwaters) campgrounds have first-come, first-serve sites. You can only make reservations in two places: the Colter Bay RV Park and the Headwaters Campground and RV Sites at Flagg Ranch. To book a site, visit www.gtlc.com or call ✆ **307/543-2861** (Headwaters) or ✆ **307/543-3100** (Colter Bay).

Otherwise, plan to arrive at your campground of choice early—campsites often fill every morning during summer, especially at the tents-only Jenny Lake Campground. Lizard Creek and Gros Ventre typically fill up last.

Most campgrounds can accommodate RVs, and Colter Bay RV Park, Headwaters, and Signal Mountain sites offer full hookups (Gros Ventre and Lizard Creek have electric hookups only). If you have a larger RV, Colter Bay RV Park, Headwaters, and Gros Ventre are your best bets; vehicle size is limited to 30 feet at Lizard Creek and Signal Mountain.

THE CAMPGROUNDS All of Grand Teton's campgrounds provide a similar (and excellent) experience: With the exception of Jenny Lake, they're all midsize to large sites with running water, flush toilets, picnic tables, and fire rings. Colter Bay and Headwaters add showers and laundry. Jenny Lake, with just 49 tent-only sites, is the park's most popular. For details on prices, opening dates, and specific amenities for each campground, see the chart on p. 152.

NORTH

Headwaters Campground at Flagg Ranch ★ Mostly an RV resort (97 of the 175 sites are earmarked for RVs), Headwaters is tucked into a spruce-fir forest near the Snake River and adjacent to a grocery store, restaurant, and hiking trails.

Lizard Creek ★ On the smaller side, this 60-site campground on the north side of Jackson Lake has a remote, away-from-it-all feel. A few sites even have lake views.

Colter Bay/Colter Bay RV Park ★ Adjacent to one of the park's busiest hubs, the Colter Bay campgrounds offer easy access to a restaurant, swimming beach, boat launch, grocery store, and guided activities. The 335-site campground, one of the park's largest, sits in an evergreen forest and is within walking distance of Jackson Lake; tent sites are nicer and more private than the RV spots.

Signal Mountain ★★ Smaller, quieter, and more intimate than nearby Colter Bay, Signal Mountain's 105 sites sit in a lovely wooded area; some have views of Jackson Lake through the trees. Two restaurants, a bar, and a grocery store are a quick stroll away.

SOUTH

Jenny Lake ★★★ The smallest, nicest campground in the Tetons sits just off Jenny Lake with grandstand views of the peaks. Get here before 10 a.m. to land a site—spots are snapped up quickly, with good reason.

Gros Ventre ★★ This expansive campground lies in a sagebrush field dotted with cottonwoods, close to the Gros Ventre River. It's a great place to spot moose and pronghorn and one of the best bets for late arrivals.

WHERE TO CAMP NEAR GRAND TETON

Several lovely campgrounds can be found along the outskirts of the park—many of them significantly cheaper than in-park sites (and a mere fraction of the cost of even the most affordable hotels in Jackson). The Bridger-Teton National Forest operates a handful of primitive (read: running water but pit toilets and no showers) campgrounds. **Curtis Canyon** is just 8 miles from Jackson, just outside the National Elk Refuge, and **Atherton Creek** and **Crystal Creek** are a bit father, just east of Kelly along the Gros Ventre Road. Just northeast of the park you'll find **Hatchet** and **Pacific Creek,** the latter poised on the edge of the Teton Wilderness. These forest

Amenities for Each Campground:
Grand Teton National Park

CAMPGROUND	TOTAL SITES	RV HOOKUPS
Inside the Park		
Colter Bay	359	Yes
Gros Ventre	341	No
Jenny Lake*	49	No
Lizard Creek	60	No
Signal Mountain	105	Yes

*Tents only are allowed here.

service campgrounds cost $10 to $12 per night and usually operate between late May and late September.

For an even more remote experience, head west on Grassy Creek Road from the Flagg Ranch area. Twenty free, primitive campsites line the road, each with a picnic table, pit toilet, and bear-resistant food storage box (BYO water).

WHERE TO EAT IN GRAND TETON

The dining options in the Tetons run the scale from quick cafeteria grub to one of the finest restaurants in the entire national park system (that'd be the Jenny Lake Lodge Dining Room), so there's something for every taste. Dinner reservations are a must at the higher-end spots during the high summer season.

Near the Northern Boundary

Looking for a kick-back meal? **Sheffields** at the Headwaters Lodge serves three meals a day, with a focus on loaded burgers, steaks, prime rib, and fish (and the chef will cook up that trout you caught for $15). For something a bit more casual, **Leek's Marina & Pizzeria** dishes up pizza with loads of toppings, plus pasta and sandwiches.

Colter Bay

This busy hub on Jackson Lake has two quick dining options—burritos, sandwiches, and salads at **John Colter Café Court**

DUMP STATION	FLUSH TOILETS	DRINKING WATER	SHOWERS	FIRE PITS/ GRILLS	LAUNDRY	ACCEPTS RESERVATIONS	FEES	OPEN
Yes	Yes	Yes	Yes	Yes	Yes	Yes	$26-$52	Mid-May to late Sept
Yes	Yes	Yes	No	Yes	No	No	$26-$52	Early May to early Oct
No	Yes	Yes	No	Yes	No	No	$26	Early May to late Sept
No	Yes	Yes	No	Yes	No	No	$24	Mid-June to early Sept
Yes	Yes	Yes	Yes	Yes	Yes	Yes	$24-$47	Mid-May to mid-Oct

and deli picks at the **General Store**—and one sit-down restaurant.

John Colter Ranch House ★ AMERICAN/BBQ   Colter Bay's signature dining room runs with the cowboy theme: wagon wheels on the walls, cattle drive scenes on the salad bar, and a bar that has been singed with the brands of local ranchers. The menu is heavy on BBQ staples like beef brisket, rotisserie chicken, and pork ribs. Herbivores will find a nice variety of salads and a few vegetarian pastas.

Colter Bay Village. ℂ **307/543-2811.** Reservations not accepted. Main courses $7–$16 (breakfast); $8–$19 (lunch); $17–$31 (dinner). Late May to early Oct daily 6:30–10:30am, 11:30am–1:30pm, and 5:30–9pm.

Jackson Lake Junction

You have several choices at both Jackson Lake and Signal Mountain Lodges, from fine dining to diner fare. Jackson Lake's **Blue Heron Lounge** is the place for casual sandwiches and creative cocktails, plus a late-night bar menu. **Signal Mountain General Store** offers the only grab-and-go food options, but they're better than most: Think quinoa bowls and veggie sandwiches. For something a little different, head to the Jackson Lake Lodge's **Pool BBQ,** where chefs grill up brisket, chicken, ribs, and pulled pork poolside and Western musicians perform live.

The Mural Room ★★ SEAFOOD/WILD GAME   You could be served a bowl of Easy Mac at Jackson Lake Lodge's marquee restaurant and still come away raving, thanks to the stunning view of the Tetons from its floor-to-ceiling windows. Luckily, the entrees aim as high as the mountain scenery: This is a place to savor impressive dishes such as espresso-rubbed elk loin, paprika-seared pheasant, rainbow trout, and burgundy-braised veal cheeks. Breakfast and lunch offer some memorable meals too, from huckleberry French toast and smoked salmon blini to buffalo steak and pork belly BLTs. Tear your eyes away from the peaks long enough to check out the historic Carl Rotors murals adorning the opposite wall.

At Jackson Lake Lodge. ℂ **307/543-3463.** Reservations recommended. Main courses $15–$25 (breakfast and lunch), $22–$46 (dinner). Mid-May to early Oct daily 7–9:30am, 11:30am–1:30pm, and 5:30–9:30pm.

Peaks ★ STEAKS/SEAFOOD   Friendly and cozy, with an inviting stone fireplace, lake view, and requisite moose head adorning the wall, Peaks is Signal Mountain Lodge's most upscale dining. The menu prioritizes local, organic, and sustainable ingredients: Expect dinner entrees such as pecan-crusted trout, bison ragout, ribeye, and an $18 burger. Tasty small plates (trout cakes, mac and cheese) and salads made from Jackson Farmers' Market veggies round out the options.

At Signal Mountain Lodge. 🕐 **307/543-2831.** Main courses $18–$34 dinner. Early May to early Oct daily 7–10am and 11:30am–10pm.

Pioneer Grill ★ AMERICAN   Jackson Lake Lodge's casual eatery is a mashup of 1950s-style diner and home-steader museum: You'll grab a stool at a high counter under displays of old wagon wheels, farm tools, and other settler essentials. The food is a similar mix of roadside-diner classics and Wyoming specialties. Think hearty breakfasts of huckleberry pancakes and trout omelets; the lunch and dinner menu features burgers, wraps, salads, and chicken wings.

At Jackson Lake Lodge. 🕐 **307/543-3100.** Reservations not accepted. Main courses $4–$13 (breakfast); $8–$22 (lunch), $11–$30 (dinner). Mid-May to early Oct daily 6am–10pm.

Trapper Grill ★ AMERICAN/MEXICAN   This more casual restaurant is next door to Peaks and shares its lovely lake view and commitment to sustainable ingredients. The wide-ranging menu should satisfy varied appetites, from baby back ribs to black bean burgers to a tofu banh mi sandwich. But the star of the show is the Mountain of Nachos, a cheesy pile of chips, beef/cage-free chicken/black beans, and all the fixins, that can certainly fill up four people. The full menu is also available in the adjacent **Deadman's Bar,** which claims one of the park's only TVs, a roaring fireplace, and a nice selection of local microbrews, wines, and cocktails.

At Signal Mountain Lodge. 🕐 **307/543-2831.** Main courses $7–$13 (breakfast); $10–$19 (lunch and dinner). Early May to early Oct daily 7–10am and 11:30am–10pm.

Jenny Lake

You can pick up snacks and limited groceries at the **Jenny Lake Store** near the visitor center on the south side of the lake, but really, there's only one game in town in this area: the top-shelf dining at Jenny Lake Lodge.

Jenny Lake Lodge Dining Room ★★★ CONTINEN-
TAL   I haven't found a restaurant in any national park that
comes close to the all-star quality of this intimate retreat.
Here, a talented chef prepares a five-course dinner starring
Jackson Farmers' Market ingredients whipped up in creative,
surprising, and delicious ways. First-course offerings might
include honey-cured quail, duck rillettes, or parsnip risotto,
followed by soup and salad. Main course options could be
rack of lamb, citrus-dusted ahi, cherry bourbon-glazed wild
boar, or a butternut squash tart. The wine list is extensive, and
service is warm and attentive. It all happens in a rustically
elegant dining room with log walls and iron chandeliers.
Reservations are essential for dinner. If you can't swing the
full culinary experience, stop by for breakfast or lunch.

At Jenny Lake Lodge. ✆ **307/543-3352.** Reservations required.
Prix-fixe breakfast $30; lunch main courses $15–$20; prix-fixe dinner
$95, not including alcoholic beverages. Early June to early Oct daily
7:30–9am, noon–1:30pm, and 6–8:45pm.

Moose Junction

The Dornan's complex has two casual and relatively affordable restaurants. The **Chuckwagon Grill,** with its outdoor
seating, dining teepee, and unimpeded Teton views is the
more fun of the two; look for grilled chicken, ribs, and trout
plus a well-stocked buffet of BBQ sides. The **Pizza Pasta
Company** offers just that, plus salads and sandwiches.

GATEWAYS TO YELLOWSTONE & GRAND TETON

You'll find civilization waiting outside almost every park entrance, but the gateway towns vary considerably in amenities and vibe, from a remote frontier outpost to a ritzy getaway packed with art galleries and high-end restaurants. Read on to choose your ideal basecamp.

WEST YELLOW-STONE, MONTANA

At the west entrance of Yellowstone National Park.

West Yellowstone has a tiny year-round population, but it bustles with travelers most of the year. It sprouted up around the Union Pacific Railroad's Yellowstone Special line starting in 1907. Though much of the town is hotels, souvenir shops, and overpriced restaurants, Yellowstone's western gateway also offers excellent access to outdoor pursuits both inside and outside the park. A few historic buildings from the early 20th century remain in town, and a surprisingly good wildlife park is probably the top in-town attraction.

Essentials

GETTING THERE For information on air service and car rentals, see "Getting There & Getting Around," in chapter 10. West Yellowstone is 90 miles from Bozeman via US 191 and 108 miles from Idaho Falls via US 20.

VISITOR INFORMATION Stop by or contact the **West Yellowstone Chamber of Commerce,**

30 Yellowstone Ave. (P.O. Box 458), West Yellowstone, MT 59758 (© **406/646-7701;** www.destinationyellowstone.com).

Getting Outside

Just a few blocks from Yellowstone's west entrance, West Yellowstone is also an easy drive from the Caribou-Targhee and Gallatin National Forests and all the outdoor opportunities therein. To the north, the Madison Range and the Lee Metcalf Wilderness offer fantastic hiking trails, and nearby Hebgen Lake hosts paddlers, sailors, boaters, and swimmers. Fly-fishing is huge here, thanks to the trout-rich waters of the Madison, Gallatin, Yellowstone, and Henrys Fork of the Snake Rivers. When the snow flies, West Yellowstone transforms into a mecca for snowmobiling and snowcoach tours, and the Rendezvous Trail system draws devoted Nordic skiers. For more details on these activities, see chapter 4.

Seeing the Sights

Beyond the attractions below, history buffs will get a kick out of the free, self-guided **Historic Walking Tour,** which guides you past hotels and railroad structures from the early 1900s (a striking number of which burned down at some point). Pick up a map and guide at the Chamber of Commerce.

Grizzly and Wolf Discovery Center ★★   The Discovery Center is no mere roadside attraction: This nonprofit houses rescued wolves, grizzly bears, and raptors and features naturalist programs, educational displays, and a small museum. The wolves are always visible in their outdoor habitats, while employees rotate the grizzlies through their enclosure, hiding food under rocks to give the bears a challenge. Kid programs, bird of prey demos, and ranger-led presentations round out the offerings. Bottom line: It's a good cause, and unlike inside the park, charismatic megafauna sightings are guaranteed.

201 S. Canyon St. (in Grizzly Park). © **800/257-2570** or 406/646-7001. www.grizzlydiscoveryctr.org. $13 adults, $8 children 5–12, free for kids under 5. Summer daily 8:30am–8:30pm; shorter hours in winter and spring.

Yellowstone Historic Center ★   Take a step back into the early days of Yellowstone travel at this museum, located inside the 1909 Union Pacific depot. Exhibits cover the development of the town and its early residents, and transportation before the age of the automobile. Highlights include several old stagecoaches and a stuffed grizzly bear nicknamed Old Snaggletooth, a once-famous dumpster bear.

104 Yellowstone Ave. ℭ **406/646-1100.** www.yellowstonehistoric center.org. $6 adults, $2 children 5–12, free for kids under 5. Mid-May to early Oct daily 9am–9pm. Closed early Oct to mid-May.

Yellowstone IMAX Theater   Located next door to the **Grizzly and Wolf Discovery Center,** the IMAX concept works pretty well here—there are things an airborne camera can show you on a giant screen that you'll never see on your own two feet. A film called *Yellowstone* plays fairly often, with swooping views of the canyon, falls, and other sights.

101 S. Canyon St. ℭ **888/854-5862** or 406/646-4100. www.yellow stoneimax.com. Admission $14/$10 premium/regular adults, $11/$7 children. Call or check the website for exact show times.

Where to Stay

As with in-park lodging, the smartest travelers book rooms well ahead of time—especially in high summer and around the holidays. Things quiet down in the spring and fall, but the popularity of the area's snowmobile trails make snowy winters quite lively. West Yellowstone is the closest gateway town to the park with a wide variety of lodging options (Cody, Wyoming, also has quite a few, but it's 50 miles from the park entrance), ranging from basic motels to swanky modern lodges to cabins and guest ranches.

Most hotels in town are independents, but a few chains have a presence. You can grab a double at **Days Inn,** 301 Madison Ave. (ℭ **406/646-7656;** www.wyndhamhotels.com), for $278 in summer. Rates are only slightly lower at the **Super 8 Motel,** 1545 Targhee Pass Hwy. 20 (ℭ **406/646-9584;** www. wyndhamhotels.com), where doubles go for $259. **Holiday Inn** is a step up in quality, with rooms for $330 to $381. **Kelly Inn,** 104 S. Canyon (ℭ **406/646-4544;** www.yellowstone kellyinn.com), is luxuriously modern, with rooms for $320 to $360. There are also two **Best Western** affiliates, with double rooms ranging from $270 to $290 in summer. Call ℭ **800/780-7234** or check www.bestwestern.com for details.

For something more unique, try **Alpine Motel,** 120 Madison Ave. (ℭ **406/646-7544;** www.alpinemotelwest yellowstone.com), an affordable and comfortable spot right downtown, with rooms from $99 to $179. The 1912 **Madison Hotel,** 139 Yellowstone Ave. (ℭ **406/646-7745;**

www.madisonhotelmotel.com), one-time host to the likes of Clark Gable and Herbert Hoover, stands out with its historic lodge and motel rooms ($74–$149) and hostel bunk rooms ($42–$45). **Moose Creek Cabins,** 220 Firehole Ave. (*©* **406/646-9546;** www.moosecreekinn.com), is a step up with its cabin-style motel rooms and kitchenette cabins for $199 to $299.

Evergreen Motel ★

It may be one of the more affordable places in town, but this is far from a generic motel: Thoughtful decor, comfortable rooms, and friendly service make this downtown spot a cut above the rest. Originally built in 1931, the rooms are a tad small by today's standards, but they're lovingly appointed with log furnishings and fake evergreen boughs, with pinecones and moose popping up on the walls and lamps. Several rooms have kitchenettes.

229 Firehole Ave. *©* **406/646-7655.** www.theevergreenmotel.com. 17 units. $149–$179 double; $180–$249 with kitchenette; 2-night minimum in summer. **Amenities:** Free Wi-Fi.

Explorer Cabins ★★

The nicest of the four Park Gate Lodges properties (the others are Yellowstone Park Hotel, Holiday Inn West Yellowstone, and Gray Wolf Inn & Suites), the Explorer Cabins offer a high-end, condo-style experience steps from downtown. The roomy cabins are tucked into a young evergreen forest, and each has a patio and kitchen. They come with giant flatscreen TVs and marble bathrooms, and most have gas fireplaces. Community fire pits are dotted around the property, and guests have access to the Holiday Inn's game room (stocked with Xbox and Netflix).

201 Grizzly Ave. *©* **877/600-4308.** www.visityellowstonepark.com. 50 units. $369 double cabin; $499 2-bedroom cabin. **Amenities:** Fire pits; s'mores kits; loaner binoculars and hiking poles; free Wi-Fi.

Hibernation Station ★★

This complex of cabins feels a bit like a Christmas village even in the middle of summer, thanks to its cozy, log-*everything* interiors, fireplaces, and rooflines adorned with wooden cutouts of horses and evergreens. Each one has its own decor theme (such as stagecoaches or mustangs), and styles range from simple, spacious doubles to 980-square-foot vacation homes complete with kitchens, jetted tubs, and dining rooms. Outside, you'll find a playground, grills, and a waterfall fountain. You can visit in winter for a real Santa's workshop vibe, but keep in mind that only a handful of cabins remain open in the off-season.

212 Gray Wolf Ave. (C) **406/646-4200.** www.hibernationstation.com. 50 units. $149–$319 cabin. Lower rates fall to spring. **Amenities:** Jacuzzi; lounge with 2 computers; free Wi-Fi (in lounge only).

Three Bear Lodge ★   One of West Yellowstone's old-timers—it was first built in the 1930s—Three Bear Lodge has had several facelifts over the years after several damaging fires, including the 2008 blaze. Today, the place features modern amenities, a Western-chic lobby with a stone fireplace and an outdoor pool. The owners salvaged much of the wood from the original building, turning it into bedframes, towel racks, and other guest room furnishings. Lodge rooms are very spacious; or at the adjoining motel, choose among simple doubles, suites, and rooms with huge Jacuzzi tubs. The lodge also arranges summertime van tours of Yellowstone and winter snowcoach and snowmobile outings.

217 Yellowstone Ave. (C) **800/646-7353** or 406/646-7353. www.threebearlodge.com. 74 units. $199–$299 double. Lower rates fall to spring. **Amenities:** Restaurant; lounge; exercise room; Jacuzzi; pool (seasonal); business center; free Wi-Fi.

Where to Eat

Morning pick-me-up? You'll find two of the best in unusual places. Head to the **Mocha Mammas** coffee bar inside the Free Heel and Wheel bike/ski shop, 33 Yellowstone Ave. ((C) **406/646-7744;** www.freeheelandwheel.com), for espresso and smoothies, or to **Book Peddler** in Canyon Square ((C) **406/646-9358**) for delicious sandwiches and salads along with the usual caffeine. For a quick bite, try one of the town's two taco buses **Taqueria Las Palmitas** at 21 N. Canyon St. ((C) **406/640-1822**), or **Taqueria Malverde,** 132 Firehole Ave. ((C) **208/403-1157**).

The Buffalo Bar ★ AMERICAN/MEXICAN   Like your watering holes lively, friendly, and adorned with as many stuffed bison as possible? Head to this local favorite, a sports bar that also hosts live poker and musical acts. The menu favors its namesake creature—you'll find bison meatballs, tacos, burritos, ribeye, and a slew of burgers, along with other meat-heavy entrees and sandwiches. There are a few wine selections, but this is more of a beer joint.

335 U.S. 20. (C) **406/646-1176.** www.thebuffalobar.com. Main courses $9–$38. Daily 10am–2am.

Café Madriz ★ SPANISH

Top-notch tapas in little West Yellowstone? *Sí!* Thank chef/owner Elena de Diego, originally from Spain, for the infusion of cultural diversity. Diners share traditional small plates, such as Spanish cheeses, *patatas* con salsa, cured meats, and tortillas *Española,* in a warm and intimate space decorated with art and tiles from de Diego's homeland; on summer nights, grab one of the front-yard café tables. Paella is a standout, and well worth the 30-minute wait; you can order a pan for two ($37) or four ($75). Pair it all with one of the Spanish wines from the curated list.

311 Canyon St. ℂ **406/646-9245.** www.cafemadriz.com. Tapas $8–$20 lunch and dinner. May–Sept Mon–Sat 11am–2pm, 5–9pm. Closed Oct–Apr.

Euro Café ★ AMERICAN

Early risers and the sleep-in crowd alike love this breakfast-and-lunch bistro, where you can tuck into specials such as egg sandwiches, biscuits and gravy, brioche French toast, and breakfast pizza (that's a delightful mixture of eggs, cheese, and gravy over a pizza crust, if you're curious) from the early hours until 3pm. There's also a full espresso bar for your caffeine fix. If you're more in the mood for lunch food, you'll also find burgers, sandwiches, soups, and salads.

237 Firehole Ave. ℂ **406/646-1170.** www.eurocafewy.com. Main courses $6–$10 breakfast, $8–$13 lunch. Daily 7am–3pm.

Madison Crossing Lounge ★★ STEAKS/SEAFOOD

By all accounts the best place in town, Madison Crossing makes for a classy night out: attentive service and excellent food in a warmly lit, Montana-chic setting. The 1918 building was the first school in town, and indeed, you'll dine where first graders of yore once practiced their lessons. The place prides itself on its extensive wine list, but the beer and cocktail menus are also lengthy (the latter heavy on fine whiskeys). Entrees are classic and well-prepared, from steaks to a huckleberry burger to a tasty Idaho trout and veggie-laden ratatouille risotto. The veggie burger is particularly creative: a mushroom, bean, and hazelnut patty with green goddess dressing.

121 Madison Ave. ℂ **406/646-7621.** Main courses $13–$39. Late Apr to Nov and Dec–Mar daily 5–10pm. Closed Apr and Nov.

GARDINER, MONTANA★

At the north entrance to Yellowstone National Park.

Yellowstone's northern gateway feels worlds away from the tourist trappings of West Yellowstone and the swanky sights of Jackson: Here you'll find just a few downtown blocks, limited dining and lodging options, deer and elk lounging in front yards, and lots of peace and quiet. The Yellowstone River cuts right through town, and unobstructed views of the scrublands and hills of north Yellowstone rise just beyond. If you're more interested in playing outside by day and stargazing by night than souvenir shopping, this laid-back town is for you—and for winter visitors, the north entrance is the only way cars can enter the park when the snow piles up.

Essentials

GETTING THERE   For information on air service and car rentals, see "Getting There & Getting Around," in chapter 10. Gardiner is 78 miles south of Bozeman on US 89.

VISITOR INFORMATION   Contact the **Gardiner Chamber of Commerce,** 216 Park St. (✆ **406/848-7971;** www.gardinerchamber.com). The nonprofit **Yellowstone Association** (✆ **406/848-2400;** www.yellowstone.org), whose headquarters are located downtown at 308 E. Park St., also has a staffed information desk, along with a gift shop and wildlife spotting scope rentals ($25/day).

Getting Outside

Proximity to the mighty Yellowstone River makes **whitewater rafting, floating,** and **fly-fishing** big in this area, and several outfitters base themselves out of Gardiner. Options range from mellow half-day floats to multiday trips with riverside camping. For rafting and floating, try **Flying Pig Adventure Company,** 511 Scott St. (✆ **888/792-9193;** www.flyingpigrafting.com), or **Wild West Whitewater Rafting,** 220 W. Park St. (✆ **406/848-2252;** www.wildwestrafting.com). **Park's Fly Shop,** 202 Second St. S. (✆ **406/848-7314;** www.parksflyshop.com), is the place to sign up for guided fly-fishing outings or fishing lessons. **Horseback riding** (including multiday pack trips) and **hiking** in the Gallatin National Forest are also popular. **Hell's A-Roarin' Outfitters,** 164 Crevice Rd. (✆ **406/848-7578;** www.hellsaroarinoutfitters.com), offers rides ranging from an hour to a full day. Come winter, you can also hop on guided **snowcoach** or **snowmobile** tours, though West Yellowstone is the true mecca for oversnow enthusiasts.

Seeing the Sights

Heritage and Research Center ★   This treasure trove of Yellowstone history houses 720,000 cultural and historic items, an archaeology lab, herbarium, research library, and the park's archives. You can drop in to see the historic exhibits anytime, but I highly recommend reserving a spot on the free, twice-weekly behind-the-scenes tour (late May to early Sept Tues and Thurs at 8:30am) for an up-close look at wildlife specimens, rare native plants, historic photos, original Thomas Moran sketches, and more.

20 Old Yellowstone Trail. © **307/344-2662.** www.nps.gov/yell/learn/historyculture/collections.htm. Free admission. Mon–Fri 8am–5pm.

Where to Stay

Gardiner has long been known for friendly, no-frills lodging, and there are still plenty of options in that category to be found. A few higher-end properties crop up in recent years, and several chain hotels maintain a presence. If you're planning on a guided tour while in town, check with your outfitter about lodging: Some of them offer rooms on the side.

Comfort Inn, 107 Hellroaring St. (© **406/848-7536;** www.choicehotels.com), makes an effort to look like it fits in, with log walls and antlered heads mounted in the lobby. Doubles go for $260 to $280. Gardiner's **Super 8,** 702 Scott St. W. (© **406/848-7401;** www.wydhamhotels.com), is the most affordable of the bunch, with doubles for $192 to $202. **Rodeway Inn & Suites,** 109 Hellroaring St. (© **406/848-7520;** www.choicehotels.com), and **Best Western Mammoth Hot Springs,** 905 Scott St. W. (© **406/848-7311;** www.bestwestern.com), are a bit spendier, with double rooms from $240 to $300.

The family-run **Hillcrest Cottages,** 400 Scott St. W. (© **406/848-7353;** www.hillcrestcottages.com), are a good bet for budget-minded travelers: You get a stand-alone cottage with a kitchenette for a nice price, but be aware some are very small. Units go for $92 to $195, May to early Oct only.

Cowboy's Lodge, 208 Stone St. (✆ **406/848-9178;** www. cowboyslodge.com), offers a variety of options, from in-town suites to log cabins to roomy villas. Prices range from $185 for a suite to $525 for a four-bedroom rental house.

Absaroka Lodge ★ Friendly, simple, affordable: Absaroka Lodge nails all three, while throwing in some of the best river views in town. Newly remodeled for 2017, the lodge sits on a bluff overlooking the Yellowstone River, and every room has a small deck or patio facing the water and the park beyond. Accommodations are basic but comfortable, and 12 rooms have kitchenettes. You're within walking distance of pretty much every restaurant and shop in town.

310 Scott St. W. ✆ **406/848-7414.** www.yellowstonemotel.com. 41 units. $85–$110 double. **Amenities:** Free Wi-Fi.

Riverside Cottages ★★ These delightful homes-away-from-home are my pick for best place to bunk in Gardiner. The larger suites feel like the guest rooms of an artsy friend, and even the motel-style efficiency rooms have fancy tile, nice furnishings, and patios. A large deck provides a common space to chill in lounge chairs, grill up a bison burger, or soak in the hot tub, and the path down the bluff is one of the only ways in town to get close to the Yellowstone River. The extremely friendly service is icing on the cake.

251 Scott St. W. ✆ **406/848-7719.** www.riversidecottages.com. 14 units. $140 efficiency; $180–$196 cottage; $226–$286 suite; lower rates fall through spring. **Amenities:** Jacuzzi; free Wi-Fi.

Yellowstone Gateway Inn ★★ Traveling with an entourage? The largest of these upscale rooms—more like high-end apartments, really—can accommodate up to eight people, and even the smallest comfortably house four. Most units have wood floors and full kitchens, plus antique-chic furniture, sleek bathrooms, and Blu-ray/DVD players (with movies available to borrow). If you're looking to shelter a group in style, you won't do better than the Gateway.

103 Bigelow Lane. ✆ **406/848-7100.** www.yellowstonegatewayinn. com. 15 units. $195 double; $315–$395 suite. **Amenities:** Free Wi-Fi.

Yellowstone Village Inn ★ The lit-up sign featuring a snoozing cowboy out front may be very retro, but inside, this family-owned property is all modern Montana. You'll find the de rigueur game animal heads and snug woodstove in the lobby—and possibly walk by a herd of elk that likes to hang out on the front lawn—plus one of the town's only pools. Double rooms meet the mid-range standard, and many have mountain views; some of the suites add kitchens and porches.

1102 Scott St. W. ℂ **406/848-7417.** www.yellowstonevinn.com. 45 units. $169–$199 double; $229–$299 suite, includes continental breakfast. Lower rates spring and fall. Closed mid-Oct to mid-Apr. **Amenities:** Indoor pool; basketball court; tetherball; free Wi-Fi.

Where to Eat

Here in sleepy Gardiner, the dining scene is all about starting your day with a hearty breakfast and ending it with burgers, steaks, and barbecue. Early wildlife-watchers can grab a quick coffee and breakfast, plus to-go lunches, at the tiny **Tumbleweed Bookstore and Café,** 501 Scott St. W. (ℂ **406/848-2225**). **The Corral Drive-In,** 711 Scott St. W. (ℂ **406/848-7627**), stands out among burger joints for its commitment to local and organic ingredients, and believe it or not, the best place for ice cream is **Yellowstone Perk** inside **Gardiner Pharmacy** at 208 E. Park St. (ℂ **406/848-9430**).

The Chico Dining Room ★★★ CONTINENTAL The motto at this remote resort 34 miles north of Gardiner is "Welcome home," and they mean it: You won't find better service or a homier atmosphere for miles around. And the food is stellar, from rich starters like bison short rib ravioli and escargot-stuffed mushrooms to entrees such as rack of lamb, king salmon, ribeye steak, and a few vegetarian mains, too. Most dishes are prepared simply and classically, some feature produce and herbs from the resort's garden, and knowledgeable servers can point you to the right bottle from the restaurant's extensive list (the cocktail menu is well worth a look, too). The Sunday brunch also draws rave reviews. Make a night of it by staying over in one of the elegant rooms or cabins (starting at $61 with shared bathrooms), or at least slip into the resort's hot springs before you go ($7.50/day).

163 Chico Rd. ℂ **406/333-4933.** www.chicohotsprings.com. Reservations recommended. Main courses $12 breakfast, $20 Sun brunch, $30–$70 dinner. Mon–Fri 7–10:30am, Sat 7–11am, Sun 8:30–11:30am; Sun–Thurs 5:30–9pm, Fri–Sat 5:30–10pm.

Cowboy's Grill ★ BBQ/STEAKS Sometimes in a place like Gardiner, a big ol' plate of BBQ feels just right—and this is the best place in town to satisfy that craving. The lengthy menu is chock-full of burgers (including bison and elk varieties, naturally), pulled pork, beef brisket, chicken, steaks, and baskets of fried fish, with classics such as mashed potatoes and baked beans on the side. Bonus: mostly local beers and tasty cobblers for dessert. You'll chow down in a casual, friendly environment, with stuffed elk and cougars peering down at you from the log walls.

208 Stone St. ✆ **406/848-9175.** www.cowboyslodge.com. Main courses $7–$32 lunch and dinner. Daily 11am–9pm.

The Raven Grill ★ AMERICAN/STEAKS This is the fanciest place in town, but you won't find dinner jackets or fine china—casual dress is just fine. The menu features hearty plates of Jamaican jerk chicken, trout, steak, elk lasagna, and creamy pastas, many served with rice or potatoes, bread, and veggies. Prices are a bit high, but the food is good and doled out in generous portions.

118 E. Park St. ✆ **406/848-9171.** Main courses $5–$16 dinner. Mon–Sat 5–10pm; Sun 4–10pm.

Yellowstone Grill ★ BREAKFAST/MEXICAN Locals love to start their day in this cheery space, where the coffee flows freely and your most important meal of the day could be an egg scramble, breakfast tacos, or a tower of blueberry pancakes—oh, and don't neglect the famous cinnamon rolls. Lunch entrees such as burritos, salads, and creative wraps (chipotle BBQ, electric Thai) take over as the day goes on, but thankfully, breakfast is served until 11:30am.

404 Scott St. ✆ **406/848-9433.** www.facebook.com/yellowstonegrill. Main courses $8–$10 breakfast, $9–$13 lunch. Tues–Sun 7am–2pm.

COOKE CITY, MONTANA ★

5 miles from the northeast entrance to Yellowstone National Park.

Rough-and-tumble Cooke City sprang up in the 1880s, when prospectors struck gold, but the mining heyday is long gone. Nowadays, the remote, tiny town (only 100 year-round residents) is all about outdoor recreation, surrounded by Yellowstone and the Custer, Gallatin, and Shoshone National Forests. Hiking, fishing, and paddling opportunities abound, and snowmobiling is huge in winter. If you're planning to cruise the ultrascenic Beartooth Highway (and you should;

see p. 49), Cooke City offers the only services until Red Lodge, 68 twisty miles away.

The **Colter Pass/Cooke City/Silver Gate Chamber of Commerce** (© 406/838-2495; www.cookecitychamber.org) operates a visitor center at 206 W. Main St. that is open daily in summer.

Cooke City and its even smaller neighbor, Silver Gate, offer the best lodging deals of any gateway town: You can snap up a midsummer room for $100 or less. The cabins and cozy lodge rooms at **Elk Horn Lodge,** 103 Main St. (© 406/838-2332; www.elkhornlodgemt.com), are traveler favorites and go for $140 to $160, some with a 3-night minimum. **High Country Motel & Cabins,** 113 W. Main St. (© 406/838-2272; www.highcountrymotelandcabins.com), is known for friendly service and a hot tub; cabin and motel rooms range from $120 to $135. The charming cabins at **Big Moose Resort,** just east of town at 715 U.S. 212 (© 406/838-2393; www.bigmooseresort.com), are a similarly great deal at $100 to $150. There are also a few private rental homes and cabins; check with the Chamber of Commerce for details.

Dining picking are slim, but tasty. Main Street's **Beartooth Café** (© 406/838-2475; www.beartoothcafe.com) has the best burgers and steaks, plus killer from-scratch desserts. Also on Main St., try **Loving Cup Café** (© 406/838-2412) for espresso, sammies, and tacos.

JACKSON, WYOMING ★★★

Near the south entrance of Grand Teton National Park.

Jackson has come a long way from the days when its only visitors were Native American tribes hunting for summer game and later, mountain men seeking beaver pelts. From the humble settlements established in the 1890s, a thriving tourism hub has sprung, catering to everyone from outdoor adventurers to glitterati on holiday. Packed with opportunities for outdoor fun, fine dining and shopping, Jackson is unlike any other gateway town and well worth a stop.

You may have heard this area referred to as Jackson Hole, and that's correct: In mountain man parlance, a "hole" was a high valley surrounded by peaks. Technically, the town itself is Jackson, while Jackson Hole is the surrounding valley. Jackson centers on the old-timey Town Square, a small park marked by four famous arches fashioned from antlers and ringed by art galleries, restaurants, and souvenir shops.

Outdoor activities are the main game in town, and you'll find no shortage of outfitters ready to set you up on your adventure. The Snake River provides easy access to whitewater rafting, float trips and trout fishing, and dude ranches can get you in the saddle. In winter, Jackson Hole Mountain Resort attracts black diamond skiers; cross-country ski trails also abound, and sleigh rides at National Elk Refuge are a classic winter excursion.

But Jackson cleans up nice, too. Climbers and hikers can come in from a day playing outside and rub elbows with the high society that frequents the town's five-star hotels, elegant restaurants, and ritzy jewelry and art galleries. If your dream national park vacation involves dropping 30 grand on a giant moose statue or indulging in elaborate spa treatments, Jackson is the place for you. More interested in microbrews beside the campfire? You'll be right at home, too.

Essentials

Air service to Jackson and rental-car agencies are discussed in chapter 10.

GETTING THERE   If you're coming south from Yellowstone, Jackson is an hour and 15 minutes' drive from the South Entrance on U.S. 89. You can also approach from points west (such as Idaho Falls) via U.S. 26 or over Teton Pass on WY 22 (a gorgeous route if the weather's nice). From the south, take U.S. 89, 189, or 191 north to reach town. For up-to-date weather information and road conditions, contact the Jackson Hole Chamber of Commerce (✆ **307/733-3316;** www.jacksonholechamber.com), call ✆ **888/996-7623** (in state) or 511 (in-state mobile), or visit www.wyoroad.info.

VISITOR INFORMATION   The **Jackson Hole Chamber of Commerce** provides up-to-date info on lodging, dining, and attractions in the area; stop by 112 Center St. The **Jackson Hole and Greater Yellowstone Visitor Center** at 532 N. Cache St. is another great resource and is staffed by rangers from surrounding parks. Open 8am to 7pm in summer and 9am to 5pm from October through Memorial Day (✆ **307/733-3316**). **Jackson Hole Central Reservations** (✆ **888/838-6606;** www.jacksonholewy.com) can help book rooms at local hotels.

GETTING AROUND Cars are the easiest way around Jackson Hole (rental cars are available at the airport and in town), but you can get away with not having one if you're flexible. The **Jackson Hole Shuttle** (© 307/200-1400; www.jhshuttle.com) and **Alltrans** (© 307/733-3135; www.jacksonholealltrans.com) provide service between the airport and Jackson or Teton Village (rates range from $20–$70 one-way), as well as private tours. Several taxis also operate in town; for a list, visit www.jacksonholeairport.com/airport-guide. Before you call a cab, remember that many of the hotels and car-rental agencies in the Jackson area offer free shuttles to and from the airport.

The **Southern Teton Area Rapid Transit** system (**START**; © 307/733-4521; www.startbus.com) offers daily bus trips around town and to/from Teton Village. Rides within town are free, and it'll cost adults $3 for a one-way fare to Teton Village (free for children 8 and under). Buses come roughly every 30 minutes and run

Whether you're a raw beginner or a seasoned pro, Jackson can make you feel at home. There's mountain biking, hiking, fishing, kayaking, and river running in the summer, and skiing, snowmobiling, and snowboarding in the winter.

SPORTS EQUIPMENT & RENTALS There's no shortage of places to gear up in this town. If you're here to climb the Tetons (or other serious endeavors), **Teton Mountaineering,** 170 N. Cache St (© 307/733-3595; www.tetonmtn.com), can equip you with top-of-the-line backpacking, climbing, and backcountry skiing gear. **Hoback Sports,** at 530 W. Broadway Ave. #3 (© 307/733-5335; www.hobacksports.com), specializes in skis, snowboards, and bikes and also offers rentals. **Skinny Skis,** 65 W. Deloney Ave. (© 307/733-6094; www.skinnyskis.com), is a popular downtown shop carrying apparel and equipment for pretty much every mountain-related sport; it also rents gear, including ice axes and crampons. Its sister shop, **Moosely Mountaineering,** 12170 Dornan Rd. in Moose (© 307/739-1801), just outside the South entrance to Grand Teton National Park, carries a more limited selection of essentials for sale and rent from early May to Sept. **Teton Backcountry Rentals,** at 565 N. Cache St. (© 307/828-1885; www.tetonbcrentals.com), rents a wide range of summer and winter gear and even delivers to your hotel. Shop for quality used gear at **Headwall Sports,** 520 U.S. 89 (℅ **307/734-8022;** www.headwallsports.com).

SUMMER SPORTS & ACTIVITIES

FISHING   Yellowstone and Grand Teton National Parks have incredible fishing in their lakes and streams; see the "Fishing" sections in chapters 4 and 6 for details.

The Snake River emerges from Jackson Lake Dam as a broad, strong river, with decent fishing from its banks in certain spots—such as right below the dam—and better fishing if you float the river. Fly-fishers should ask advice at local stores on recent insect hatches and good stretches of river, or hire a guide. Outdoor gear stores will provide all the tackle and more information on fishing conditions than you can likely process. **JD High Country Outfitters,** at 50 E. Broadway (℅ **307/733-7210;** www.highcountryflies.com), stocks all the fishing gear and fly-tying supplies you'd ever need and also runs guided trips on six local rivers. For more in-the-know local insight into the best places to cast, book a trip with **Grand Teton Fly Fishing,** 225 W. Broadway (℅ **307/690-0910;** grandtetonflyfishing.com), or **Grand Fishing Adventures,** PO Box 582 in Teton Village (℅ **307/734-9684**). Both are licensed concessionaires with Grand Teton National Park. Expect to pay $450 to $575 for a half-day trip.

GOLF   It's hard to imagine a golf course with more impressive views than the swanky **Jackson Hole Golf & Tennis Club,** 5000 Spring Gulch Rd. (℅ **307/733-3111;** www.jhgtc. com), with its vista of the Tetons (not to mention the occasional grazing bison or moose). The 18-hole, Robert Trent Jones II course also offers fine dining at **North Grille** and a pool. Daily greens fees range from $165 to $190, cart included. The other public option in town, **Teton Pines Country Club and Resort,** 3450 N. Clubhouse Dr. (℅ **307/733-1733;** www.tetonpines.com), is no slouch in the scenery department, either, and also features a tasty restaurant and tennis. Daily greens fees at the Arnold Palmer– and Ed Seay–designed 18-hole course are $140 to $160, cart included.

HIKING   Grand Teton National Park is a hiker's paradise (see chapter 6), but the trails can get a mite crowded during the high season. Fortunately, the 3.4-million-acre **Bridger-Teton National Forest** extending north, south, and east of Jackson encompasses equally gorgeous mountain scenery—with a fraction of the people, and without the same permit red tape. The **Shoshone National Forest,** just east, and the **Caribou-Targhee National Forest,** northwest, add to the embarrassment of riches in the area. Those who strike out to explore the Bridger-Teton trails will 13,000-plus-foot peaks, turquoise lakes, glaciers, and abundant wildlife. Options are nearly endless, but one standout is the Teton Crest Trail, a high-altitude route that winds for 40 miles between Teton Pass and Grand Teton's String Lake. For details, other hike suggestions, and trail conditions, head over to the **Jackson Hole and Greater Yellowstone Visitor Center** at 532 N. Cache St. to chat with rangers, or contact the forest service directly (© **307/739-5500;** www.fs.usda.gov/btnf).

HORSEBACK RIDING   Besides the stables inside Grand Teton National Park (see chapter 6), several Jackson outfitters offer rides ranging from 2-hour jaunts to multiday trips. Try the family-owned **Mill Iron Ranch** (© **307/733-6390;** www.millironranch.net) and **A-OK Corral at Horse Creek Ranch** (© **307/733-6556;** www.horsecreekranch.com). Half- to full-day rides range from $85 to about $150.

KAYAKING, CANOEING & PADDLEBOARDING The Snake River attracts river rats from the world over, but several local lakes also offer excellent paddling. For lessons and guided tours in river and lake kayaking, canoeing, and stand-up paddleboarding, check out **Rendezvous River Sports,** 945 W. Broadway (© **307/733-2471;** www.jackson holekayak.com).

RAFTING   Rafting trips on the Snake River come in two flavors: wild and mild. The Grand Canyon of the Snake, a deep gorge about 20 miles south of Jackson, hosts the area's classic whitewater trip—an 8-mile stretch of turbulent water, featuring up to 10 Class II and III (on a scale of I–VI) rapids. The mellower float trips take place in and near the national park and also west of Jackson on the Snake's flatwater sections. Where whitewater trips are all about adrenaline and splashy action, float trips focus on scoping the banks for moose, bald eagles, bears, otters, and more aquatic wildlife. Several operators run float trips in the park (see chapter 6).

If you have to pick just one, go for the whitewater: The wild ride is great for older kids but still plenty thrilling for adults, and it's great fun to grab a paddle and row like crazy through the rapids. Jackson is practically lousy with top-notch rafting outfitters, so chances are you'll have an excellent time no matter which one you choose. Some of the very best are **Barker-Ewing** (© 307/733-1000; www.barker-ewing.com), **Mad River Boat Trips** (© 307/733-6203; www.mad-river.com), **Sands Whitewater** (© 307/733-4410; www.sandswhitewater.com), **Dave Hansen Whitewater** (© 307/733-6295; www.davehansenwhitewater.com), and **Lewis and Clark River Expeditions** (© 800/824-5375; www.lewisandclark riverrafting.com). Eight-mile, 3-hour whitewater trips usually cost $75 to $85 for adults.

ROPES COURSES & ZIPLINES Channel your inner Indiana Jones on one of Jackson's aerial adventure courses: You'll catwalk across hanging logs, scramble up rope nets, and zip through the trees (all securely clipped in to safety cables, of course). The **Treetop Adventure** at Snow King Resort, 400 E. Snow King Ave. (© 307/201-5666; www.snowkingmountain.com), features an adult course that gets progressively more challenging, plus a closer-to-the-ground kids' version ($70 for adults and $40 for children 7–13). Jackson Hole Mountain Resort, 3395 Cody Lane, Teton Village (© 307/733-2292; www.jacksonhole.com), has its **Aerial Adventure Course,** part of a Grand Adventure Park that also boasts a bungee trampoline, freefall drop tower, climbing wall, and mountain bike courses (admission prices were not final at press time).

WINTER SPORTS & ACTIVITIES

CROSS-COUNTRY SKIING Though it's best known for its superlative alpine ski resorts, Jackson offers fantastic opportunities for skinny-skis, too. Classic and skate skiers can hit groomed trails at several Nordic centers, while those with a bit more wanderlust can glide into the backcountry of the Bridger-Teton National Forest or Grand Teton (see chapter 6).

Teton County Parks and Recreation (© 307/733-5056; www.tetonparksandrec.org) grooms several areas for free Nordic skiing from mid-December to mid-March, including Cache Creek Canyon and the Snake River Dike. A bit farther afield, just outside Wilson, you'll find **Trail Creek Nordic Center** (© 307/733-6433; www.jhskiclub.org), an excellent spot for skate skiing. The Jackson Hole Ski and Snowboard

Club maintains its 10 miles of groomed trails, and day passes cost $15. Also near Wilson, the Teton Pines golf course becomes **Teton Pines Nordic Center** (℗ **307/733-1733;** www.tetonpines.com) in winter, with 9.9 miles of groomed, Teton-view trails; day passes are $15. On the other side of the valley, **Turpin Meadow Ranch** (℗ **307/543-9147;** www.turpinmeadowranch.com) operates a Nordic Ski Touring Center with 12 miles of rolling terrain near Moran; day passes cost $15. And on the other side of the mountains, $10 grants access to **Grand Targhee Resort**'s (℗ **307/353-2300;** www.grandtarghee.com) 9.3-mile Nordic Trail System. Check the Jackson Hole Nordic website at www.jhnordic.com for grooming details for these and other local areas.

Looking for a guided experience? **Jackson Hole Mountain Resort,** 3395 Cody Lane, Teton Village (℗ **307/733-2292;** www.jacksohole.com), can take you on private half- ($210) and full-day ($335) tours in the valley and inside Grand Teton.

DOG SLEDDING   No need to fly to the Yukon to careen over the snow behind a team of huskies—**Jackson Hole Iditarod Sled Dog Tours** (℗ **307/733-7388;** www.jhsleddog.com) can make that happen right here in Jackson. Run by eight-time Iditarod racer Frank Teasley, the outfitter offers half- and full-day trips through the Bridger-Teton National Forest for groups of four, plus a guide, and yes, you get to try your hands at the reins. A half-day trip costs $245, covers 12 miles, and includes a light picnic lunch. If you can, go for the full-day option ($355), which cruises to Granite Hot Springs (a 20-mile round trip) for a soak and a hot lunch.

DOWNHILL SKIING   Alpine skiers the world over dream about Jackson's slopes: Three resorts within striking distance (two of them top-tier destinations), abundant snow, and a reputation for exhilarating black diamond runs make it a true skier's paradise. No wonder locals and travelers alike turn ski-obsessed the moment the first flakes fall.

The crown jewel of the Jackson ski scene is **Jackson Hole Mountain Resort ★★**, 3395 Cody Lane, Teton Village (℗ **307/733-2292;** www.jacksonhole.com). Long known as an expert's mountain, half of the resort's runs are single or double black diamonds, and thrill seekers come to challenge themselves on supersteep trails such as the infamous Corbet's

Couloir, a daunting chute. But the resort has expanded and improved its blue runs in recent years, too. Twelve lifts grant access to 2,500 acres of in-bounds snow. The Sweetwater Gondola whisks you from base to peak in 7.5 minutes; also be sure to check out the iconic Aerial Tram, a 100-skier sky bus to Rendezvous Bowl. Adult lift tickets are $130/day, though you can sometimes pre-buy them online for a slight discount.

Grand Targhee Resort ★★, 3300 Ski Hill Rd., Alta (✆ **307/ 353-2300;** www.grandtarghee.com), offers a mellower experience over on the west side of the Teton Range. This much smaller ski area (5 lifts and 2,602 acres) is blessed with killer views and more than 500 inches of powder a year, and with lift tickets for $80/$85 holidays, it's quite the deal compared to its ritzier neighbor.

Then there's the locals' hill, **Snow King Mountain,** at 402 E. Snow King Ave., Jackson (✆ **307/201-5464;** www.snowking mountain.com). The hill (the smallest of the area ski resorts) anchors the south side of town, and indeed, you walk there from downtown Jackson; the runs trend toward the steep end of the spectrum. Snow biking trails, an ice climbing wall, inner tube slide, and hockey rink round out the activities. Lift tickets cost a mere $55.

SNOWMOBILING Although West Yellowstone is the most popular base for snowmobiling in the Yellowstone area, Jackson has a growing contingent of snowmobile aficionados and outfitters keen on exploring Grand Teton, Yellowstone, Bridger-Teton National Forest, the Continental Divide Snowmobile Trail, and especially Togwotee Pass.

Several outfitters run guided day or multiday trips near Jackson and as far north as Yellowstone. Check out **Scenic Safaris,** 1255 S. U.S. 89 (✆ **888/734-8898;** www.scenic-safaris. com); **Togwotee Snowmobile Adventures,** 1050 S. U.S. 89 (✆ **307/733-8800;** www.togwoteelodge.com); and **Old Faithful Snowmobile Adventures,** Jackson (✆ **307/733-9767;** www.snowmobilingtours.com). Tours range from $250 to $395 per driver (passengers cost a bit less). If you're just looking to rent your own sled, **Leisure Sports,** 1075 S. U.S. 89 (✆ **307/733-3040;** www.jacksonholefun.com), provides a variety for $135 to $225 per day, plus helmets, suits, and other essentials.

A BIRD'S-EYE VIEW

AERIAL TOURING The Tetons are gobsmacking enough from the valley floor—so imagine the view from high above. Get a vista even climbers don't see with a scenic flight tour: You'll glide over the area's major peaks and the wild back-country, gaining a perspective unlike any other. **Fly Jackson Hole,** 1250 E. Jackson Hole Airport Rd. (© **844/395-5499;** www.flyjacksonhole.com), offers sightseeing and photography tours ranging from $295 to $395 per person.

BALLOONING Add an extra shot to your latte for one of **Wyoming Balloon Company**'s (© **307/739-0900;** www.wyomingballoon.com) 6am "float trips" over a private ranch with in-your-face Tetons views (winds are calmest early in the day). The hour-long hot air balloon rides soar up to 4,000 feet. Prices are $325 for adults and $285 for children ages 6 to 12 (kids 5 and under not allowed).

WILDLIFE-WATCHING

National Elk Refuge ★ In summer, when green vegetation blankets the landscape, Jackson Hole's elk scatter throughout the high country of Grand Teton and Yellowstone National Parks and the Bridger-Teton National Forest. But as cold temps and snow arrive, they creep down from the mountains and gather on the lower-elevation plains of the National Elk Refuge in a kind of 7,000-strong elk family reunion. You can watch thousands of the antlered animals tussle, forage, and most often, just hang out in this protected space measuring 10 miles long and 6 miles wide at its fattest point. The U.S. Fish and Wildlife Service keeps the population happy by feeding them alfalfa pellets when deep snow makes grazing difficult, a tradition dating back to 1910. Besides essentially guaranteed elk sightings from late fall to April or May, you might spy bison (who like the elk's alfalfa, too), coyotes, bald eagles, trumpeter swans, and the occasional wolf.

You can drive the Refuge Road yourself, but the most fun way to see the refuge's wintering elk is on one of Double H Bar's winter **horse-drawn sleigh rides ★**. Bundle up for the hour-long rides, which will get you up close to thousands of the majestic animals. Pick up tickets at the Jackson Hole and Greater Yellowstone Visitor Center at 532 N. Cache St. ($21 adults; $15 for children 5–12; 4 and under free), then hop the free shuttle to the departure point. Rides depart from 10am to 4pm daily and are first-come, first-served.

Located 3 miles north of Jackson on U.S. Hwy. 26/89. © **307/733-9212.** www.fws.gov/refuge/national_elk_refuge. Free admission. Visitor center: summer daily 8am–7pm; winter daily 9am–5pm.

Area Attractions

One could almost be forgiven for neglecting the actual vacation destination—Grand Teton and Yellowstone—and getting caught up in all of Jackson's activities, shops, restaurants, and attractions instead. That's how lively this upscale mountain town is. (We did say *almost:* Don't let Jackson's charms divert you away from the parks entirely.)

Town Square is a fine place to begin your Jackson explorations; show up at 6pm in summer and you'll be treated to a free Old West shootout reenactment from the Chamber of Commerce and Jackson Hole Playhouse. History buffs can dig even deeper into the lives of the Native Americans, ranchers, and homesteaders of Jackson Hole's past at the **Jackson Hole Historical Society and Museum,** 1 block north at 225 N. Cache St. (© **307/733-2414;** www.jacksonholehistory.org). Admission is $5 for adults, free for children under 10. Also worth a stop: the three-story hydroponic greenhouse at **Vertical Harvest,** 155 W. Simpson Ave. (© **307/201-4452;** www.verticalharvestjackson.com), an innovative approach to urban farming. Free tours Weds, Fri, and Sat at 1pm.

Jackson Hole Aerial Tram ★ The same cherry-red tram that carries skiers to the top of Jackson Hole Mountain Resort's Rendezvous Mountain in winter remains in operation for hikers and sightseers in the warmer months—and though it's pricey, the 12-minute ride to 10,449 feet is one of Jackson's iconic thrills. You'll get unbeatable views of the Teton Range, Jackson, and the Snake River Valley, plus easy access to a network of trails along ridgelines and through wildflower meadows. At the top, **Corbet's Cabin** serves loaded waffles—peanut butter and bacon or lemon glaze and whipped cream are popular toppings) and beer. Hike, ride or even paraglide down with **Jackson Hole Paragliding** (© **307/739-2626;** www.jhparagliding.com).

3265 Village Dr., Teton Village (at Jackson Hole Ski Resort). © **307/739-2753.** www.jacksonhole.com. Tickets $29/$37 seniors/adults, $22 children 6–17, free for children 5 and under. Early Sept to early Oct and late May to mid-June daily 9am–5pm; mid-June to early Sept daily 9am–6pm. Tram runs approximately every 15 min.

National Museum of Wildlife Art ★★ This unique museum perched on a hill opposite the National Elk Refuge asks a provocative question: How do we see the animals that share our world? A series of well-curated galleries then goes about answering it with everything from 19th-century oil paintings of bighorn sheep and grizzlies to a stone sculpture of a sloth as the Madonna. Carl Rungius, the "premier painter of North American wildlife," dominates one gallery with examples of his work from the late 1800s to the 1940s, but you'll also find contributions from Georgia O'Keefe, Charles M. Russell, Henri Rousseau, and John Gutzon de la Mothe Borglum (of Mt. Rushmore fame). A children's gallery lets little ones channel their inspiration through drawings, stuffed animals, and costumes. The museum also houses a small café.

2820 Rungius Rd. (3 miles north of town on U.S. 89). © **307/733-5771.** www.wildlifeart.org. $14 adults, $6 first child 5–18, $2 additional children, kids 4 and under free. Tues–Sat 9am–5pm; Sun 11am–5pm.

ART GALLERIES

Jackson is home to more than 30 galleries, most of them clustered around Town Square. And while the town's reputation as a hotbed for Western art is well-deserved—you'll find soulful mustangs, romanticized cowboys and Native Americans, and bronze moose in droves—more surprising works pop up in some of the edgier galleries.

Rare Gallery, 60 E. Broadway (© **307/733-8726;** www.raregalleryjacksonhole.com), features modern paintings, sculpture, photos, and jewelry. **Tayloe Piggott Gallery,** 62 S. Glenwood St. (© **307/733-0555;** www.tayloepiggottgallery.com), exhibits contemporary work from noted artists in a sleek space. **Cayuse Western Americana,** 255 N. Glenwood St. (© **307/739-1940;** www.cayusewa.com), specializes in antiques such as Native American beadwork and weavings, vintage belt buckles and spurs, and early national park photography. The **Jackson Hole Gallery Association** (www.jacksonholegalleries.com) is a great resource.

Where to Stay

The good news: There's no shortage of excellent places to lay your head in Jackson and Teton Village. The bad news: It'll

Jackson

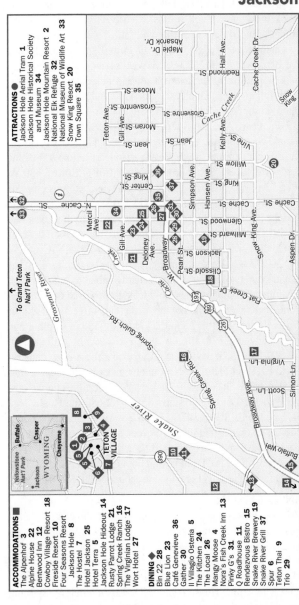

ATTRACTIONS ●

Jackson Hole Aerial Tram **1**
Jackson Hole Historical Society and Museum **34**
Jackson Hole Mountain Resort **2**
National Elk Refuge **32**
National Museum of Wildlife Art **33**
Snow King Resort **20**
Town Square **35**

ACCOMMODATIONS ■

The Alpenhof **3**
Alpine House **22**
Bentwood Inn **12**
Cowboy Village Resort **18**
Fireside Resort **10**
Four Seasons Resort Jackson Hole **8**
The Hostel **7**
Hotel Jackson **25**
Hotel Terra **5**
Jackson Hole Hideout **14**
Rusty Parrot Lodge **21**
Spring Creek Ranch **16**
The Virginian Lodge **17**
Wort Hotel **27**

DINING ◆

Bin 22 **28**
Blue Lion **23**
Café Genevieve **36**
Gather **30**
Il Villagio Osteria **5**
The Kitchen **24**
The Local **26**
Mangy Moose **4**
Nora's Fish Creek Inn **13**
Pinky G's **31**
Q Roadhouse **11**
Rendezvous Bistro **15**
Snake River Brewery **19**
Snake River Grill **37**
Spur **6**
Teton Thai **9**
Trio **29**

179

cost you. In high season, rates at even the mediocre hotels soar into the high $200s and the finest properties can set you back thousands. Book rooms as early as possible, and ask about reduced rates in spring and fall.

On the western edge of town, the **Pony Express Motel,** 1075 W. Broadway (© **307/733-3835;** www.ponyexpressmotel.com), is a step up from the average motel, including some rooms with full kitchens. Doubles go for $217 and suites for $327 in high season. A couple of blocks off Town Square, **Antler Inn,** 43 W. Pearl Ave. (© **307/733-2535;** www.townsquareinns. com), is a good bet, with a big hot tub and knotty wood bedframes. In summer, doubles range from $170 to $200 (some have fireplaces). Sister property **49er Inn & Suites,** 330 W. Pearl Ave. (© **307/733-7550;** www.townsquareinns.com), is similarly well-kept, with a stylish rusted exterior and an indoor pool, plus a hot tub; expect to pay a high-season rate of $219 to $269 (pricier rooms have fireplaces) for a double.

On the north side of town, **The Lexington,** 285 N. Cache St. (© **307/733-2648;** www.lexingtonhoteljacksonhole.com), has a wide variety of rooms, from standard doubles to suites to a full apartment. Complimentary hot breakfast is served on a mezzanine, there's a pool and hot tub, and you get free use of cruiser bikes during your stay. Doubles start at $350 in summer and mini-suites at $370. **Inn on the Creek,** 295 N. Millward St. (© **307/739-1565;** www.innonthecreek.com), is a cozy, country-style B&B on Flat Creek; room amenities might include fireplaces, patios, Jacuzzis, or kitchens. Summertime doubles cost $289 to $359 and studio suites $359 to $668. And **Rustic Inn,** 475 N. Cache St. (© **307/733-2357;** www.rusticinnatjh.com), sits on its own aspen- and evergreen-shaded property against Saddle Butte and Flat Creek; the 12-acre space includes fire pits, a teepee, plus a pool, sauna, and hot tub. Guest rooms ($349–$499 for doubles) and stand-alone cabins ($439–$569) are luxe.

IN JACKSON

Alpine House ★★ This intimate, Scandinavian-style inn just might be the friendliest lodging in town. With 22 unique rooms (plus five cottages on Flat Creek, a few blocks away), a library with a crackling fireplace, and a sunny atrium where the chef serves local bread and homemade granola for breakfast, The Alpine House is more B&B than hotel. Every room is different, but all share a bright white color scheme, blond wood, and touches such as antique furniture or lofted beds. Perks include free use of cruiser bikes and a 24-hour "honor bar" stocked with wine and whiskey. Owners Hans and Nancy Johnstone are former Olympians and great resources for planning outdoor adventures in Jackson Hole.

285 N. Glenwood St. ✆ 307/739-1570. www.alpinehouse.com. 27 units. $265–$340 double; $370 suite; $350–$520 cottage, includes full breakfast (inn, not cottages). Lower rates Oct–May. **Amenities:** Lounge; sauna; spa; free Wi-Fi.

Cowboy Village Resort ★ Set slightly apart from the bustle of downtown, this unassuming complex has the feel of a summer camp—except *these* cabins come with comfy beds and cable TV. The small but nicely decorated log cabins all have kitchenettes, private bathrooms, and pullout couches. There are also two lodge rooms, one of which is a family suite with bunk beds and a full kitchen. The village is one of the best deals in town for budget-minded travelers.

120 S. Flat Creek Dr. ✆ 307/733-3121. www.townsquareinns.com. 84 units. $134–$269 double; $188–$314 family suite, includes continental breakfast (winter only). Lower rates in winter. **Amenities:** Pool; Jacuzzi; gym; business center; free Wi-Fi.

Hotel Jackson ★★★ Staying at the Hotel Jackson is like sleeping inside of an issue of *Dwell* magazine: From the walls paneled with salvaged Wyoming barnwood to the custom-photo-printed curtains and pillows, every meticulously considered design detail comes together perfectly. Rooms in the LEED-certified boutique hotel are done up in a chic brown and white palette, and include gas fireplaces; some have mountain views, and suites include private patios and soaking tubs. If you're looking for the coolest lodging in town, this is it. The restaurant, Figs, serves creative Mediterranean fare.

120 N. Glenwood St. ✆ 307/733-2200. www.hoteljackson.com. 64 units. $399–$499 double; $699–$999 suite. Lower rates spring and fall. **Amenities:** Restaurant; Jacuzzi; free ski shuttle to Teton Village (winter); free Wi-Fi.

Rusty Parrot Lodge ★★ If you could somehow pick up a stately manor from the English countryside and plop it in the middle of Jackson, it would surely look and feel a whole lot like the Rusty Parrot. This family-run luxury lodge has tons of charm: Think wood-paneled library, a cozy den with leather chairs and a stained-glass window, outdoor fire pits, and an intimate restaurant, the Wild Sage. Every room is a little different, but all feature custom-made wood furniture and giant soaking tubs (some have fireplaces, too). The pampering Body Sage Spa is right on the premises.

175 N. Jackson St. © **307/733-2000.** www.rustyparrot.com. 32 units. $465–$495 double; $755 suite. Lower rates spring and fall. **Amenities:** Restaurant; lounge; Jacuzzi; spa; free ski shuttle to Teton Village (winter); free Wi-Fi.

Virginian Lodge ★ In a town stuffed with A-list accommodations for A-list prices, the friendly, unpretentious Virginian is a breath of fresh air. The owners have purposely kept rates affordable to make sure the 99 percent still have a place to stay in Jackson. The place is unapologetically old-school Western, with a taxidermied wildlife and a chandelier fashioned from a wagon wheel and antlers in the lobby; guests can also warm up by the giant fireplace, play arcade games, swim in the outdoor pool, or hang out in the expansive courtyard (there's even a liquor store and a hair salon on site). Rooms are simple and decorated with retro posters; kitchenette, Jacuzzi rooms, and suites are available. The Virginian also offers an RV park.

250 W. Broadway. © **307/733-2792.** www.virginianlodge.com. 170 units. $149–$159 double; $189 w/kitchenette; $169–$239 suite. **Amenities:** Restaurant; lounge; pool; Jacuzzi; free Wi-Fi.

Wort Hotel ★★★ Part elegant historic hotel, part art gallery, and part lively bar/music space, the Wort Hotel is one of a kind. The stately stone building in the center of downtown has been hosting guests since the family of late 19th-century homesteader Charles Wort opened it in 1941 (with one glitch in the 1980s, when it nearly burned down), and it remains one of Jackson's iconic buildings. The lobby's grand staircase leads to one of two cozy fireplaces, and more than 200 paintings, sculptures, furniture, and photos are on display. The rooms are done in "New West" style, with leather chairs and cowboy-themed art, and some have wet bars; the Grand Rooms and suites are enormous (the largest, the Silver Dollar Suite, spans 850 sq. ft.), with sitting areas and posh bathrooms. The hotel's **Silver Dollar Bar** is a Jackson institution, named for the 2,032 silver dollars inlaid in the bar.

50 N. Glenwood St. (at Broadway). © **307/733-2190.** www.worthotel. com. 55 units. $429–$489 double; $899 suite. Lower rates fall–spring. **Amenities:** Restaurant; lounge; gym; Jacuzzi; free Wi-Fi.

NEAR JACKSON

Bentwood Inn ★★ Ever wished you had a wealthy friend with a gorgeous mountain getaway? Until you manage to widen your social circle, there's the Bentwood Inn. This warm, welcoming B&B (built from logs felled during the 1988 Yellowstone fire) offers five themed rooms, each with a private bathroom and fireplace. A lounge starring a stone fireplace and piano invites idling, and the wide front porch is the perfect spot to kick back on a summer night. Innkeepers Bob and Virginia Schrader can help you plan your itinerary and arrange for activities and dining; they prioritize environmentally friendly practices. The included hot breakfast often features homemade breads and fresh fruit, and you also get evening wine and hors d'oeuvres. A few times a week, the owners whip up a four-course dinner, too.

4250 Raven Haven Rd., Wilson. ℰ **307/739-1411.** www.bentwood inn.com. 5 units. $429 double, includes full breakfast. **Amenities:** Restaurant; free Wi-Fi.

Fireside Resort ★ If you're into ultramodern architecture, you'll love this collection of sleek, wooden modular cabins on wheels on the highway between Jackson and Teton Village. Each features a fireplace, full kitchen, small deck, pullout couch, and très cool furniture (pony-print ottomans, iron-accented coffee tables). A few have lofts with platform beds. Fire pits provide still more hangout space, and the creek winding through the property makes for frequent moose sightings. There's also an RV park on site ($79–$125 per night), and you can arrange for rental Jeeps through the resort.

2780 N. Moose Wilson Rd, Wilson. ℰ **307/733-1177.** www.fireside jacksonhole.com. 23 units. $432–$482 cabin (3-night minimum in summer). Lower rates fall through spring. **Amenities:** Free Wi-Fi.

Jackson Hole Hideout ★★ Though it's just 15 minutes from downtown Jackson, this delightful B&B on the top of a steep, winding forest road feels a world away. Formerly known as A Teton Tree House, the sprawling inn resembles the Weasley House of Harry Potter fame with its many edges, corners, nooks, and crannies; new owners Greg and Beth McCoy updated the place inside and out in 2015. Each of the five plush rooms has a private bathroom and all but one have a private deck with valley views (the Wrangler Room even has a swing). An outdoor fire pit and indoor fireplace offer more cozy corners for lounging. The tasty breakfast menu might include frittatas, waffles or baked French toast, and you'll be treated to drinks and hors d'oeuvres at check-in.

6175 Heck of a Hill Rd., Wilson. © **307/733-3233.** www.jackson holehideout.com. 5 units. $340–$375 double, includes full breakfast. Lower rates fall through spring. **Amenities:** Free Wi-Fi.

Spring Creek Ranch ★★★

For a positively opulent experience, look up—about 1,000 feet above the valley floor, where Spring Creek Ranch sits atop East Gros Ventre Butte, on a 1,000-acre wildlife sanctuary. The Teton views from up here are incredible, and you could spot deer or moose wandering past your windows. Accommodations range from deluxe (rooms with fireplaces and balconies) to lavish (studio to four-bedroom townhomes with sunken living rooms and fancy full kitchens) to downright sumptuous (mountain villas that start at 4,000-plus sq. ft.). Guests also enjoy **The Granary,** an upscale restaurant serving steak and seafood entrees, and extensive fitness options such as tennis courts and a big outdoor pool. Staff naturalists lead guided hikes around the preserve and excursions to Yellowstone and Grand Teton.

1600 N. East Butte Rd., Jackson (on top of the East Gros Ventre Butte). © **307/733-8833.** www.springcreekranch.com. 117 units. $360 double; $395–$2,600 condo or home, includes breakfast at The Granary. Lower rates fall–spring. **Amenities:** Restaurant; lounge; Jacuzzi; pool; spa; tennis; free Wi-Fi.

IN TETON VILLAGE

You can take advantage of the attractions of Jackson, to the south, and Grand Teton, to the north, without suffering the crowds by journeying to Teton Village, which is approximately equidistant from both. Located at the foot of Jackson Hole Mountain Resort, the village and surrounding area offer several fine dining establishments, and activities nearby include skiing, ballooning, and hiking in Grand Teton National Park. During winter months, this is the center of activity in the valley. While lodging in the town of Jackson tends to be a little cheaper in the winter than the summer, Teton Village is reversed—rooms by the ski hill get more expensive after the snow falls. For a wide range of basic condos and deluxe vacation homes, contact **Jackson Hole Resort Lodging** (© **307/733-3990;** www. jhrl.com) or check out Airbnb's numerous options.

The Alpenhof ★★ Teton Village's oldest and most unique lodge has been bringing a touch of Bavarian flavor to the mountain since 1965. The lodge's original owners were Swiss and German, and they designed the Alpenhof to echo the country inns of their home in the Alps: gingerbread-house balusters, roaring fireplaces, and ornately carved wooden beams. Similarly, the in-house **Alpenrose Dining Room** (winter only) serves up all manner of strudels, schnitzels, and raclettes. Rooms are all a little different, featuring hard-carved Bavarian-style furnishings and stenciled art on the walls; some have their own fireplaces and/or balconies. The suites are particularly nice, with lots of space and roomy decks.

3255 W. Village Dr. ✆ **307/733-3242.** www.alpenhoflodge.com. 42 units. $209–$359 double; $430–$600 suite. Lower rates spring (Mar and May) and fall (Oct). Closed Oct–Nov and Apr. **Amenities:** 2 restaurants (1 in summer); lounge; Jacuzzi; pool; sauna; free Wi-Fi.

Four Seasons Resort Jackson Hole ★★★

If nothing but the best will do, you can't beat this posh resort perched right at the foot of a pair of ski lifts. From the opulent stone fireplace in the lobby to the ultra-comfortable, stylish rooms to the top-notch service, the Four Seasons oozes swanky comfort—all with a Western flavor that fits perfectly with its surroundings. There's an on-site salon, an elaborate spa, a kids' room stocked with a pool table and Xbox games, rental bikes and stand-up paddleboards, and a concierge service that can set you up with guided activities such as horseback riding, rafting, and hot-air ballooning. Even the most "basic" rooms here are spacious and thoughtfully appointed, with decks, soaking tubs, and fireplaces, and you can really live it up in a suite or enormous private residence. The three restaurants range from high-end to a poolside café, and there's an elegant lobby bar.

7680 Granite Loop. ✆ **307/732-5000.** www.fourseasons.com/jackson hole. 158 units. $799–$1,259 double; $1,409–$4,700 condo or suite. Lower rates spring and fall. **Amenities:** 3 restaurants; lounge; concierge; gym; Jacuzzis; pool; sauna; spa; free Wi-Fi.

The Hostel ★

Ski bum paradise meets European-style travelers' hub in this low-key lodge. Considering its prime location just steps from the ski mountain, it's shockingly affordable, and by far the best value in Teton Village. Privacy-seekers can book private rooms with one king bed or four twins (plus bathrooms), while those who want rock-bottom prices can crash in simple shared quads. When not out playing, guests gather in a lively common area reminiscent of a

1970s rec room, with board games, ping pong, foosball, and comfy couches; as well as flatscreen TVs and DVD/Blu-ray players. There's also a ski waxing station and ski storage, and in summer, BBQ grills, horseshoes, and croquet.

3315 Village Dr. ⓒ **307/733-3415.** www.thehostel.us. 55 units. $79–$139 double/private quad; $34–$45 bunk. Lower rates spring–fall. **Amenities:** Free Wi-Fi.

Hotel Terra ★★   With its mismatched modern furniture, nouveau-West accents, and stark wildlife photography adorning the walls, Hotel Terra is the hippest lodge in the village. The sleek property prides itself on its sustainable touches; the building is LEED-certified. Boutique shops, a spa, the rooftop infinity pool and hot tub, and excellent dining (including standout **Il Villagio Osteria**) keep the vibe quite luxurious. Rooms are well-appointed; the standard options boast rain showers, soaking tubs, and heated bathroom floors, studios add kitchens and fireplaces, and one- to three-bedroom suites can put up the whole family. Some rooms have balconies or small terraces, too. Winter bonus: Hotel Terra recently added a ski valet with on-site rentals.

3335 W. Village Dr. ⓒ **307/739-4000.** www.hotelterrajacksonhole.com. 132 units. $350–$380 double; $500–$1,480 suite. Lower rates spring and fall. **Amenities:** 2 restaurants; lounge; concierge; gym; Jacuzzi; pool; spa; free Wi-Fi.

Where to Eat

Unlike some of the other gateway towns, Jackson has more quality restaurants than you'd ever fit into a single vacation. Like most everything else around here, options tend to be upscale and pricey, but you can also find a few gems in the casual category. This is a meat town, so expect all kinds of steak, elk, and bison to grace local menus, plus seafood and locally sourced ingredients. For a quick breakfast, try **Cowboy Coffee Co.,** 125 N. Cache St. (ⓒ **307/733-7392**), for egg sandwiches and huckleberry espresso drinks, or the charming **Persephone Bakery,** 145 E. Broadway (ⓒ **307/200-6708**), a purveyor of delicate pastries, rustic breads, and hot sandwiches.

EXPENSIVE

The Blue Lion ★★ NEW AMERICAN   Homey and cozy, the Blue Lion is a Jackson institution that has been housed in the same 1930s home since it opened in 1978.

Tables are grouped under stained glass windows, and in summer, the shady front patio hosts live acoustic music. The place is known for its rack of lamb with jalapeño mint sauce, plus its tenderloins (beef, bison, and elk) and grilled fish. French onion soup and buffalo ravioli appetizers are stand-outs.

160 N. Millward St. ⓒ **307/733-3912.** www.bluelionrestaurant.com. Reservations recommended. Main courses $19–$43. Summer daily 5:30–10pm; winter daily 5:30–9pm.

Gather ★★ NEW AMERICAN Executive chef Clark Myers left the outstanding Jenny Lake Lodge (see chapter 7) for this new-in-2015 spot. Gather shares Jenny Lake's commitment to local, seasonal ingredients, but this downtown Jackson restaurant has a much sleeker, modern feel. The menu is a combination of elevated comfort food (cheddar broccoli grits), international inspirations (grilled Spanish octopus), creative veggie dishes (cauliflower risotto, toasted quinoa), and classic Wyoming fare. There's also an extensive wine list, and on Tuesdays at 2pm, you can pop in to taste the week's special with the chef.

72 S. Glenwood St. ⓒ **307/264-1820.** Reservations recommended. Main courses $23–$40. Mon–Sat 5–10pm; Sun 5–9pm (closed Tues in Oct–Nov).

Il Villaggio Osteria ★★ ITALIAN This high-end pizza and pasta spot brings a true taste of Italy to Teton Village: Chef Serge Smith trained and worked there, and it shows. Expect indulgent fresh-made pastas; mains like lamb shoulder, elk T-bone, trout, and boar shank; wood-fired pizzas topped with the likes of pulled mozzarella, anchovy, and potato or mushrooms and béchamel cheese; and a variety of inventive antipasti. The wine list is long and varied, with plenty of Italian bottles, plus an impressive cocktail menu. Il Villaggio Osteria lives in the sustainability-minded Hotel Terra, so it makes sense that they've partnered with the Monterey Bay Aquarium Seafood Watch program to put responsibly sourced fish on the menu.

3335 W. Village Dr., Teton Village (in the Hotel Terra). ⓒ **307/739-4100.** Reservations recommended. Main courses $12–$22 lunch; $22–$48 dinner. Daily 7–10am, 11:30am–4pm, 5–10pm.

The Local ★★ STEAK/SEAFOOD Jackson is a steak lover's town, and this swanky downtown stop is one of the best places around to enjoy a lovingly prepared slab of meat. The Local partners with area ranchers to serve grass-fed, hormone-free steaks. Trout, fried chicken, buffalo medallions, and an excellent (if $18!) burger round out the menu, and there's a nice selection of charcuterie and a raw bar. The bar serves a long list of tasty small bites alongside its cool cocktails and whiskey flights. The lunch menu leans more to burgers, sandwiches, and salads.

55 N. Cache St. ☎ **307/201-1717.** www.localjh.com. Reservations recommended. Main courses $9–$19 lunch, $18–$39 dinner. Mon–Sat 11:30am–close; Sun 5:30pm–close (usually 10:30–11:30pm).

Snake River Grill ★★★ NEW AMERICAN   This rustic-yet-fancy restaurant on Town Square is all about consistency: It has been a mainstay of the dining scene for more than 20 years, and it's perennially touted as the town's best restaurant by adoring locals and travelers alike. The eats are inventive and wide-ranging: You might start with tuna tartare, butter-basted quail, or Southern-style veal sweetbreads, then move on to a Korean hot bowl, Wagyu flat iron steak, or tuna served with soba noodles. Favorites include onion rings served stacked on a branding iron and the featured-on-the-Food-Network Eskimo ice cream bars. The impressive wine list has more than 300 choices, plus a great cocktail menu.

84 E. Broadway (on the Town Square). ☎ **307/733-0557.** www.snakerivergrill.com. Reservations recommended. Main courses $23–$54. Daily 5:30pm–close (usually 9–10pm). Closed Nov and Apr.

Spur ★★ NEW AMERICAN   All shiny, dark wood, flickering firelight, and modern lines, Spur fits right into the contemporary design of its host, the Teton Mountain Lodge. Chef Kevin Humphreys offers a thoughtfully curated menu that showcases local and organic ingredients. Look for appetizers such as tuna tartare tacos and buffalo pastrami sausage, plus charcuterie and cheese boards; main dishes might include cod and steelhead fish options and surprises like venison filet. The lunch menu's loaded nachos have legions of fans, and Spur also offers breakfast and Sunday brunch.

3385 Cody Lane (at Teton Mountain Lodge). ☎ **307/732-6932.** Reservations recommended. Main courses $12–$18 lunch, $22–$33 dinner. Mon–Sat 7–10am and 11:30am–9pm; Sun 11am–9pm.

Trio ★★ NEW AMERICAN   Jackson's dining scene can be a web of interconnections, with top chefs hopping between restaurants or branching out from established favorites to open their own hot spots. So it is with Trio, started by three chefs from the excellent Snake River Grill. The spinoff has earned its stripes as one of the best upscale restaurants in town. Dishes tend toward well-executed classics such as New York strip steak, halibut, buffalo tenderloin, and wood-fired chicken, plus a selection of pizzas. Locals rave about the waffle fries, topped with bleu cheese fondue and scallions.

45 S. Glenwood St. © **307/734-8038.** www.bistrotrio.com. Reservations recommended. Main courses $15–$46. Sun–Fri 5:30–9pm; Sat 5:30–9:30pm.

MODERATE

Bin 22 ★★ TAPAS   Owner Gavin Fine (a sommelier and co-owner of The Kitchen, Q Roadhouse, Il Villaggio Osteria, and Rendezvous Bistro) envisioned Bin 22 as a one-stop shop: a laid-back place to pick up a bottle of wine and a few groceries as well as sit down to Spanish- and Italian-style small plates. Here, you can choose a bottle from the well-stocked wine shop and take it to your table to pair with tasty tapas: salumi, cheeses, and excellent shareables such as charred octopus, baked egg, and the house-pulled mozzarella with several toppings. On top of all the wine options, Bin 22 also serves up pints from Jackson's Roadhouse Brewing.

200 W. Broadway. © **307/739-9463.** www.bin22jacksonhole.com. Shared plates $10–$17. Mon–Sat 11:30am–10pm; Sun 3–10pm.

Café Genevieve ★★ NEW AMERICAN   The log cabin housing this welcoming café doesn't just look old—a couple of early settlers built it in the early 1900s. Today, the café serves Southern-inspired food with a local, seasonal flair. Every day kicks off with a hearty brunch, served until 3pm, which stars fried chicken and waffles, Cajun eggs benedict, and biscuits and gravy. Lunch consists of soups, salads, and burgers, while dinner gets more upscale with dishes such as brick chicken, pork neck ragu, or a duck ramen bowl. Don't leave without sampling the café's specialty, pig candy—rich candied bacon crumbled over a salad or served as an appetizer. The lovely patio makes for fine al fresco dining in summer.

135 E. Broadway. © **307/732-1910.** www.genevievejh.com. Reservations recommended. Main courses $9–$15 breakfast; $12–$18 lunch; $20–$39 dinner. Daily 8am–3pm; Tues–Sat 8am–close (usually 9–10pm).

The Kitchen ★★ NEW AMERICAN   Visiting the Kitchen is a bit like dining inside a warm, inviting spaceship, thanks to its streamlined architecture and curved wall aglow with soft lighting. One of Jackson's favorite restaurants, the place's artfully presented dishes draw from a variety of culinary influences, from Asian to Mountain West flavors. Fish have a major role on the menu, from the crudo bar to entrees of seared ahi tuna or halibut. You'll find a nice mix of classics (pork chops, fish and chips, burgers) and more fanciful meals (wild boar ravioli, smoked arctic char). There's also a long list of specialty cocktails and wines by the glass.

155 N. Glenwood St. ☎ **307/734-1633.** www.thekitchenjackson hole.com. Reservations recommended. Main courses $18–$34. Thurs–Mon 5–10pm.

Mangy Moose ★ AMERICAN This venerable slopeside institution commands the Jackson Hole après-ski scene. Celebrating its 50th anniversary in 2017, the enormous, two-story Mangy Moose is *the* place to be when your shaking legs can't handle one more run on the mountain; conveniently, you can ski directly to it. A lively atmosphere awaits, with moose heads and old-school posters on the walls, microbrews on tap, and live music that fires up just as the slopes shut down. The menu favors carnivores, with chops, prime rib, burgers, and steaks; sides like fries and mac and cheese add a comfort-food touch. You can also fuel up here midday on wraps, burgers, and pizza, or swing by the affiliated RMO Café for breakfast.

3295 Village Dr., Teton Village. ☎ **307/733-4913.** www.mangymoose. com. Reservations recommended for groups. Main courses $6–$10 breakfast; $9–$15 lunch; $15–$42 dinner. Daily 7am–2pm (cafe), 11am–2am (saloon), 5–10pm (dining room).

Q Roadhouse ★ AMERICAN Those with peanut allergies should steer clear of this casual local favorite between Teton Village and Jackson: The (free) nuts are served out of barrels, and it's customary to just toss your shells on the floor. Follow them with stick-to-your-ribs, Southern-style choices like a po' boy, shrimp and grits, or catfish; you might also find a few outliers, such as Indian lamb stew, pasta, and a Korean breakfast bowl. Q's own Roadhouse brews are on tap, along with a long wine list, and in summer an ice cream shack sets up right outside.

2550 Moose-Wilson Rd. ☎ **307/739-0700.** www.qjacksonhole.com. Reservations recommended. Main courses $10–$19. Daily 5–9:30pm. Bar open later (usually 11pm).

Rendezvous Bistro ★★ FRENCH/AMERICAN Rendezvous Bistro was conceived to offer a top-shelf dining experience without the sky-high price tag. And the place delivers the best of both worlds: a sunny, casual space with excellent service and cooking. Sophisticated eaters gravitate toward the raw bar, which serves oysters on the half shell and tuna tartare, or to apps like escargot in garlic-herb butter. The French influence permeates the main courses, too, with dishes such as cassoulet, steak frites, and *croque madame,* but you might also find more Americanized flavors: roasted chicken, meatloaf, and pasta. The bistro also sources some veggies from Vertical Harvest, the local multistory greenhouse.

380 S. Broadway. © **307/739-1100.** www.rendezvousbistro.net. Reservations recommended. Main courses $12–$34. Daily 5:30–10pm.

INEXPENSIVE

Nora's Fish Creek Inn ★ AMERICAN It's easy to find this beloved diner 7 miles west of Jackson: Just look for the giant trout on the roof. Locals flock to this longtime favorite for its famed breakfasts; the place is usually bustling, but it's worth the wait. Friendly staffers serve up trout and eggs, biscuits and gravy, omelets, and pancakes in a cozy log cabin with a crackling fireplace, and the bar slings bloody marys, mimosas, and screwdrivers. Specials include Mexican-inspired plates such as *huevos rancheros* and the banana bread French toast, which Guy Fieri highlighted on a 2014 episode of *Diners, Drive-Ins, and Dives.* Nora's also serves lunch on weekdays.

5600 W. Wyo. 22, Wilson. © **307/733-8288.** www.norasfishcreekinn. com. Main courses $7–$16 breakfast, $9–$15 lunch. Mon–Fri 6:30am–2pm; Sat–Sun 6:30am–1:30pm.

Pinky G's ★ PIZZA Looking for a late-night bite? Pinky G's is there for you until 2am, offering up big slices of New York-style pizza. Build your own or go for one of the specialty pies, including the Abe Froman (spicy sausage and buffalo mozzarella) and the BBQ Porky G'ZA (pulled pork with peppers); you'll also find chicken wings and calzones on the menu. Exposed brick walls and a giant gumball machine give the place a hip, casual vibe, and there's a full bar.

50 W. Broadway © **307/734-7465.** www.pinkygs.com. Pizzas $12–$23. Daily 11am–2am.

Snake River Brewing Co. ★★ MICROBREWERY Foosball, first-rate beers, and food that's a significant cut above your average pub fare—is it any wonder this casual brewery is hopping most nights? Jacksonites pack the place to scarf down rich pastas, loaded pizzas, burgers, pan-fried trout, plus an impressive array of hearty salads and starters (try the sausage sampler). Wash it down with one of their popular beers: The Jenny Lake Lager, Snake River Pale Ale, and Pako's EYE-P-A have all taken home awards. Arcade games, darts, and frequent community events make this a family-friendly place to spend an evening.

265 S. Millward St. ⓒ **307/739-2337.** www.snakeriverbrewing.com. Main courses $13–$23. Daily 11am–11pm. Bar stays open later.

Teton Thai ★ THAI   Five-alarm flavor devotees love this family-owned joint in Teton Village for its very spicy options (milder palates won't want to go past 2 on the spice scale), while everyone appreciates its summer patio. The extensive menu features Thai classics, from stir-fries to noodles to soups to curries; meat options include crispy duck on top of the usual proteins and veggies. Also look for starters such as fried tofu, chicken satay, and egg rolls. The bar menu offers sake and tropical cocktails along with local microbrews and wine.

7342 Granite Loop Rd. ⓒ **307/733-0022.** www.tetonthaivillage. com. Main courses $11–$18 lunch, $14–$18 dinner. Mon–Sat 11:30am–9:30pm (summer); daily 11:30am–9pm (winter).

Jackson After Dark

Jackson packs a whole lot of culture into a small mountain town. It's always worth checking out what's going on at the **Center for the Arts,** 265 S. Cache St. (ⓒ **307/734-8956;** www.jhcenterforthearts.org), a collaboration between 19 local and state nonprofits. The campus includes a 500-seat theater and puts on dance performances, art shows, plays, live music, comedy shows, and lectures—Reggie Watts, Willie Nelson, and David Sedaris have all dropped by in recent years.

In summer, the **Grand Teton Music Festival** (ⓒ **307/733-1128;** box office during the festival; www.gtmf.org) showcases talent from all over the country, plus Canada. The classical music celebration extends for 7 weeks, with performances taking place in an amphitheater in Teton Village. Tickets range from $25 to $55 (students are free). Find still more live music at the **Pink Garter Theatre,** 50 W. Broadway (ⓒ **307/733-1500;** www.pinkgartertheatre.com), host to local and national touring acts, or at the summer weekly free **Music on Main** shows in Victor, Idaho (ⓒ **208/399-2884;**

www.tetonvalleyfoundation.org). Jackson's START bus can take you straight there for about $8.

As for more traditional nightlife, the **Million Dollar Cowboy Bar,** 25 N. Cache St. (© 307/733-2207; www.million dollarcowboybar.com), is Jackson's quintessential watering hole. The bar stools are saddles, the pillars knotty pine, and the scene raucous, thanks to frequent live country music shows and dancing—what's not to love? Fuel up for the night at the excellent **Million Dollar Cowboy Steakhouse** located directly under the bar. For a more chilled-out vibe, **Sidewinders Tavern,** 945 W. Broadway (© 307/734-5766; www. sidewinderstavern.com), is the town's favorite sports bar, with 30 flat-screen TVs and 28 beers on tap. **Thai Me Up,** 75 E. Pearl Ave. (© 307/733-0005; www.thaijh.com), pours 20 different pints from the award-winning nano-brewery Melvin Brewing and plays kung fu movies over the bar. And you can't go wrong at the **Stagecoach Bar,** 5755 W. Hwy. 22 (© 307/733-4407; www.stagecoachbar.net), Wilson's favored place to party since 1942. Thursday nights bring a disco dance-a-thon, and every Sunday, the Stagecoach Band gets an enthusiastic crowd dancing to country western tunes.

CODY, WYOMING ★★

53 miles from the east entrance to Yellowstone

Welcome to the Wild West: More than any other Yellowstone gateway town, Cody has staked its identity on keeping the era of cowboys and Indians alive and kicking. No wonder, considering the town's history: The famed Old West showman William F. "Buffalo Bill" Cody helped found the place in the 1890s, and his work securing a railroad stop and dam spurred the town's growth. Today, that Wild West flavor still permeates Cody, from the main drag shootout reenactments to the rebuilt historic Old Trail Town to the cowboy hats and belt buckles you'll spy downtown.

Set in the gorgeous Bighorn Basin and ringed by three sets of mountains (the Bighorns, Absarokas, and Owl Creeks), this area would be an outdoor haven even without its proximity to Yellowstone. The Shoshone River flows right through town, and the 50-mile scenic drive from Cody through the Wapiti Valley to Yellowstone is by far the most visually stunning way to approach the park. After you're through playing outside, Cody makes a primo basecamp for browsing galleries, catching a rodeo, and checking out a collection of stellar museums. Buffalo Bill would be proud.

Essentials

For information on air service to Cody and rental-car agencies see "Getting There & Getting Around," in chapter 10.

GETTING THERE   Cody is a 4-hour, 177-mile drive from Jackson if you take U.S. 89 north and U.S. 14/16/20 east through Yellowstone; it's another hour if you go via U.S. 26 east and WY 120 west outside the park borders (which you'll have to do fall through early summer). From Sheridan, it's 147 miles and 3 hours away on U.S. 14 west. If you're traveling from Cheyenne, take I-25 north and U.S. 20 west 392 miles and nearly 6 hours to get to Cody. Be aware winter storms can quickly make the roads treacherous: Call ℂ **888/996-7623,** or 511 (in state) or 307/772-0824 for road and travel information. Online, visit www.wyoroad.info.

VISITOR INFORMATION   The **Cody Chamber of Commerce,** 836 Sheridan Ave. (ℂ **307/587-2777;** www.cody chamber.org), visitor center is open daily 8am to 7pm in summer (to 5pm Mon–Fri fall–spring). The **Park County Travel Council** (ℂ **307/587-2297;** www.yellowstonecountry. org) is also a great source of info.

Getting Outside

The very best outdoor recreation opportunities around Cody are in Yellowstone itself. Beyond that, the **Shoshone National Forest** lies between the park and town and offers trails that grant access to the North Absaroka and Washakie Wildernesses, plus a number of peaceful campgrounds along the North Fork of the Shoshone River. Closer to town there's **Buffalo Bill State Park,** a small preserve on the shores of **Buffalo Bill Reservoir.** If water sports such as boating, fishing, waterskiing, and windsurfing are your thing, it's well worth a stop; two campgrounds accommodate RVs and waterfront picnic areas abound. In winter, **Sleeping Giant Ski Area** attracts local alpine skiers, Nordic fans glide several groomed trails, and ice climbers flock to the South Fork Valley. **Sunlight Sports,** 1131 Sheridan Ave. (ℂ **307/587-9517;** www.sunlightsports.com), carries a full suite of camping, climbing, and skiing equipment plus rentals. **Sierra Trading**

Post, 1402 8th St. (© **307/578-5802;** www.sierratradingpost. com), sells top-brand gear and apparel for steep discounts.

Several Cody outfitters also run tours into Yellowstone, which are great for people who don't want to deal with mountain driving over Sylvan Pass or high-season traffic hassles in the park. Among them: **Cody Wyoming Adventures** (© **307/ 587-6988;** www.codywyomingadventures.com), **Experience Yellowstone** (© **307/272-6671;** www.experienceynp.com), and **Grub Steak Expeditions** (© **307/527-6316;** www.tourto yellowstone.com). Expect to pay anywhere from $175 to $550, depending on tour length.

CLIMBING   The canyon of the Shoshone River on the way to Yellowstone is a magnet for rock and ice climbers, offering routes ranging from rookie-friendly to challenging. **Jackson Hole Mountain Guides** (© **307/733-4979;** www.jhmg.com) runs day climbs in summer ($185–$245 per person) and ice climbs in winter ($220–$290). Major ice fans should plan their trips to coincide with the **Cody Ice Festival** (www.codyicefest.com), which hosts climbing clinics, speakers, and plenty of parties.

FISHING   Trout-laden waters and dependable solitude make Cody an angling heaven. Fly-fishing is tops on the easy-access **Shoshone River,** including its **North Fork** and **South Fork.** The **Clark's Fork of the Yellowstone,** Wyoming's only Wild & Scenic River, is another favorite. About 80 miles south of town, the slow-moving **Big Horn River** appeals to beginners. And boat fishermen cast into the waters of **Buffalo Bill Reservoir,** home to lake trout, browns, cutthroats, and rainbows. **Tim Wade's North Fork Anglers,** 1107 Sheridan Ave. (© **307/527-7274;** www.northforkanglers. com), carries all the equipment you'll need and can lead you right to the fish on a variety of guided trips, from floats to riverside strolls (rates start at $300–$350 for a half-day trip).

FLOAT TRIPS/RAFTING   The supremely scenic and relatively mild (most sections are Class II or III on a 5-point scale) Shoshone River makes Cody a fine place to get out on the water. The longstanding outfitter **Wyoming River Trips,** 233 Yellowstone Ave. (© **307/587-6661;** www.wyomingriver trips.com), guides in the lovely Red Rock Canyon, the Lower Canyon, and the North. **Red Canyon River Trips,** 1119 12th St. (© **307/587-6988;** www.codywyomingadventures.com), offers floats and rafting trips in those areas, plus the Clark's

Fork of the Yellowstone. Shorter trips cost about $30 and half-day outings about $75.

GOLF Sneak in a game at the 18-hole course at **Olive Glenn Golf and Country Club,** 802 Meadow Lane (✆ **307/ 587-5551;** www.oliveglenngolf.com), Cody's lone option. Fees are $45 for 9 holes and $68 for 18, cart included.

HIKING There's no shortage of excellent trails around Cody. Closer to town, hoof up the steep **Sheep Mountain** or **Heart Mountain** trails for big views of the Bighorn Mountains. The **Shoshone National Forest** also offers several hikes along mountain creeks, into wildlife-packed basins, and up to the high-elevation Beartooth Plateau.

SKIING **Sleeping Giant Ski Area,** 348 North Fork Hwy. (✆ **307/587-3125;** www.skisg.com), is a fraction of the size of the resorts around Jackson, but lift tickets also cost a fraction ($36) of what you'd pay there, and this two-lift operation is a great spot for families. Cross-country skiers find almost 12 miles of track at **North Fork Nordic Trails,** 183 North Fork Hwy. (www.nordicskiclub.com), near Pahaska Teepee Resort, just outside Yellowstone's East entrance.

SNOWMOBILING Private permits for snowmobiling inside Yellowstone are tough to get, so sledding on a guided tour is often your best bet. **Gary Fales Outfitting,** 2768 North Fork Hwy. (✆ **307/587-3970;** www.garyfalesoutfitting. com), is the only Cody-area park concessionaire and leads day trips among the geysers and along Yellowstone Lake; trips cost $375 per double snowmobile. DIY sledders can explore an extensive trail network in the Beartooth Mountains, the Bighorns, the Wyoming Range, and stretching along the Continental Divide; check out the **Wyoming State Trails Program** website (www.wyotrails.state.wy.us) for trail maps.

WINDSURFING Wyoming's strong winds make the 8-mile-long, 4-mile-wide **Buffalo Bill Reservoir** a popular windsurfing destination. It's best experienced from June to September. There is a boat ramp near the campground on the north side of the reservoir, just off U.S. Hwy. 14/16/20. There are no places to rent a windsurf board in the vicinity.

Special Events

The Buffalo Bill Center of the West's five museums hold several fun and fascinating events throughout the year. Tops among them are the June **Plains Indian Museum Powwow,** where traditional Native American dancers compete for prizes, and the September **Rendezvous Royale,** a Western art show and auction with seminars and artist studio tours. Contact the center (℃ **307/587-4771;** www.centerofthewest. org) for details. And if you've never been to a rodeo (and even if you have), don't miss the annual **Cody Stampede** (℃ **307/587-5155;** www.codystampederodeo.com), held leading up to the Fourth of July: It's a classic Western good time, complete with a parade, craft fair, and plenty of ropin' and ridin'.

Seeing the Sights

Buffalo Bill Dam and Visitor Center ★ Stand on the top of the 325-foot Buffalo Bill Dam to watch the North Fork of the Shoshone River unfurl at your feet, winding its way through a plunging canyon toward Cody, 6 miles to the east. Completed in 1910, the Buffalo Bill supports irrigation projects throughout the Bighorn Basin—and forms **Buffalo Bill Reservoir,** an oasis for boating, windsurfing, and fishing. The visitor center plays a short movie about the dam project and displays exhibits on the history of the dam, Wyoming wildlife, and prehistoric life in the Bighorn Basin (did you know an *Allosaurus* was discovered in nearby Greybull?).

4808 North Fork Hwy., 6 miles west of Cody. ℃ **307/527-6076.** www.bbdvc.com. Free admission. Visitor Center: May and Sept Mon–Fri 8am–6pm, Sat–Sun 9am–5pm; June–Aug Mon–Fri 8am–7pm, Sat–Sun 9am–5pm. Closed Oct–Apr.

Buffalo Bill Historical Center ★★★ Undeniably the top attraction in Cody (and one of the best cultural centers in Wyoming), this complex of five museums can easily absorb you for an entire day, if not more. The center is affiliated with the Smithsonian and aims to interpret the story of the American West through science, art, history, and culture.

The **Buffalo Bill Museum** ★★ is the complex's flagship, and it has come a long way since its humble beginnings as a log cabin in 1927. Trace the life, work, and family of William F. "Buffalo Bill" Cody, the famous Army scout, frontiersman, showman, and entrepreneur; exhibits include footage of his Wild West Show and personal artifacts. Get up close with the Greater Yellowstone Ecosystem's flora and fauna at the

Draper Natural History Museum ★★★, which features everything from the tiny pika to the enormous grizzly bear. Staff naturalists and interactive exhibits bring the region to life—stop by here before your Yellowstone trip, if possible. At the **Whitney Western Art Museum** ★★, giant bronze elk share space with paintings and prints from both contemporary and historically significant artists, including Albert Bierstadt, Thomas Moran, and Charles M. Russell, for a look at the landscapes, animals, people and legends that make up the Western art genre. The highly interactive **Plains Indian Museum** ★★ displays beautiful examples of beadwork, headdresses, and moccasins. Listening booths and videos delve into what life is like for modern tribal members, too. And the **Cody Firearms Museum**'s ★ 7,000-plus guns represent the world's most comprehensive collection of American firearms, from old muzzle-loaders to Winchesters and Colts to more modern examples.

Rotating special exhibits, a research library, educational programs, and demos (like the popular live raptor show) complete the experience. A small café and coffee bar can revive you should museum overload set in.

720 Sheridan Ave. ✆ **307/587-4771.** www.centerofthewest.org. $19 adults, $12 children 6–17, kids 5 and under free. Admission is good for 2 consecutive days. May to mid-Sept daily 8am–6pm; mid-Sept to Oct daily 8am–5pm; Nov daily 10am–5pm; Dec–Feb Thurs–Sun 10am–5pm; Mar–Apr daily 10am–5pm.

Cody Nite Rodeo ★★ If barrel racing, saddle bronc and bull riding sound like something you'd like to see, don't miss the nightly rodeo action at Stampede Park. Taking place every summer night since 1938, Cody Nite Rodeo bills itself as the world's longest-running rodeo. Get there early for a chance to take a picture with a rodeo bull, learn real roping skills, or get your face painted courtesy of a rodeo clown.

Stampede Park (421 W. Yellowstone Ave.). ✆ **307/587-5155.** www. codystampederodeo.com. $20 adults, $10 children 7–12, kids 6 and under free. June–Aug nightly at 8pm; gates open at 7pm.

Cody Trolley Tours ★ What's this Cody place all about, anyway? There's no more entertaining way to answer that question than by hopping on one of these restored trollies for an hour's cruise. Guides will walk you through Cody highlights of the past and present, with an emphasis on town founder Buffalo Bill. You'll hear about unsolved mysteries, bygone bank robberies, and modern life in Cody while touring past historic homes, public art, and the Buffalo Bill Dam and Reservoir. You can save a few bucks by combining your trolley ticket with admission to the Buffalo Bill Center of the West (and start and end your tour from the museums).

1192 Sheridan Ave. (at the Irma Hotel). ℰ **307/527-7043.** www. codytrolleytours.com. $27 adults, $15 children 6–17, kids 5 and under free. Tours late May to late Sept daily 11am and 3pm.

Heart Mountain Interpretive Center ★★ Between 1942 and 1945, almost 11,000 Japanese-Americans were forced to live in barracks here—part of the U.S.'s dark chapter on WWII Japanese internment camps. This engaging and sobering interpretive center walks you through that era with historic photos, original writings, newspaper and film clips, and artifacts from the camp. Home movies of forced removals in the aftermath of Pearl Harbor and video interviews with survivors breathe life into the past, and you can walk inside a reconstructed barracks building to imagine life in such cramped quarters. Heart Mountain is one of only a handful of internment camps now open to the public and a potent reminder of the dangers of racism and xenophobia.

1539 Rd. 19, Powell (13 miles north of Cody on U.S. 14). ℰ **307/754-8000.** www.heartmountain.org. $7 adults, kids 11 and under free. Mid-May to early Oct daily 10am–5pm; Oct to mid-May Wed–Sat only.

McCullough Peaks Wild Horse Herd Management Area ★ Here's something most of us don't see every day: wild mustangs running free! The hundred-plus wild horses who call this high desert preserve home are descended from the ones the Spanish brought to America in the 1500s, and they come in a multitude of colors—black, white strawberry roan, and everything in between. Chances of spotting them grazing, galloping, or even sparring are quite good, but even if you don't, you might see coyote, pronghorn, or great horned owls among the badlands and steep cliffs. Check with the Bureau of Land Management for details on the likeliest places to look. **Cody Wyoming Adventures** (www.cody wyomingadventures.com) also offers guided tours of the area for $33.

12 to 27 miles east of Cody on U.S. 14/16/20. ℰ **307/578-5900.** www.blm.gov. Free admission.

Old Trail Town ★ Part ghost town and part museum, this assemblage of weathered old storefronts and clapboard cabins from the Wyoming and Montana of the late 1880s makes it easy to imagine yourself back in the era of mountain men and frontier settlers. A wooden boardwalk takes you past several notable old structures, including an 1883 cabin where Butch Cassidy and the Sundance Kid once conspired; the cabin of a Crow scout who worked with General Custer's expedition; and the 1897 home of Cody's first mayor. There's also a museum filled with relics, a suite of old wagons, and the relocated graves of many Western notables.

1831 DeMaris Dr. ⓒ **307/587-5302.** www.oldtrailtown.org. $9 adults, $5 children 6–12, kids 5 and under free. Mid-May to Sept daily 8am–7pm.

Where to Stay

Cody's lodging options include high-class inns, historic hotels, and budget-friendly basics. If you're in the market for a larger cabin or rental home, check out the 80-plus choices managed by **Cody Lodging Company,** 1302 Alger Ave. (ⓒ **307/587-6000;** www.codylodgingcompany.com). The **Airbnb** (www.airbnb.com) game in Cody is also strong, with a variety of affordable choices, and **VRBO** (www.vrbo.com) offers several upscale homes in the Shoshone River canyon.

Buffalo Bill Village: Holiday Inn, Comfort Inn, and Buffalo Bill Cabin Village ★ It's not so much a "village" as it is a convenient cluster of accommodations within walking distance of downtown, but this three-hotel complex has a lot going for it. The stand-alone log cabins at Buffalo Bill Cabin Village look rustic on the outside, but each one features modern hotel amenities and private bathrooms. The Holiday Inn and Comfort Inn are standard examples of their chains and a half-step up from the cabins in caliber. The three share an outdoor heated pool, restaurant, and bar; the Holiday Inn adds a fitness center. There's also an old-timey gift shop on-site.

1701 Sheridan Ave. ⓒ **307/587-5555.** www.blairhotels.com. Comfort Inn: 74 units. $238 double. Holiday Inn: 186 units. $215–$219 double. Historic Cabins: 83 units. $79–$159. Cabins closed Oct–Apr. **Amenities:** Restaurant; bar; gym (Holiday Inn); pool; free Wi-Fi.

The Chamberlin Inn ★★★ Utterly charming and packed with historic bona fides, the Chamberlin is Cody's finest hotel.

First opened as a boarding house in 1903 and lovingly restored since then, the boutique hotel is now full of elegant nooks and crannies: a leafy conservatory, a sun porch, and a lobby with a fireplace and tin ceiling. There's also a large courtyard with stately trees and summer croquet games. Ernest Hemingway famously stayed here as he finished *Death in the Afternoon* in 1932; you can even sleep in his room, the Hemingway King Studio. Rooms range from doubles to suites to apartments to the expansive Courthouse, all different and featuring historic furniture, exposed brick walls, and wrought iron accents.

1032 12th St. ✆ **307/587-0202.** www.chamberlininn.com. 21 units. $225–$295 double; $325–$375 suite or apt. **Amenities:** Lounge; free Wi-Fi.

The Cody ★★   This deluxe hotel on the west side of town (near the rodeo grounds) is one of Cody's finest options. From the moment you step into the expansive lobby, the place sets a warm, inviting tone: dark, heavy woods; comfy couches set in small groups; and Western-style paintings and accents. Or hang out on the outdoor patio, where a fire pit makes al fresco relaxation an option year-round. Rooms are simple and chic: Some doubles have patios or balconies (the ones on the west side have the best views of Shoshone River Canyon), and the suites boast kitchenettes and Jacuzzis. Nice touch: a free shuttle to downtown Cody.

232 W. Yellowstone Ave. ✆ **307/587-5915.** www.thecody.com. 75 units. $239–$249 double; $269 suite, includes buffet breakfast. Lower rates fall–spring. **Amenities:** Gym; Jacuzzi; pool; free Wi-Fi.

Cody Legacy Inn & Suites ★   Looking for an excellent value? This welcoming spot near Beck Lake Park offers a lot of bang for your buck: spacious rooms filled with log cabin-style pine furniture, plus bonuses like an outdoor pool, hot tub, sauna, and fitness center. Even more generously sized suites sleep up to six, and some have kitchenettes and fireplaces. Like the rest of Cody, the Legacy fully embraces the town's colorful history—but with better credentials than most, as co-owner Kellie Edwards is Buffalo Bill's great-great-granddaughter. Check out her display of historic photos and portraits of Buffalo Bill in the lobby, where there's also a snug stone fireplace to gather around.

1801 Mountain View Dr. ✆ **307/587-6067.** www.codylegacyinn. com. 52 units. $168–$178 double; $198–$258 suite. **Amenities:** Pool; Jacuzzi; sauna; gym; free Wi-Fi.

The Irma Hotel ★   Naturally, the town that Buffalo Bill built contains one of his hotels—first opened in 1902 to cater to early Yellowstone tourists, hunters, and ranching barons, and named after his youngest daughter. The man himself kept a couple of private suites here (one of which you can still bunk in today). The Irma has taken steps to preserve the historic nature of the place, from the old-fashioned guest room options to the elaborate cherrywood bar anchoring the on-site Silver Saddle Saloon—a gift from Queen Victoria, and a longtime draw for curious travelers. You have two choices for rooms: standards, which are modern and unremarkable, or the much more character-filled historic rooms, which feature period touches such as rose wallpaper, ornate tasseled curtains, and pull-chain toilets. Among its other charms: the free shootout reenactment that takes place daily in summer right outside, and the popular prime rib buffet at the **Irma Restaurant.**

1192 Sheridan Ave. ✆ **307/587-4221.** www.irmahotel.com. 39 units. $147 double; $170 historic double; $198 suite. Lower rates fall–spring. **Amenities:** Restaurant; lounge; free Wi-Fi.

Ivy Inn & Suites ★★   Those looking for thoroughly modern accommodations will do well at this Best Western Premier property, one of Cody's nicest options. Contemporary design is the name of the game, with rooms boasting arty black-and-white cowboy photography and funky patterned rugs and the soaring lobby centering around a sleek stone fireplace. Standard rooms are comfortable, with upscale bathrooms and dreamy beds; upgrade to a suite for a separate living area. The **8th Street Restaurant** serves up three meals daily, and there's also a large-for-a-hotel pool plus hot tub.

1800 8th St. ✆ **307/587-2572.** www.mayorsinn.com. 70 units. $243–$261 double; $284–$311 suite. Lower rates fall–spring. **Amenities:** Restaurant; lounge; pool; Jacuzzi; gym; free Wi-Fi.

Where to Eat

Cody has a rep as a steak-and-potatoes kind of town—and you'll certainly have no trouble finding a burger or a T-bone—but recently, more variety has been creeping into the dining scene. For a morning bite, **Peter's Café & Bakery,** 1219 Sheridan Ave. (✆ **307/527-5040**), attracts locals with traditional breakfasts and fresh-baked pastries, plus lunch and dinner. Locals say the best espresso in town can be had at the **Beta Coffeehouse,** 1450 Sheridan Ave. (© **307/ 587-7707**). And one of the liveliest rodeo hangouts you're likely to visit, the **Proud Cut Saloon,** 1227 Sheridan Ave. (© **307/587-6905**), offers monster steaks and burgers. And that name? It's an homage to a stallion that stays feisty even after gelding.

Annie's Soda Saloon ★ SANDWICHES/DESSERT This new-in-2016 establishment manages to feel both old-fashioned and cutting-edge at the same time. Barnwood-style paneling and a tin ceiling put you in the mood for Annie's signature treats, ice cream sodas like the ones you used to get at the five and dime—and what a treat they are. Choose from more than 30 soda flavors, from butter beer to mango to strawberry, then add ice cream, or go with one of the suggested pairings (like the Cowboy Rickey, limeade soda plus cherry ice cream). You can also cool off with a shake, sundae, or plain old cone. But don't skip right to dessert: The creative panini and salads (some of which are served in a mason jar) are mighty tasty, too.

1202 Sheridan Ave. © **307/578-8400.** www.anniessodasaloon.com. Main courses $7–$8; ice cream sodas $4. Mon–Sat 11am–7pm.

Cassie's Supper Club ★★★ STEAKS/SEAFOOD A town like Cody wouldn't be complete without a place like Cassie's: stuffed with cowboy memorabilia, a menu full of enormous steaks, and home to a raucous dance floor with live country and swing bands playing their hearts out. Cassie's has been an institution since the 1920s; once a "house of ill repute," it remains a one-of-a-kind spot to spend an evening. Grab a table in the three-floor dining room and tuck into well-prepared steaks, seafood, ribs, burgers, or pizza; brews and shots flow from the three distinct bars. The live music and dancing here are legendary, headlined on Friday and Saturday nights by owner/head chef Steve Singer's outfit West the Band.

214 Yellowstone Ave. © **307/527-5500.** www.cassies.com. Reservations recommended. Main courses $7–$25 lunch, $9–$46 dinner. Daily 11am–10pm. Bar open until 2am.

The Local ★★ NEW AMERICAN This warm, candlelit spot just off downtown's main drag stands out from the rest with its chic, upscale atmosphere and commitment to local, organic, and/or humanely raised ingredients. The seasonal menu might include such deliciousness as mushroom toasts with fig jam, rainbow trout served with veggie slaw and sea-weed, or rabbit in brandy-honey sauce; less adventurous eaters will find well-executed burgers, steak, or fish tacos. It's also a safe haven for vegetarians, who can look forward to entrees like a quinoa lentil bowl or black-eyed pea burger. Exposed brick walls and subway tiles add to the ambiance, making this the kind of place you'll want to linger over.

1134 13th St. ℭ **307/586-4262.** Reservations recommended. Main courses $10–$13 lunch, $12–$38 dinner. Tues–Sat 8:30am–2pm (espresso bar and lunch) and 5–8:30pm.

Wyoming's Rib & Chop House ★ STEAKS/SEAFOOD

Yes, it's a chain, but a good one. With a handful of locations, mostly in Wyoming and Montana, the Rib & Chop House scratches that upscale steakhouse itch. The multipage menu has something for every meat-eater, including fried chicken, steaks, ribs, salmon, and shrimp entrees; the generous salads and the gumbo also win fans. Gluten-free eaters will find plenty of options.

1367 Sheridan Ave. ℭ **307/527-7731.** www.ribandchophouse.com. Main courses $8–$13 lunch, $8–$41 dinner. Sun–Thurs 11am–9pm; Fri–Sat 11am–10pm.

Cody After Dark

Cody hosts a pair of dinner-and-music shows. One, **Cody Cattle Company,** 1910 Demaris St. (ℭ **307/272-5770;** www.thecodycattlecompany.com), is more family-friendly and features a chuckwagon-style buffet dinner and a live "cow-boy band." Open early June to mid-September; shows start at 6:30pm. **Dan Miller's Cowboy Music Revue,** at the Buffalo Bill Center of the West at 720 Sheridan Ave. (ℭ **307/578-7909;** www.cowboymusicrevue.com), takes the music side of the show a bit more seriously; performances run early June to late September at 6:30pm. There's no better place to warm up your dancin' boots than **Cassie's Supper Club** (see above). The **Silver Dollar Bar,** 1313 Sheridan Ave. (ℭ **307/527-7666**), is another local favorite watering hole with pool tables, but be aware the scene can get a bit colorful late at night. For a more relaxed evening, sample the local suds at **Pat O'Hara Brewing Company,** 1019 15th St. (ℭ **307/586-5410;** www.patoharabrewing.com).

A PARKS NATURE GUIDE

Yellowstone and Grand Teton National Parks have distinct differences. One is an immense wilderness plateau that sits atop a caldera seething with molten lava; the other is a striking set of peaks rising from a broad river plain. One encloses some of the most remote backcountry in the lower 48 and provides crucial habitat for rare species; the other is a short drive from a chic resort town and includes an airport and grazing cattle in its mixed-use approach. What they *do* share is the affection of millions of visitors who come here annually to renew their ties to nature through the parks' mountains, alpine lakes, majestic elk, and astonishing geysers.

The **Greater Yellowstone Ecosystem** is an interdependent network of watersheds, mountain ranges, wildlife habitats, and other components extending beyond the two parks into seven national forests, an Indian reservation, three national wildlife refuges, and nearly a million acres of private land. It is one of the largest intact temperate ecosystems on the planet, and covers an area as vast as Connecticut, Rhode Island, and Delaware combined.

It's also a massive source of water. West of the Continental Divide, snowmelt trickles into creeks, streams, and rivers that run through Yellowstone before draining into the Snake River, traveling through Grand Teton National Park and Idaho, and running into the Columbia River, which winds its way west through Oregon and into the Pacific Ocean. Water on the eastern slopes of the divide passes through Yellowstone in the form of the

Madison and Gallatin rivers, which meet the Jefferson River west of Bozeman, Montana, and merge into the Missouri, which flows into the Mississippi and, ultimately, the Gulf of Mexico.

THE PARKS TODAY

It has long been a challenge for park managers to make the parks accessible to more than 4 million annual visitors. This necessitates the construction of new facilities and ongoing road maintenance and repair. At the same time, the parks are wild preserves, and the National Park Service must cope with the impact of eight million feet on the forests, meadows, and thermal areas, as well as on the lives of the millions of animals that inhabit the area.

Some of the pivotal issues in the parks today include the impact of snowmobiles; the reintroduced gray wolves and the resulting livestock losses in and around the parks; the inadequacy of the park's infrastructure to cope with the crush of visitors each year; invasive species; and the reduction of habitat surrounding the parks, coupled with elk and bison seeking forage beyond park boundaries and possibly infecting cattle with a disease called brucellosis, which, when transmitted, causes cows to abort fetuses.

Possible solutions are often "too little, too late," layering complex management strategies on an ecosystem that might do better if it were allowed to work things out naturally. The problem is that Grand Teton and Yellowstone have already been altered significantly by humans, so "natural" becomes a relative concept.

As the world awakens to the accelerating loss of vital species in shrinking wild habitats, it becomes ever more imperative to find ways to preserve the relatively unspoiled ecosystems, like that of Greater Yellowstone.

LANDSCAPE & GEOLOGY

The Yellowstone and Grand Teton region is one of the most dynamic seismic areas in the world—wracked by earthquakes, cracked by water boiling to the surface, and littered with the detritus of previous volcanic eruptions. Today, the bowels of the Yellowstone caldera are again filling with magma. Geologic studies show that, for the past 2 million years, the plateau has blown its top every 600,000 years or so—and the last explosion was about 640,000 years ago. That means that a titanic blow—bigger than anything seen in recorded history—could happen, well, any century now, give or take thousands of years. The good news is that the big one is not imminent; geologists say things need to heat up considerably first.

As you'll learn when you visit the exhibits on the park's geology at Moose, Mammoth, and the various geothermal areas, what you see on the surface—great layers of ash and the core of volcanic vents, such as Mount Washburn and Bunsen Peak—is only a fraction of the story of Yellowstone and Grand Teton.

On 2.2 million acres, Yellowstone is significantly larger than its sister to the south. Encompassing 3,472 square miles, Yellowstone has 310 miles of paved roads and 1,000 miles of backcountry trails, and it is home to more geysers and hot springs than the combined total in the rest of the world.

Although it can't match Yellowstone's size, Grand Teton National Park is nothing to sneeze at. It has towering mountain spires, which have been compared to cathedral towers, reaching almost 14,000 feet skyward; picturesque glacial lakes; and a great deal of interesting topography. The roughly 500 square miles of Grand Teton contain about 160 miles of paved roads and over 250 miles of hiking trails.

The Faces of Yellowstone

By the end of the 1872 Hayden expedition, explorers had identified several distinct areas in the park, each with its own physical characteristics. Less spectacular than the craggy mountain scenery of Grand Teton, and less imposing than the vast expanses of the Grand Canyon in Arizona, Yellowstone's beauty is subtle, reflecting the changes it has undergone during its explosive past.

Although Yellowstone has its share of mountains, much of the park is a high mountain plateau. The environment changes dramatically as you ascend the mountain slopes from the foothill zones in the valleys—the elevation at the entrance at West Yellowstone is 6,666 feet, for example, compared to 5,314 feet at the Gardiner entrance. Because the park lies about halfway between the equator and the North Pole, its summers consist of long, warm days that stimulate plant growth at the lower elevations.

At the lowest elevations, down around 5,300 feet above sea level, you'll find **grassy flats** and sagebrush growing on dry, porous soils, with creeks and rivers cutting through to form wildlife-rich **riparian zones.** The **foothills,** sloping upward toward peaks, are sometimes dotted by deposits of glacial moraine. Douglas fir, pine, and other conifers, as well aspen clad these slopes, and are marshes and ponds are fed by the spring snowmelt. Shrubs and flowers, such as huckleberry and columbine, favor these wet, shady spots.

Then comes the **mountain zone** (6,000–7,600 ft.), thickening forests dominated by lodgepole pine, broken by meadows where deer, elk, and moose often graze. The transition area between the highest forest and the bare surface above timberline is known as the **subalpine zone** (7,600–11,300 ft.). Finally, we come to the bare rock at the very top of the continental shelf, where small, hardy plants bloom briefly after the annual thaw.

Although the park is most famous for its geysers, visitors can choose among very different environments, reflections of the long-term effects of geologic activity and weather.

The limestone terraces at **Mammoth Hot Springs** give testimony to the region's subsurface volcanic activity. The park sits atop a rare geologic hot spot where molten rock rises to within 2 miles of the Earth's surface, heating the water in a plumbing system that still mystifies scientists.

The **northern section of the park,** between Mammoth Hot Springs and the Tower-Roosevelt region, is a high-plains area that is defined by mountains, forests, and broad expanses of river valleys that were created by ice floes.

The road between the Tower-Roosevelt junction and the northeast entrance winds through the **Lamar Valley,** an area that has been covered by glaciers three times, most recently during an ice age that began 25,000 years ago and continued for 10,000 years—in geologic terms, just yesterday. Because this area was a favorite of Theodore Roosevelt, it is often referred to as "Roosevelt Country." The beautiful valley where elk, bison, and wolves interact is dotted with glacial ponds and strewn with boulders deposited by moving ice.

Farther south are **Pelican** and **Hayden Valleys,** the two largest ancient lake beds in the park. They feature large, open meadows with abundant plant life that provides food for a population of bison and elk.

In the warm months, you'll enjoy the contrast between the lush green valleys and **Canyon Country,** in the center of the park. Canyon Country is defined by the Grand Canyon of

Yellowstone, a colorful, 1,000-foot-deep, 24-mile-long gorge—in many opinions, just as dramatic as its cousin in Arizona. The Yellowstone River cuts through the valley, in some places moving 64,000 cubic feet of water per second, and creating two waterfalls, one of which is more than twice the height of Niagara Falls.

When you arrive at the **southern geyser basins,** you might feel that you've been transported through a geologic time warp. Here you will find the largest collections of thermal areas in the world—there are perhaps 600 geysers and 10,000 geothermal features in the park—and the largest geysers in Yellowstone. The result: boiling water that is catapulted skyward and barren patches of sterile dirt; hot, bubbling pools that are unimaginably colorful; and, of course, the star of this show, the geyser **Old Faithful.**

You'll see the park's volcanic activity on a 17-mile journey east to the **lake area,** the scene of three volcanic eruptions that took place more than 600,000 years ago. When the final eruption blasted more than 1,000 square miles of the Rocky Mountains into the stratosphere, it created the Yellowstone caldera, a massive depression measuring 28 by 47 miles, and Yellowstone Lake basin, some 20 miles long and 14 miles wide, reaching depths of 390 feet. The landscape here consists of flat plateaus of lava that are hundreds of feet thick.

The Spires of Grand Teton

Your first sight of the towering spires of the **Cathedral Group**—the *trois tetons* (three breasts), as lonesome French trappers called them—will create an indelible impression. A bit of history makes them even more interesting.

Their formation began more than 2.5 billion years ago when sand and volcanic debris settled in an ancient ocean that covered this entire area. Scientists estimate that roughly 40 million to 80 million years ago, a compression of the Earth's surface caused an uplift of the entire Rocky Mountains from Mexico to Canada. This was just the first step in an ongoing series of events that included several periods during which a miles-thick crust of ice covered the area. Then, 6 million to 9 million years ago, the shifting of the Earth's tectonic plates caused movement along the north-south Teton fault that produced a tremendous uplift. The valley floor also dropped precipitously. These simultaneous forces pushed the rock that is now the **Teton Range** to its present site, from a position 20,000 to 30,000 feet *below* what is today the floor of Jackson Hole. The west block of rock tipped upward to create the Teton Range, and the eastern block swung downward to form the valley that is now called **Jackson Hole**—kind of like a pair of horizontal swinging doors that moved the Earth 5 miles.

After this upheaval, and after eons of erosion and glacier activity, **Grand Teton,** the centerpiece of this 40-mile-long fault area, towered 13,770 feet above sea level—more than a mile above the visitor center at Moose Junction. There are eleven other peaks over 12,000 feet high in the park today, with conditions that support mountain glaciers. As you gaze upward at this magnificent range, you will notice that many of the cliffs are more than half a mile in height.

During geologic explorations of **Mount Moran** (elevation 12,605 ft.), it was discovered that erosion had removed some 3,000 feet of material from its summit, meaning that it once must have been more than 15,000 feet high. Equally remarkable is the fact that the thin layer of Flathead sandstone on top of this peak is also found buried at least 24,000 feet below the valley's surface—further evidence of the skyward thrust of the mountains.

Although this is the youngest range in the Rockies, the rocks here are some of the oldest in North America, consisting of granitic gneisses and schists, which are the hardest and least-porous rocks known to geologists.

The Teton area experienced a cooling trend about 150,000 years ago, during which glaciers more than 2,000 feet thick flowed from higher elevations, and an ice sheet covered Jackson Hole. When it melted for the final time, some 60,000 to 80,000 years ago, it gouged out the 386-foot-deep, 16-mile-long depression now known as **Jackson Lake.**

The receding layers of ice also left other calling cards. Several beautiful **glacial lakes** were created, including Phelps, Taggart, Bradley, Jenny, String, and Leigh. The sides of **Cascade Canyon** were polished by receding ice. Glacial lakes, called **cirque lakes,** were carved at the heads of canyons, and the peaks of the mountains were honed to their present jagged edges. Five glaciers have survived on Mount Moran. The best trail for glacial views is the Cascade Trail, which leads to the Schoolroom Glacier. But you shouldn't walk on the Mount Moran glaciers unless you are experienced and have

Landscape & Geology

A PARKS NATURE GUIDE

the proper gear; the terrain is icy and can be unstable. Like glaciers in many parts of the world, Grand Teton's glaciers are retreating due to climate change.

PLANT LIFE IN THE PARKS

When it comes to the variety of plants in the two parks, the only limiting factor is the high altitude—otherwise, the diversity of terrain, weather, and soils permits a fairly wide range of vegetation. Estimates vary, but there are more than 1,500 native plant varieties in the Greater Yellowstone ecosystem. Some species are found living on the dry valley beds in hostile soil, close to other species that predominate in lush meadows and riverbeds. Some thrive in thermal areas, while others do well in alpine areas, near mountain lakes, and in cirques near glaciers.

Examination of plant fossils indicates that life began during the Eocene epoch, approximately 55 million years ago, and continued for 17 million years. The inspection of petrified tree stumps in Yellowstone's Lamar Valley led to the identification of 27 distinct layers of forests, one atop the other. Climatic conditions during the Eocene period were similar to those in the southeastern and south-central United States. Difficult as it might be to imagine, the area was once a warm, temperate zone in which rainfall might have averaged 50 to 60 inches per year at what was then an elevation of 3,000 feet above sea level.

These days, the elevation ranges from 5,000 to 13,000 feet, the average low temperature is approximately 30°F (–1°C), and hundreds of inches of snow fall each year. Plants have adapted to a growing season that is a mere 60 days in duration. As a consequence, forests once populated with hardwoods, such as maple, magnolia, and sycamore, are now filled with conifers, the most common of which are pine, spruce, and fir. A smattering of cottonwood and aspen also thrive in the cool park temperatures.

The parks have several growing zones. Above 10,000 feet in the alpine zone, plants adapt to wind, snow, and lack of soil by growing close to the ground, flowering soon after the snows melt. You'll find such flora on trails near Dunraven Pass in Yellowstone and in Cascade Canyon in Grand Teton.

In Yellowstone, the canyon and subalpine regions, at 7,000 to 10,000 feet, are known for **conifer forests** and open meadows of **wildflowers.** As elevation increases, wildflowers are abundant and healthy, while trees are stunted and shrublike.

In the valley in Grand Teton, at 6,400 to 7,000 feet, the porous soil supports plants that tolerate hot and dry summer-time conditions. **Sagebrush, wildflowers,** and **grasses** thrive and predominate. Plants bloom in a pageant of colors from early June to early July.

Identifying the plants described below does not require a degree in botany, but Kurt F. Johnson's *A Field Guide to Yellowstone and Grand Teton National Parks* (Farcountry Press, 2013) is a handy addition to your trip kit.

Trees

Coniferous trees are most common in the parks because of the high altitude and short growing season, but there are some hardy deciduous trees as well, such as cottonwood and aspen. The most common cone-bearing trees in the parks are lodgepole pines, which cover as much as 80% of Yellowstone, and Douglas fir, subalpine fir, Engelmann spruce, blue spruce, and whitebark pine. The key to identification is the trees' basic shape, the shape of their needles, and various characteristics of their cones.

Lodgepole Pine   This familiar tree grows tall and slender, with bare trunk at the bottom and needles near the top resulting in dense stands that look like the spears of a closely ranked army. The needles of the lodgepole are clustered in pairs, typically around 3 inches long. You'll see logs from this tree supporting tepees and forming the walls of cabins.

Lodgepole Pine

Douglas Fir   "Doug fir" is actually a member of the pine family, with prickly cones and dark, deeply etched bark. This tree has flat, flexible, single needles that grow around the branch, giving the tree the appearance of fullness. Another giveaway is that its cones hang downward and do not disintegrate aloft, but litter the forest floor. These trees like the north-facing side of the mountain.

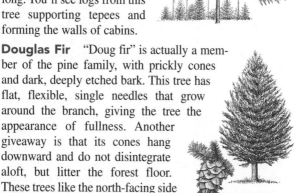

Douglas Fir

Subalpine Fir You can distinguish firs by their needles, which sprout individually from branches instead of in clusters, like a pine; and by their cones, which grow upright on the branch until they dry up and blow away. Look for the slender, conical crown of this tree. When heavy snows weigh down the lower branches, they often become rooted, forming a circle of smaller trees called a snow mat. You'll find subalpine fir at high elevations near the timberline.

Subalpine Fir

Engelmann Spruce This tree also likes the higher elevations, growing in shaded ravines and in the canyons of the Teton Range above 6,800 feet and sometimes much higher. Look for it near Kepler Cascades, Spring Creek, and the south entrance of Yellowstone National Park. It is distinguished by single needles that are square and sharp to the touch, and by cones with papery scales that are approximately 1½ inches long.

Engelmann Spruce

Blue Spruce The Engelmann spruce's cousin, this tree is most commonly found along the Snake River near Jackson. True to its name, it is characterized by its bluish appearance; and cones that are twice the size of the Engelmann's.

Blue Spruce

Other Plants

Here's a brief listing of some of the most common and interesting plants found in the ecosystem.

Plantastic Photos

To successfully record your discovery of the parks' flora, consider using a microlens that will allow you to focus within 6 inches of blossoms. Speeds of 200 ISO or faster will add to the chances of proper exposure, even on cloudy days.

Glacier Lily   A member of the lily family with a nodding bloom on a 6- to 12-inch stem, this bright yellow spring flower is found in abundance in both parks at elevations of more than 7,500 feet. Also known as the fawn lily, trout lily, and adder's-tongue, it is especially common near Sylvan Pass and on Dunraven Pass.

Glacier Lily

Indian Paintbrush   This is the Wyoming state flower. It has a distinctive narrow, bright scarlet bloom that is most commonly found from mid-June to early September in the Snake River bottomland. Other species are white, yellow, orange, and pink.

Indian Paintbrush

Plains Prickly Pear   This member of the cactus family is only one of two such species found in the park, usually in the Mammoth area and near the Snake River. It is distinguished by thick, flat green stems armed with spines and, during midsummer, a conspicuous yellow flower with numerous petals. American Indians, who recognized prickly pear's medicinal qualities, treated warts by lacerating them and then applying juice from the plant.

Plains Prickly Pear

Fringed Gentian   This member of the gentian family is the official flower of Yellowstone Park, where it is common and blooms throughout the summer. Its purple petals are fused into a 2-inch-long corolla and sit atop 1- to 3-foot-tall stems. It is also found below Jackson Lake Dam in Grand Teton.

Fringed Gentian

Silky Phacelia   This is one of the most photogenic and easily recognized species in the parks. Growing in purple clumps alongside the road at Dunraven Pass, the flower derives its name from the silvery pubescence that covers its stems and leaves. It's best photographed in July and August.

Silky Phacelia

Shooting Star The shooting star is characterized by pinkish ½- to 1-inch-long flowers that dangle earthward like meteorites from a 12-inch stem; they bloom in June. It is commonly found near thermal areas, streambeds, and Yellowstone Lake.

Shooting Star

Yellow Monkey Flower This flower exhibits a bright yellow petal that, together with orange spots, attracts insect pollinators near streambeds at elevations of 7,000 to 9,000 feet all summer. It is also found near thermal areas and Yellowstone Lake.

Yellow Monkey Flower

Fairyslipper (also known as the Calypso Orchid) Finding this beautiful orchid might require some serious detective work. It is one of 15 orchid species found in the parks and is considered by many to be the most beautiful and striking. Seen during May and June, it usually has one small, green leaf and a red-pink flower that resembles a small lady's slipper. It is found in cool, deep-shaded areas and is becoming rare because its habitat is disappearing.

Fairyslipper
(aka Calypso Orchid)

Bitterroot The state flower of Montana, the bitterroot makes its first appearance in early June in dry, open, sometimes-stony soil and in grassy meadows. Its fleshy rose and white petals extend up to 1 inch in length. It was a source of food for Indians, who introduced it to Captain Meriwether Lewis of Lewis and Clark fame, hence its botanical name, *Lewisia rediviva*.

Bitterroot

Columbia Monkshood This purple flower has a hood-shape structure with two sepals at its side and two below (all of which make up the calyx, the leafy parts surrounding the flower). It varies in height from 2

Columbia Monkshood 215

to 5 feet. You'll find these flowers in wet meadows and stream banks from June to August, often near thermal areas and Yellowstone Lake.

WILDLIFE IN THE PARKS

For many, the primary reason for a visit to these parks is the wildlife: bears, bighorn sheep, bison, elk, bald eagles, river otters, and moose all wandering free, often near roadsides. Yellowstone and Grand Teton are home to the largest concentration of free-roaming wildlife in the lower 48. This includes one of the largest herds of elk in North America, the largest free-roaming herd of bison in the U.S., and the only significant population of grizzly bears south of Canada.

Also in the parks are pronghorns, mountain goats, and two species of deer (totaling eight species of ungulates, or hoofed mammals); black bears; three species of wildcats; coyotes; wolverines; pine martens; about 60 smaller species of mammals; and 322 species of birds. Add to that the gray wolves reintroduced in 1995—they now number about 530 in the entire ecosystem—and you have a rich array of wildlife. Most of these creatures steer clear of humans. But humans want to get ever closer to the animals, and that can cause problems. Unlike the critters that inhabit petting zoos, the animals in the Greater Yellowstone Ecosystem are wild and pose an unpredictable threat to the safety of visitors.

Death is a day-to-day affair in the parks. In the spring, you'll see carcasses of elk and bison that died during the long winter, attracting bears and other carnivores looking for a free lunch. That's part of the picture when you vow to interfere as little as possible with nature's way.

Park naturalists generally agree that every major vertebrate wildlife species that was present during the most recent ice

Ready for Their Close-Ups

Photographers need a telephoto lens, preferably a zoom, to get good shots of wildlife. Even the biggest animals in the park present minimal risks to humans, unless you move in for a close-up. Invest in a 300-millimeter lens, or 100- to 300-millimeter zoom, and you should get some good shots without disturbing the wildlife or putting yourself at risk.

BLACK bear OR GRIZZLY bear?

Because a black bear can be black, brown, or cinnamon, here are some identifiers. The grizzly is the larger of the two: typically 3½ feet at the shoulder with a dish-face profile and a pronounced hump between the shoulders. The black bear's ears are rounder. The grizzly's color is typically yellowish brown, but the coat is sometimes recognized by its cinnamon color, often highlighted by silver tips. In terms of tracks, the black bear's toes follow an arc around the foot pad while the grizzly's toes are arranged in a nearly straight line. The grizzly's claws are also considerably longer.

Caution: Park rangers attempt to keep track of grizzlies to prevent human/bear encounters. However, it is best to assume that they are always around; make noise when traveling in isolated spots.

age (more than 10,000 years ago) is a resident of the parks today, as are several rare or endangered species, the most notable being the grizzly bear and the bald eagle.

Mammals

Bear (Black & Grizzly)   In recent years, grizzly bears have enjoyed a comeback, in part because of the reintroduction of gray wolves, which create plenty of carcasses for bears to scavenge. But unless you have the patience to spend weeks outdoors in bear country, such as the Lamar and Hayden Valleys, your chances of seeing a grizzly in Yellowstone or Grand Teton aren't all that good—you might have to go to the zoo in West Yellowstone.

Estimates vary, but there are probably about 700 grizzly bears in the Greater Yellowstone Ecosystem today, and an equal or greater number of black bears. Rangers say you're more likely to spot the black bears, especially during the spring months after they emerge with new cubs from their winter dens. However, the black bears are probably more visible because they are more likely to venture near human development than are grizzlies, meaning that an encounter with a grizzly is most likely to occur in the backcountry. Bears that get a taste for human food, or get too comfortable around human campsites, are relocated to the depths of the wilderness. Black bears are most commonly sighted in the Canyon-Tower and Madison–Old Faithful areas, where they feed on green grass, herbs, berries, ants, and carrion.

Grizzly bears are most commonly seen in the northeast area of the park, in the meadows on the hillsides of the Lamar Valley, or wandering the Hayden Valley north of Yellowstone Lake. They also feed on trout spawning in Yellowstone Lake tributaries during the late spring (campgrounds by these streams are closed during spawning). They are most active in spring, when they emerge from hibernation hungry, and in the fall, when they busy themselves fattening up for winter.

Grizzly bears can do you the most damage, particularly when their cubs are around or when they think you're after their food.

Black Bear

Grizzly Bear

Bighorn Sheep   If there's a hint of a foothold, a bighorn sheep will find it. Its hooves are hard and durable on the outside but soft and clamplike underneath—perfect for steep, rocky terrain. You'll often hear them clattering before you spot their stocky, gray-brown bodies and white rumps. Six feet long, the males weigh up to 300 pounds. Their horns are coiled; the females' are straight. Look for them on Mount Washburn, along Specimen Ridge, and in the Gallatin Range in Yellowstone; they are also seen occasionally in the Heart Mountain area in southern Yellowstone. In Grand Teton, smaller herds are found in the Gros Ventre Valley, as well as the western slopes of the Teton Range. In the winter, a large herd of bighorn sheep congregates south of the town of Dubois in Whiskey Basin, in the Wind River Range east of the Teton Range.

Bighorn Sheep

Bison

Bison Bison (commonly, but incorrectly, called buffalo) appear indifferent to humans as they wander the roads and go about their grazing, but don't think for a minute that they're docile. Their prodigious size, cute calves and fearless nature ensure that bison are very visible symbols of Yellowstone. On ballerina-thin ankles, these burly brown animals carry as much as 2,000 pounds, concentrated in thick shoulders and massive chests. Those big heads help them clear snow for winter grazing, but during harsh winters they instinctively migrate to lower elevations (some biologists insist that both grizzlies and bison were driven up on the plateau from their natural home on the prairie). Bison are very easy to spot in the summer; you'll see them munching grass and wallowing in dust pits in Hayden Valley, Pelican Valley, the Madison River area, and the geyser areas near the Firehole River. In the winter, snowmobilers often have to make way for the shaggy beasts because bison take advantage of the snow-packed roads to travel around.

Coyote The wily coyote is the predator most often spotted by park visitors. Looking like lanky shepherd dogs with grizzled, gray-brown coats, coyotes make their homes in burrows and caves. Numbers have dropped some since the gray wolf reintroduction, but coyotes are very adaptable. Active hunters year-round, they feast on small animals, such as squirrels and rabbits, as well as the carcasses of animals that died naturally or were killed by larger carnivores. They are seen near park roads, in the meadows, and in the sagebrush. Coyote pups are considered a delicacy by great horned owls, eagles, mountain lions, and bears.

Coyote   *Gray Wolf*

Gray Wolf In a controversial move, gray wolves were reintroduced to Yellowstone in 1995 for the first time since

WOLF OR coyote?

Wolves and coyotes both bear a striking resemblance to large dogs. Here are some ways to distinguish them.

o Coyotes grow to a height of 20 inches; wolves often grow to 34 inches and are far more massive.

o Coyotes have long, pointed ears; wolf ears are rounded and relatively short.

o Coyotes have thin, delicate legs, similar to those of a fox; wolves' legs are thick and long.

the 1920s, when they were eliminated by hunters operating under a federal predator control program designed to protect cattle herds. The population of Canadian gray wolves is thriving in its new environment, though numbers are still down after a bout with deadly distemper virus in 2008 (the population was estimated at about 100 in 2016). They are high-profile occupants of the Lamar Valley, under constant observation by visitors with binoculars or spotting scopes.

Elk   It is estimated that the Yellowstone herd has 10,000 to 20,000 elk (also called wapiti) in summer and 5,000 in winter, and other herds spend time in the park as well. The most common large animal in both parks, elk are rather sociable and travel in small groups. Males are easily identifiable by a massive set of antlers. Although they shed them every spring, by early summer, bulls are beginning to display prodigious racks that, by year's end, are the envy of their cousins in the deer family. The elk's grayish brown body, which typically weighs as much as 900 pounds, is accented by a chestnut brown head and neck, a shaggy mane, a short tail, and a distinctive tan patch on the rump.

One herd can often be located in the vicinity of Mammoth Hot Springs, often on the lawn of the main square. Others are found throughout each park. During winter months, the northern Yellowstone herd heads to a winter grazing area near Gardiner, while their cousins in Grand Teton head for the National Elk Refuge, just north of Jackson, where the Forest Service supplements their diet with bales of alfalfa.

Elk

Moose

Moose   Perhaps because of their size, their homely appearance, or their broad antler racks that can grow to 6 feet across, moose elicit unequaled excitement from park visitors. A typical adult male moose weighs 1,000 pounds and is most easily recognizable by a pendulous muzzle and fleshy dewlap that hangs beneath its neck like a bell.

Sightings are most frequent on the edges of ponds and in damp, lush valley bottoms, where moose feed on willows and water plants, especially along the Moose-Wilson Road and near the Jackson Lake Lodge in Grand Teton.

The plodding, nibbling moose in a meadow is not to be approached. Cows will charge any perceived threat to a calf, and bulls become particularly ornery in the fall, so give both a wide berth.

Mountain Lion   After their near-eradication in the early 1900s, today there are probably up to 40 mountain lions (also known as cougars, panthers, or pumas) in Yellowstone, and a smaller number in Grand Teton. Adults weigh 100 to 150 pounds, making them the largest feline in the parks and the Rocky Mountains. Largely opportunistic predators, the parks' mountain lions hunt deer, elk, and porcupine. They are seldom seen in Yellowstone but more often heard: Listeners often mistake their high-pitched wails for a human.

Mountain Lion

Antlers or Horns?

Most of the larger, four-legged animals roaming the parks have lavish headpieces that are either horns or antlers. But what's the difference? Antlers are shed every year; horns last a lifetime. Male deer, elk, and moose shed their antlers every spring, so they're as bald as cue balls when the parks open. By early June, though, new velvet-covered protuberances are making their appearance. In comparison, both sexes of bison and pronghorn grow only one set of horns during their lifetimes.

Mule Deer   Not to be outnumbered by their larger cousins, an estimated 1,900 mule deer live within park borders in summer. They are most often spotted near forest boundaries or in areas covered with grass and sagebrush. Their most distinguishing characteristics are their huge ears and a black tip on their tail that contrasts with their white rump. When they run, they bounce, with all four legs in the air. Fawns are typically born in late spring, often in pairs.

Mule Deer

Pronghorn

Pronghorn   The often-sighted pronghorns graze near the north entrance to Yellowstone and on the valley floors of Grand Teton, but they are shy and difficult to approach or photograph because of their excellent vision and speed. Often mistakenly referred to as antelope—they're actually The pronghorn is identified by its short, black horns, tan-and-white body, and black accent stripes. They can run 45 mph, but they can't clear fences. Yellowstone's pronghorn population reached about 450 in 2015, its highest since 1992.

BIRDS IN THE PARKS

The skies above the parks are filled with predators on the wing, including eagles and 27 species of hawks, not to mention ospreys, falcons, and owls.

Bald Eagle The bald eagle holds a position in the pecking order that parallels that of the grizzly. Of all the birds in the park, visitors are most interested in spotting this photogenic species, once almost wiped out by the pesticide DDT. The Yellowstone and Grand Teton National Parks are now home to one of largest populations of eagles in the continental United States; in Yellowstone alone, there are at least 19 active nests, and 18 young were born in 2015. Bald eagles are most recognizable by a striking white head, tail feathers, and wingspans up to 7 feet. The Yellowstone Plateau, Snake River, Yellowstone Lake, and headwaters of the Madison River are prime spotting areas for this spectacular bird.

Bald Eagle

Golden Eagle

Golden Eagle The bald eagle's cousin, the golden eagle, is similar in appearance, although it is smaller and does not have a white cowl. The golden eagle goes after small

Birding Spot

Take a picnic lunch or a relaxing break at the **Oxbow Bend** overlook in Grand Teton. Weather permitting, you can soak up some sunshine and observe the great blue herons, ospreys, pelicans, cormorants, and maybe a bald eagle. Although it's a popular spot, there's always room for one more vehicle.

mammals, such as jack rabbits and prairie dogs. They hunt in open country; sometimes you'll find one feeding on roadkill.

Osprey   The osprey, nicknamed the "fish eagle" on account of its diet, is the eagle's smaller relative, growing from 21 to 24 inches and with a white underbody and a brown topside. Ospreys tend to create large nests made of twigs and branches on the tops of trees and power poles. Look for this handsome, interesting bird in the Snake River area and the Grand Canyon of the Yellowstone River, a popular nesting area.

Osprey

Raven

Raven   Sporting a 50- to 60-inch wingspan, the raven is jet black and markedly larger than the crow. The most intelligent bird in the parks, the raven plays an interesting role in the Greater Yellowstone Ecosystem: Biologists have observed ravens communicating with wolves, leading them to carcasses, and even playing with pups. Ravens benefit from wolf kills because they are scavengers, so this relationship is symbiotic. They can be seen just about everywhere in both parks.

Trumpeter Swan   The trumpeter swan, one of the largest birds on the continent, has made the Greater Yellowstone Ecosystem a sanctuary. Easily recognizable by its long, curved neck, snowy white body, and black bill, it is found in marshes and on lakes and rivers, namely the Madison River in Yellowstone and Christian Pond, Swan Lake, and Cygnet Pond in Grand Teton.

Trumpeter Swan

Other Raptors **American kestrels, prairie falcons,** and **red-tailed hawks** are seen on Antelope Flats–Kelly Road in Grand Teton, where they search for small rodents.

American Kestrel   *Prairie Falcon*   *Red-Tailed Hawk*

Other Aquatic Birds The **great blue heron,** a skinny, long-legged wading bird, is found in wetlands and rocky outcrops, especially near the end of Jackson Lake. Yellowstone Lake is a prime viewing area for the best fishers in the park, the **American white pelicans** that capture fish in their long, yellow-pouched bill. The **American dipper,** the only aquatic songbird in North America, revels in cold, fastflowing mountain streams. The **slate-gray dipper** is tiny, only 7 to 8 inches tall, and is recognized by its long bill and stubby tail.

Great Blue Heron

PLANNING YOUR TRIP

I t's no one's idea of a fun vacation to end up inhaling exhaust behind a long line of cars waiting to access Yellowstone's east entrance, or wearing a T-shirt in a late-season Montana snowstorm. Few things can do more to ruin a much-anticipated vacation than poor planning. So look over some of the crucial information in this chapter before you hit the road—it might make the difference between a trip you'll never forget and one you'd rather not remember. For additional help in planning your trip and for further on-the-ground resources in Yellowstone and Grand Teton, see "Fast Facts," later in this chapter.

GETTING THERE & GETTING AROUND

The automobile is the main method of transport within the parks. You won't find any trains or buses with regular schedules in the parks, although many tour operators use buses. Bikes are a common sight on park roads, but both riders and drivers should exercise extreme caution here: Roads are twisty and rife with wildlife, pulled-over vehicles, and jaw-dropping scenery.

By Plane

The closest airport to Yellowstone is **Yellowstone Airport** (© 406/646-7631; www.yellowstone airport.org), just 1 mile north of the town of **West Yellowstone,** Montana (and 2 miles north of the west entrance to the park), on U.S. 191. The airport has commercial flights seasonally, late May

10

through the end of September only, on **Delta Airlines,** connecting through Salt Lake City.

American Airlines, Delta, SkyWest, and **United** all have flights to and from **Jackson Hole Airport** (℡ 307/733-7682; www.jacksonholeairport.com), which is right in Grand Teton National Park in **Jackson,** Wyoming, and only 56 miles of scenic driving from the southern entrance of Yellowstone.

To the north, **Bozeman Yellowstone International Airport** (℡ 406/388-8321; www.bozemanairport.com) in **Bozeman,** Montana, provides service via **Alaska, Allegiant, American Airlines, Delta, Frontier,** and **United,** as well as private jet service through **Jet Suite.** From Bozeman, you can drive 87 miles on U.S. 191 to the West Yellowstone entrance, or you can drive 20 miles east on I-90 to Livingston and then 53 miles south on U.S. 89 to the Gardiner entrance.

Also to the north, **Billings Logan International Airport** (℡ 406/247-8609; www.flybillings.com), Montana's busiest airport, is only 2 miles north of downtown **Billings,** Montana. Service is provided by **Allegiant, Alaska, Delta, Cape Air,** and **United.** From Billings, it's a 65-mile drive south on U.S. 212 to Red Lodge, and then 30 miles on the Beartooth Highway to the northeast Yellowstone entrance in Cooke City.

Yellowstone Regional Airport (℡ 307/587-5096; www. flyyra.com) in **Cody,** Wyoming, serves the Bighorn Basin as well as the east and northeast entrances of Yellowstone with year-round commercial flights via **Delta/SkyWest** and **United Express.** From Cody, it's a gorgeous 53-mile drive west along U.S. 14/16/20 to the east entrance of Yellowstone.

Airfares to the small airports surrounding the parks can be pricey, so if you like to drive, consider flying into **Salt Lake City,** Utah, and driving about 300 miles to Grand Teton National Park, a route that has some nice scenic stretches. Even **Denver,** a drive of roughly 500 miles, is an alternative, although the route is not nearly as scenic.

By Car

If interstate highways and international airports are the measure of accessibility, then Yellowstone is as remote as Alaska's Denali National Park. But more than four million people make it here every year, on tour buses, in family vans, on bicycles, and astride snowmobiles—even from the other side of the world. Car is the most common method of travel in and around the parks, and the most convenient. Public transportation is sparse in these parts, and the lack of trains make it nearly impossible to even get near the parks without a vehicle.

Grand Teton's gateways are from the north, south, and east. Drivers naturally enter from whichever side they approach the parks. From the west, U.S. 20 or U.S. 191 takes you to West Yellowstone, Montana. From the south, U.S. 191 runs through Jackson and the length of Jackson Hole before entering Yellowstone. From the east, U.S. 20 bisects Cody, Wyoming, and continues west 53 miles to the east entrance of Yellowstone. The northeast entrance of Yellowstone is accessible from U.S. 212 via Cooke City, Montana. Finally, the north entrance is just outside Gardiner, Montana, on U.S. 89.

Most of the major auto-rental agencies have operations in the gateway city airports. Visit each airport's rental car page for details, national reservation phone numbers, and local rental desk phone numbers. Also consider using a third-party booker such as **Hotwire** (www.hotwire.com) or **Kayak** (www.kayak.com) for substantial savings on your rates. You'll find the most car rental companies at Billings Logan International (www.flybillings.com/815/car-rentals) and Bozeman Yellowstone International (www.bozemanairport.com), with eight each. Jackson Hole Airport and the town of Jackson together host eight options, with three at the airport itself (www.jacksonholeairport.com/airport-guide). Five outfits operate out of Cody's Yellowstone Regional Airport (www.flyyra.com/parking-transportation), and three are based in West Yellowstone's Yellowstone Airport (www.yellowstone airport.org/airport-info.shtml).

Driving Distances to Yellowstone National Park*	
Salt Lake City	390 miles
Denver	563 miles
Las Vegas	809 miles
Seattle	827 miles
Portland	869 miles
Omaha	946 miles
Washington, D.C.	2,081 miles

*The difference in distance to Grand Teton is about 70 miles, depending on your route.

One U.S. gallon equals 3.8 liters or .85 imperial gallons. Gasoline is sold in the gateway cities, but at only a select few locations in the park; fill up well before empty. International visitors should note that insurance and taxes are almost never included in quoted rental car rates in the U.S. Be sure to ask your rental agency about additional fees for these. They can add a significant cost to your car rental.

By Bus or Shuttle

Public transportation options are fairly limited around the parks, but there are a few companies that will haul you from selected airports to gateway towns. For long-distance bus travel, check **Greyhound** (✆ **800/231-2222**; www.greyhound. com) schedules for Bozeman, Jackson, and Idaho Falls. From the Bozeman airport, you can catch a ride to West Yellowstone with **Karst Stage** (✆ **406/556-3500**; www.karst stage.com) for $95 one-way (prices drop if you have more passengers) or **Yellowstone Roadrunner** (✆ **406/640-0631**; www.yellowstoneroadrunner.com). The latter also serves Jackson and Idaho Falls; call for rates. And in winter, **Xanterra Parks & Resorts** (✆ **307/344-7311**; www.yellowstone nationalparklodges.com) runs a daily shuttle from Bozeman airport to Mammoth for $75 one-way (advance booking required).

Tips for RVers

You love 'em, or you hate 'em—the large, lumbering vehicles that serve some travelers as both transport and home. There are some retirees, self-named "full-timers," who sell their homes and most of their possessions and spend the rest of their lives chasing comfortable weather down the highway. Others might see it as a cost-saving way to vacation in the West—by renting a rolling room for the whole family at perhaps $1,000 per week plus gas. Is that a better deal than an economy car and inexpensive motels? You do the math.

You don't have to carry your bags, or even unpack them, and you'll sleep in campgrounds instead of motels, hear the sounds of the night outside, and have great flexibility in planning your itinerary. The trade-off is horrid gas mileage, making your own beds, and preparing your own meals most of the time.

A few years back, Yellowstone officials considered closing the RV campground at Fishing Bridge, on the north end of Yellowstone Lake. The outcry was enormous, testimony to the immense popularity of RV travel, so the Fishing Bridge facility remains open today. You can drive most of the major roads in both parks with an RV or a trailer; but there will be some areas where large vehicles are prohibited, and most of the camping areas don't provide hookups—Colter Bay, Flagg Ranch, and Fishing Bridge are the exceptions.

TIPS ON ACCOMMODATIONS

Inside the parks, your options for lodging are fairly limited; the finite number of rooms and seemingly limitless number of peak-season visitors makes for high occupancy and rates. And the fact that many of the parks' hostelries have historic designations might mean they don't fit some visitors' modern tastes. In the gateway cities, there is more variety, from dorm-style hostels to luxury ski resorts. House swapping is a possibility in Jackson and Cody, but less likely in the smaller gateways. In Yellowstone, information regarding lodging is available from **Xanterra Parks & Resorts,** P.O. Box 165, Yellowstone National Park, WY 82190 (© **307/344-7311;** www.yellowstonenationalparklodges.com). In Grand Teton, lodging information is available from park concessionaires: **Grand Teton Lodge Company,** P.O. Box 250, Moran, WY 83013 (© **307/543-2811;** www.gtlc.com), and **Signal Mountain Lodge Co.,** P.O. Box 50, Moran, WY 83013 (© **307/543-2831;** www.signalmountainlodge.com). For more information about where to stay, see chapters 7 and 8.

SPECIAL PERMITS
Backcountry Permits

If you want to sleep in the Yellowstone or Grand Teton backcountry, you must get a permit, follow limits for length of stay and campfires, and stay in a designated area. The permit costs $3 per person per night in Yellowstone (with a maximum group fee of $15) and $25 total in Grand Teton.

Alternatively, you can reserve a site by paying a $35 fee to Grand Teton or $25 to Yellowstone. At Yellowstone, reservations must be made through fax, mail, or in person; at Grand Teton, they go through the site www.recreation.gov. Even when you get reservations, you still need to pick up your permit in person upon your arrival in the park. Yellowstone begins processing reservations for the current year starting on April 1, but accepts requests from January 1 to October 31. In Grand Teton, you can reserve a permit only from the first Wednesday in January to May 15; thereafter all permits are first-come, first-served. If you're going during the parks' busy season, you'd be wise to make a reservation.

In Yellowstone, permits can be obtained at any ranger station (most of which are open 8am–4:30pm during the summer) and most visitor centers, no more than 2 days before embarking on a trip. To make a reservation by mail, send an application (available at www.nps.gov/yell/planyourvisit/backcountryhiking.htm) to the **Backcountry Office,** P.O. Box 168, Yellowstone National Park, WY 82190. Phone reservations are not accepted, but if you want information about the system, call © **307/344-2160.**

In Grand Teton, permits are issued at the Craig Thomas (Moose) and Colter Bay visitor centers and the Jenny Lake Ranger Station. Phone reservations are not accepted, but information is available by calling © **307/739-3602.**

Boating Permits

For motorized craft in Yellowstone, the cost is $20 for annual permits and $10 for 7-day permits. Fees for nonmotorized boats are $10 for annual permits and $5 for 7-day permits. Boating permits are required for all vessels. Motorized boating is restricted to designated areas. Boating is prohibited on all of Yellowstone's rivers and streams except for the Lewis River Channel, where hand-propelled vessels are permitted. In Grand Teton, the fees are $40 for motorized boats and $10 for nonmotorized. Powerboats are permitted on Jenny and Jackson Lakes; nonmotorized boats are allowed on most park lakes and the Snake River. Sailboats, windsurfers, and jet skis are allowed only on Jackson Lake. U.S. Coast Guard–approved personal flotation devices are required for each person boating.

Fishing Permits

In **Yellowstone,** park permits are required for anglers ages 16 and over; the permit costs $18 for 3 days, $25 for 7 days, and $40 for the season. Children 15 and under don't need a permit if they are fishing with an adult, but they need to pick up a free permit if they're fishing without supervision. Permits are available at any ranger station, any visitor center, Yellowstone Park General Store, and most fishing shops in the gateways. The season usually begins on the Saturday of Memorial Day weekend and continues through the first Sunday in November. Exceptions to this rule are Yellowstone Lake, its tributaries, and sections of the Yellowstone River, which have shorter seasons.

In **Grand Teton,** state of Wyoming fishing licenses are required for everyone ages 14 years and over. An adult nonresident license costs $14 per day and $92 for the season. Nonresident youth fees (ages 14–18) are $15 for the season. A $12.50 Conservation Stamp is also required for all licenses except the 1-day variety. Jackson Lake is closed all of October.

PLANNING A BACKCOUNTRY TRIP

While I've given the particulars for both Yellowstone and Grand Teton National Parks in their respective chapters (see chapters 3 and 5), the following tips are useful when planning a backcountry trip.

Regulations

The theme in the backcountry is "leave no trace," and that means packing out any garbage you take in, not taking pets, and avoiding leaving scars on the landscape by staying on designated trails and reusing existing campsites. Fires are allowed only in established fire rings, and only dead and downed material may be used for firewood; fires are prohibited in some areas, but backpacking stoves are allowed throughout the parks. You must have a park permit for overnight stays in the backcountry. There's a complete list of do's and don'ts in the *Backcountry Trip Planner,* available at most visitor centers. For more information on "leave no trace" ethics, see **www.lnt.org**.

Backpacking for Beginners

Be sure to wear comfortable, sturdy hiking shoes that will resist water if you're planning an early-season hike; cotton socks are not a good idea because the material holds moisture, whereas wool and synthetics, such as fleece, wick it away from your body. Your sleeping bag should be rated for the low temperatures found at high elevations; if you bring a down bag, keep it dry or suffer the consequences. A lightweight sleeping pad is a must. An internal frame backpack with good padding, a lumbar support pad, and a wide hip belt helps ensure a comfortable trip. Be sure that you've tried out the pack and boots—wear them around the house!—before you take it on a long trip with heavy loads, so that you'll have time to break them in.

Personal Safety Issues

It's best not to backpack alone, but if you must, be sure that you have told park rangers and friends where you'll be and how long you'll be gone. Don't leave the parking lot without the following gear: a compass, topographical maps, a first-aid kit, bug repellent, toilet paper, a headlamp, matches, a knife, food supplies, a bear-resistant food container (required in Grand Teton) if your campsite doesn't have a bear pole, bear spray, as well as a tent, a stove, and a sleeping bag. At this altitude, sunscreen and sunglasses with UV protection are also wise. You'll also need water treatment pills or a good water filter, because that seemingly clear stream could be filled with parasites that are likely to cause intestinal disorders. If you don't have either, bring water to a boil before you drink it. For more details, see "The 10 Essentials+1," p. 83.

RECOMMENDED READING

The following books are interesting, informative, and easy to find: *A Ranger's Guide to Yellowstone Day Hikes,* by Roger Anderson and Carol Shiveley Anderson (Farcountry Press, 2013); *Empire of Shadows: The Epic Story of Yellowstone,* By George Black (St. Martin's Griffin, 2013); *The Art of Yellowstone Science: Mammoth Hot Springs as a Window on the Universe,* by Brad W. Fouke and Tom Murphy

(Crystal Creek Press, 2016); *Death in Yellowstone,* by Lee H. Whittlesey (Roberts Rinehart Publishers, 2014); *Yellowstone: The Official Guide to Touring the World's First National Park,* by the Yellowstone Association (Yellowstone Association, 2014); *Creation of the Teton Landscape: A Geologic Chronicle of Jackson Hole & the Teton Range,* by J. David Love, John C. Reed, Jr., and Kenneth L. Pierce (Grand Teton Association, 2016); *Peaks, Politics & Passion: Grand Teton National Park Comes of Age,* by Robert W. Righter (Grand Teton Association, 2014); and *Grand Teton National Park Fishing Guide,* by Dave Shorett (LakeStream Publications, 2004). **Falcon Press** also publishes a long list of hiking, fishing, climbing, and other guides to the Yellowstone/Grand Teton region.

If you cannot find these publications in your local bookstore, many can be ordered from either **Yellowstone Forever** (✆ **406/848-2400;** www.yellowstone.org) or the **Grand Teton Association** (✆ **307/739-3403;** www.grandtetonpark.org).

[FastFACTS] YELLOWSTONE & GRAND TETON NATIONAL PARKS

Area Codes **Yellowstone** is almost entirely in Wyoming, with the area code **307.** The park also extends slightly into Montana (area code **406**) and Idaho (area code **208**). **Grand Teton** is entirely in Wyoming, and its area code is also **307.**

Car Rental See "Getting There & Getting Around," earlier in this chapter.

Cellphones See "Mobile Phones," later in this section.

Crime See "Safety," later in this section.

Customs International visitors may carry in or out up to $10,000 in U.S. or foreign currency with no formalities; larger sums must be declared to U.S. Customs and Border Protection on entering or leaving, which includes filing form FinCen105. For details regarding U.S. Customs and Border Protection, consult your nearest U.S. embassy or consulate, or **U.S. Customs and Border Protection** (www.cbp.gov).

Disabled Travelers Both parks are becoming increasingly user-friendly for travelers with disabilities. Those who are blind or have permanent disabilities can obtain a free **Interagency Access Pass,** which allows lifetime access to all national parks and federal fee areas. The pass must be obtained in person and is available at any entrance point to Yellowstone or Grand Teton.

YELLOWSTONE **Wheelchair-accessible accommodations** are available in all park lodges. For detailed information about accessible features throughout the park, visit www.nps.gov/yell/planyourvisit/accessibility.htm). All campgrounds *except* Fishing Bridge, Pebble Creek, Slough Creek, and Tower Fall have at least one **wheelchair-accessible campsite.**

Wheelchair-accessible restrooms with sinks and flush toilets are located at all developed areas except West Thumb. Accessible vault toilets are located at West Thumb and Norris, all campgrounds, and in most scenic areas and picnic areas.

Many of Yellowstone's **roadside attractions,** including the south rim of the Grand Canyon of the Yellowstone, West Thumb Geyser Basin, much of the Norris and Upper Geyser basins, Mammoth Hot Springs, and parts of the Mud Volcano and Fountain Paint Pot areas, are negotiable by wheelchair. **Visitor centers** at Old Faithful, Grant Village, Mammoth, and Canyon are wheelchair accessible, as are the Norris Museum and the Fishing Bridge Visitor Center.

Wheelchair-accessible parking is available at all major developed areas and some overlooks and picnic areas.

GRAND TETON **Campsites** at Colter Bay, Jenny Lake, and Gros Ventre campgrounds are on relatively level terrain; Headwaters Lodge & Cabins at Flagg Ranch also offers accessible campsites and RV sites. Lizard Creek and Signal Mountain are hilly and less accessible.

Wheelchair-accessible dining facilities are located at Flagg Ranch, Leeks Marina, Colter Bay, Signal Mountain Lodge, Jackson Lake Lodge, and Jenny Lake Lodge.

Visitor centers at Moose, Colter Bay, Jenny Lake, and Flagg Ranch provide interpretive programs, displays, and visitor information in several forms, including visual, audible, and tactile.

Wheelchair-accessible parking spaces are located close to all visitor center entrances; curb cuts are provided, as are **accessible restroom facilities.**

More information is available from **Grand Teton National Park** at www.nps.gov/grte/planyourvisit/accessibility.htm.

Doctors In Yellowstone, the **clinic at Mammoth Hot Springs** (📞 307/344-7965) is open year-round except some holidays. **Lake Clinic** (📞 307/242-7241) and **Old Faithful Clinic** (📞 307/545-7325) are open during the summer. In Grand Teton, the **Grand Teton Medical Clinic** at Jackson Lake Lodge (📞 307/543-2514) is open daily in the summer from 9am to 5pm. The next-closest clinic is in Jackson, Wyoming: **St. John's Medical Center,** 625 E. Broadway (📞 307/733-3636), has a 24-hour emergency room.

Drinking Laws The legal age for the purchase and consumption of alcoholic beverages is 21; proof of age is required and often requested at bars, nightclubs, and restaurants, so it's always a good idea to bring ID when you go out. Do not carry open containers of alcohol in your car or any public area that isn't zoned for alcohol consumption. The police can fine you on the spot. Don't even think about driving while intoxicated. Alcohol is widely available at stores in both parks and in the gateway cities. Bars in both Montana and Wyoming close at 2am.

Driving Rules See "Getting There & Getting Around," earlier in this chapter.

Electricity Like Canada, the U.S. uses 110 to 120 volts AC (60 cycles), compared to 220 to 240 volts AC (50 cycles) in most of Europe, Australia, and New Zealand. Downward converters that change 220–240 volts to 110–120 volts are difficult to find in the U.S., so bring one with you.

Embassies & Consulates All embassies are in the nation's capital, Washington, D.C. Some consulates are in major U.S. cities, and most nations have a mission to the United Nations in New York City. If your country isn't listed below, check **www.embassy.org/embassies**.

The embassy of **Australia** is at 1601 Massachusetts Ave. NW, Washington, DC 20036 (© **202/797-3000;** www.usa.embassy.gov.au). Consulates are in Chicago, Honolulu, Houston, New York, Los Angeles, and San Francisco.

The embassy of **Canada** is at 501 Pennsylvania Ave. NW, Washington, DC 20001 (© **202/682-1740;** www.can-am.gc.ca/washington). Canadian consulates are in 12 cities throughout the U.S., including Atlanta, Boston, Chicago, New York, Los Angeles, Miami, and Seattle.

The embassy of **Ireland** is at 2234 Massachusetts Ave. NW, Washington, DC 20008 (© **202/462-3939;** www.dfa.ie). Irish consulates are in Austin (Texas), Atlanta, Boston, Chicago, New York, and San Francisco,

The embassy of **New Zealand** is at 37 Observatory Circle NW, Washington, DC 20008 (© **202/328-4800;** www.mfat.govt.nz). New Zealand consulates are in Los Angeles, Honolulu, and New York.

The embassy of the **United Kingdom** is at 3100 Massachusetts Ave. NW, Washington, DC 20008 (© **202/588-6500;** www.gov.uk/government/world/organisations/british-embassy-washington). British consulates are in Atlanta, Boston, Chicago, Houston, Miami, New York, San Francisco, and Los Angeles.

Emergencies Call © **911.** In Yellowstone, you can also call the park's main information number (© **307/344-7381**), which is staffed 24 hours a day. In Grand Teton, dial © **307/739-3300.**

Family Travel One useful guide to traveling with the kids is *An Outdoor Family Guide to Yellowstone and Grand Teton National Parks* (Mountaineers Books, 2006). Older children can learn about nature by enrolling in the **Junior Ranger Program** at both Yellowstone (p. 68) and Grand Teton (p. 112).

Gasoline   See "Getting There & Getting Around," earlier in this chapter.

Health   Health hazards range from mild headaches to run-ins with wild animals, but the latter happens less frequently than car accidents in the parks. To be safe, you might want to keep a first-aid kit in your car or luggage, and have it handy when hiking. It should include at least butterfly bandages, sterile gauze pads, adhesive tape, an antibiotic ointment, pain relievers for children and for adults, alcohol pads, a pocket knife with scissors, and tweezers. Healthcare is available at clinics in both parks; hospitals with 24-hour emergency rooms are located in Jackson and Cody, Wyoming, as well as in Bozeman, Montana.

Altitude Sickness   The most common health hazard in the parks is discomfort caused by altitude sickness. Adjusting to the parks' high elevations is a process that can take a day or more. Symptoms of altitude sickness include headache, fatigue, nausea, loss of appetite, muscle pain, and lightheadedness. Doctors recommend that, until acclimated, travelers should avoid heavy exertion, consume light meals, and drink lots of liquids but little caffeine or alcohol.

Bugs, Bites & Other Wildlife Concerns   Wildlife are to be treated with utmost respect in both parks. Keep your distance—at least 300 feet if possible—from any wild animal in either park. Mosquitoes, spiders, and ticks are the most bothersome biters, aside from the occasional rattlesnake you might see around Gardiner, Montana.

Waterborne Illnesses   See "Water," below.

Internet & Wi-Fi   When it comes to modern telecommunications, Yellowstone and Grand Teton National Parks have extremely limited infrastructure: Lack of connectivity is the rule, not the exception. These are not destinations for those who need to check e-mail every few minutes—or even every day. Some Yellowstone lodges have begun to add Wi-Fi for a fee in recent years, sometimes only in the lobby or other public spaces: They are Mammoth Hot Springs Hotel, Lake Lodge Cabins, Lake Yellowstone Hotel, Grant Village, and Old Faithful Snow Lodge. In Grand Teton National Park, Wi-Fi is available in public areas at Colter Bay Village, Jackson Lake Lodge, Signal Mountain Lodge, and Jenny Lake Lodge. Internet access is widely available in all of the gateways, but can be notably slow in Gardiner and West Yellowstone.

Legal Aid   While driving, if you are pulled over for a minor infraction (such as speeding), never attempt to pay the fine directly to a police officer; this could be construed as attempted bribery, a much more serious crime. Pay fines by mail, or directly into the hands of the clerk of the court. If accused of a more serious offense, say and do nothing before consulting a lawyer. In the U.S., the burden is on the state to prove a person's guilt beyond a reasonable doubt, and everyone has the right to remain silent, whether he or she is suspected of a crime or actually arrested. Once arrested, a person can make one telephone call to a party of his or her choice. The international visitor should call his or her embassy or consulate.

LGBT Travelers   While Wyoming and Montana have earned reputations as intolerant destinations in the past, Yellowstone and Grand Teton National Parks are generally gay-friendly. However, gay culture and nightlife are very limited in Jackson and nearly nonexistent in other gateways.

Mail   At press time, domestic postage rates were 34¢ for a postcard and 49¢ for a letter. For international mail, letters and postcards start at $1.15. For more information visit www.usps.com.

If you aren't sure what your address will be in the U.S., mail can be sent to you, in your name, c/o General Delivery at the main post office of the city or region where you expect to be. (Call ℂ **800/275-8777** for information on the nearest post office.) The addressee must pick up mail in person and must produce proof of identity (a driver's license or passport, for example). Most post offices will hold mail for up to 1 month and are open Monday to Friday from 8am to 6pm and Saturday from 9am to 3pm.

Always include a zip code when mailing items in the U.S. If you don't know the zip code, visit www.usps.com/zip4.

Medical Requirements   Unless you're arriving from an area known to be suffering from an epidemic (particularly cholera or yellow fever), inoculations or vaccinations are not required for entry into the U.S. See "Health," above.

Mobile Phones   The parks have several cell towers in developed areas. Cell service is widely available on the floor of Jackson Hole throughout Grand Teton National Park; in Yellowstone, it is available in Canyon, Grant, Lake, Mammoth Hot Springs, and Old Faithful villages but largely unavailable on the roads and in wilderness areas. Cell service is available in all of the gateway cities. International travelers may want to buy a pay-as-you-go phone for the trip.

Money & Costs   Throughout this guide, Frommer's lists prices in the local currency. See the table below for currency conversions. These conversions were accurate at press time. Rates fluctuate, however, so before departing consult a currency exchange website such as www.oanda.com/currency/converter to check up-to-the-minute rates.

THE VALUE OF THE U.S. DOLLAR VS. OTHER POPULAR CURRENCIES

US$	A$	C$	Euro €	NZ$	UK£
1.00	1.32	1.33	0.94	1.43	0.80

ATMs are widely available in the gateway cities and developed areas in both parks. Beware of hidden credit card fees while traveling.

WHAT THINGS COST IN YELLOWSTONE & GRAND TETON

	US$
Admission to both parks for a week	50.00
Double motel room in the parks, peak season	93.00–438.00
Cabin (private)	90.00–310.00
Dinner main course in a full-service hotel restaurant	10.00–46.00
Horseback riding	43.00–80.00
Basic lake cruise	19.00–32.00
Bus sightseeing tour (Yellowstone)	75.00–114.00
Round-trip snowcoach to Old Faithful	234
1 gallon/1 liter of regular gas	2.50/1.52

If you are visiting from outside the U.S., check with your credit or debit card issuer to see what fees, if any, will be charged for overseas transactions.

For help with currency conversions, tip calculations, and more, download Frommer's convenient Travel Tools app for your mobile device. Go to www.frommers.com/go/mobile and click on the Travel Tools icon.

Newspapers & Magazines The primary papers in the region are the *Billings Gazette, Bozeman Daily Chronicle,* and the *Cody Enterprise.* In **Yellowstone,** the best source of park information is the free *Yellowstone Summer* (or whichever season you're visiting), the free park newspaper available at all entrances and visitor centers. In **Grand Teton,** the free *Grand Teton Guide* is full of park information. In **Jackson,** the newspaper is the *Jackson Hole News & Guide.*

Packing Nothing will ruin a trip to the parks faster than sore or wet feet. Bring comfortable walking shoes, even if you plan to keep walking to a minimum. **Bring shoes that are broken in,** and if you plan to do some serious hiking, get sturdy boots that support your ankles and protect against water. Early in the season, trails might be wet or muddy; late in the fall, you can get snowed on. The more popular trails are sometimes also used by horses, which can make stream crossings a mucky mess.

Wear your clothing in layers, and bring a small, empty backpack or fanny pack so that you have somewhere to put the clothes as you take those layers off and on as temperature, altitude, and your level of physical exertion change. Cotton is a no-no in the backcountry; synthetic fabrics are recommended because they dry much faster. Gloves or mittens are useful before the park heats up, or in the evening when it cools down again, *even in summer.*

The atmosphere is thin at higher altitudes, so protect your skin. Bring a strong sunblock, a hat with a brim, and sunglasses. I also recommend bringing insect repellent, water bottles, and a first-aid kit.

Take into account that elevations at the parks are between 5,000 and 11,000 feet; in campgrounds and on hiking trails, you'll want clothing appropriate to the temperatures—in summer, 40°F (4°C) in the evening, 75°F (24°C) during the day.

For more helpful information on packing for your trip, download our convenient Travel Tools app for your mobile device. Go to www.frommers.com/go/mobile and click on the Travel Tools icon.

Passports   Virtually every air traveler entering the U.S. is required to show a passport. All persons, including U.S. citizens, traveling by air between the U.S. and Canada, Mexico, Central and South America, the Caribbean, and Bermuda are required to present a valid passport. *Note:* U.S. and Canadian citizens entering the U.S. at land and sea ports of entry from within the Western Hemisphere must now also present a passport or other documents compliant with the Western Hemisphere Travel Initiative. Children 15 and under may continue entering with only a U.S. birth certificate, or other proof of U.S. citizenship.

Petrol   Please see "Getting There & Getting Around," earlier in this chapter.

Police   Call ✆ **911.**

Safety   The roads are the most dangerous places in Yellowstone, so be especially cautious while driving. Lightning and falls are also killers, but wildlife is the most unique peril in the parks. The most dangerous animal in either park might well be the grizzly bear, but all wildlife has the potential to injure a human. Keep a safe distance from buffalo, deer, moose, and other animals—at least 300 feet. Most people have a healthy respect for bears and are content to view them from a distance. But because a close encounter can happen unexpectedly, you need to know what to do in this situation. First, be aware that what matters most to a bear are food and cubs. If you get between a sow and her cubs, you could be in trouble. If a bear thinks that the food in your backpack is his, you also have a problem.

Unless bears have already developed a taste for human food, though, they won't come looking for you. Make a lot of noise on the trail through bear habitat, and *Ursus arctos horribilis* will give you a wide berth. Don't camp anywhere near the carcass of a dead animal; grizzlies sometimes partially bury carrion and return to it. Hang your food bag from your campsite's pole or use a bear-resistant food container, keep your cooking area distant from your campsite, and don't keep any food or utensils in your tent—or even clothes worn while cooking. Soaps and other perfumed items can also be attractants.

Avoid hiking at night or in the meadows of mountain areas if visibility is poor. Bears have an extremely good sense of smell but poor eyesight. Always carry bear spray.

If you encounter a bear, here are some things you should and should not do:

- **Do not run.** Anything that flees looks like prey to a bear, and it might attack. Bears can run at more than 30 mph. The bear might bluff charge, but you're best off holding your ground.
- Avoid direct eye contact.
- If the bear is unaware of you, **stay downwind** (so that it doesn't catch your scent) and **detour away from it slowly.**
- If the bear is aware of you but has not acted aggressively, **slowly back away.**
- **Do not climb a tree.** Although black bears have more suitable claws for climbing, grizzly bears can climb trees, too.
- Make noise and act intimidating if the bear does not retreat.
- If you're attacked, drop to the ground face down, clasp your hands over the back of your neck, tuck your knees to your chest, and **play dead.** Keep your backpack on—it can help protect your body. Only as a last resort should you attempt to resist an attack and fight off a bear.
- Always carry **bear spray,** be sure that it's handy when you're in possible bear habitat, not buried in a backpack. If you use it, aim for the bear's face and eyes. After you use it, leave the area: Bears have been seen returning to sniff about an area where spray has been used.

Smoking Montana has a statewide smoking ban; Wyoming does not, but smoking is banned in most public places in the park and Jackson Hole.

Taxes Lodging and sales tax in Yellowstone and its gateways varies from 4% to 8%. Tax is 6% in Grand Teton Park and 6% to 8% in Jackson Hole. The U.S. has no value-added tax (VAT) or other indirect tax at the national level. Every state, county, and city may levy its own local tax on all purchases, including hotel and restaurant bills and airline tickets. These taxes do not appear on price tags.

Telephones Many convenience stores and packaging services sell **prepaid calling cards** in denominations up to $50. Many public pay phones at airports accept American Express, MasterCard, and Visa. **Local calls** made from most pay phones cost either 25¢ or 35¢. Most long-distance and international calls can be dialed directly from any phone. **To make calls within the U.S. and to Canada,** dial 1 followed by the area code and the seven-digit number. **For other international calls,** dial 011 followed by the country code, city code, and the number you are calling.

Calls to area codes **800, 888, 877,** and **866** are toll free. Calls to area codes **700** and **900** (chat lines, bulletin boards, "dating" services, and so on) can be expensive, with charges of 95¢ to $3 or more per minute. Some numbers have minimum charges that can run $15 or more.

For **reversed-charge or collect calls,** and for person-to-person calls, dial the number 0 then the area code and number; an operator will come on the line, and you should specify whether you are calling collect, person-to-person, or both. If your operator-assisted call is international, ask for the overseas operator.

For **directory assistance** ("Information"), dial 411 for local numbers and national numbers in the U.S. and Canada. For dedicated long-distance information, dial 1, then the appropriate area code plus 555-1212.

Time   Both parks are in the **Mountain Standard Time** zone. **Daylight saving time (summer time)** is in effect from 1am on the second Sunday in March to 1am on the first Sunday in November. Daylight saving time moves the clock 1 hour ahead of standard time.

For help with time translations and more, download our Travel Tools app. Go to www.frommers.com/go/mobile and click on the Travel Tools icon.

Tipping   In hotels, tip **bellhops** at least $1 per bag ($2–$3 if you have a lot of luggage) and tip the **chamber staff** $1 to $2 per day (more if you've left a big mess for him or her to clean up). Tip the **doorman** or **concierge** only if he or she has provided you with some specific service (for example, calling a cab for you or obtaining difficult-to-get theater tickets). Tip the **valet-parking attendant** $1 every time you get your car.

In restaurants, bars, and nightclubs, tip **service staff** and **bartenders** 20% of the check, tip **checkroom attendants** $1 per garment, and tip **valet-parking attendants** $1 per vehicle.

Tip **cab drivers** 15% of the fare; tip **skycaps** at airports at least $1 per bag ($2–$3 if you have a lot of luggage); and tip **hairdressers** and **barbers** 15% to 20%.

For help with tip calculations, currency conversions, and more, download our convenient Travel Tools app for your mobile device. Go to www.frommers.com/go/mobile and click on the Travel Tools icon.

Toilets   You won't find public toilets or "restrooms" on the streets in most U.S. cities, but they can be found in hotel lobbies, bars, restaurants, museums, department stores, railway and bus stations, and service stations. Large hotels and fast-food restaurants are often the best bet for clean facilities. Restaurants and bars in resorts or heavily visited areas may reserve their restrooms for patrons. Both Yellowstone and Grand Teton have vault (flushless) toilets at numerous pullouts along the roads, and there are toilets at some trail heads, though not all.

VAT   See "Taxes," above.

Visas   The U.S. Department of State has a **Visa Waiver Program (VWP)** allowing citizens of the following countries to enter the U.S. without a visa for stays of up to 90 days: Andorra, Australia, Austria, Belgium, Brunei, Chile, Czech Republic, Denmark, Estonia, Finland, France, Germany, Greece, Hungary, Iceland, Ireland, Italy, Japan,

Latvia, Liechtenstein, Lithuania, Luxembourg, Malta, Monaco, Netherlands, New Zealand, Norway, Portugal, San Marino, Singapore, Slovakia, Slovenia, South Korea, Spain, Sweden, Switzerland, Taiwan, and the United Kingdom. (**Note:** This list was accurate at press time; for the most up-to-date list of countries in the VWP, consult https://travel.state.gov.) Even though a visa isn't necessary, in an effort to help U.S. officials check travelers against terror watch lists before they arrive at U.S. borders, visitors from VWP countries must register online through the Electronic System for Travel Authorization (ESTA) before boarding a plane or a boat to the U.S. Travelers must complete an electronic application, providing basic personal and travel eligibility information. The Department of Homeland Security recommends filling out the form at least 3 days before traveling. Authorizations will be valid for up to 2 years or until the traveler's passport expires, whichever comes first. Currently, there is a $14 fee for the online application. Existing ESTA registrations remain valid through their expiration dates. **Note:** As of April 1, 2016, you must have an enhanced e-passport to qualify for the VWP. Citizens of these nations also need to present a round-trip air or cruise ticket upon arrival. E-Passports contain computer chips capable of storing biometric information, such as the required digital photograph of the holder. Canadian citizens may enter the U.S. without visas, but will need to show passports and proof of residence.

Citizens of all other countries must have (1) a valid passport that expires at least 6 months later than the scheduled end of their visit to the U.S.; and (2) a tourist visa.

For information about U.S. visas, go to http://travel.state.gov/visa.

Visitor Information   The primary entries to Yellowstone and Grand Teton are through Montana and Wyoming, so if you want information about the surrounding areas, contact these states' travel services: **Montana Office of Tourism** (② **800/847-4868;** www.visitmt.com); and **Wyoming Office of Tourism,** 5611 High Plains Rd., Cheyenne, WY 82007 (② **800/225-5996** or 307/777-7777; www.travelwyoming.com).

To receive maps and information before your arrival, contact Yellowstone directly, P.O. Box 168, **Yellowstone National Park,** WY 82190 (② **307/344-7381;** www.nps.gov/yell), and **Grand Teton National Park,** P.O. Drawer 170, Moose, WY 83012 (② **307/739-3300;** www.nps.gov/grte). For information about educational programs at the Yellowstone Forever Institute and other resources, contact **Yellowstone Forever,** P.O. Box 117, Yellowstone National Park, WY 82190 (② **406/848-2400;** www.yellowstone.org). The **Grand Teton Association** is a not-for-profit organization that provides information about the park through retail book sales at park visitor centers; you can also buy books about the park from the organization by mail. Contact the association at P.O. Box 170, Moose, WY 83012 (② **307/739-3406;** www.grandtetonpark.org).

National forests and other public lands surround the parks. For information about national forests and wilderness areas in Montana, contact the **U.S. Forest Service Northern Region,** 26 Fort Missoula Rd., Missoula, MT 59804 (📞 **406/329-3511;** www.fs.usda.gov/r1). For information on Wyoming's national forests, turn to the **U.S. Forest Service Intermountain Region,** 324 25th St., Ogden, UT 84401 (📞 **801/625-5306;** www.fs.usda.gov/r4), and the **U.S. Forest Service Rocky Mountain Region,** 740 Simms St., Golden, CO 80401 (📞 **303/275-5350;** www.fs.usda.gov/r2).

The federal **Bureau of Land Management** also manages millions of acres of recreational lands and can be reached at its Wyoming state office, 5353 Yellowstone Rd. (P.O. Box 1828), Cheyenne, WY 82009 (📞 **307/775-6256;** www.blm.gov/wy); or its Montana state office, 5001 Southgate Dr., Billings, MT 59101 (📞 **406/896-5000;** www.blm.gov/montana-dakotas).

Water   Two waterborne hazards are *Giardia* and *Campylobacter,* with symptoms that wreak havoc on the human digestive system. If you pick up these pesky bugs, they might accompany you on your trip home. Untreated water from the parks' lakes and streams should be boiled before consumption, pumped through a fine-mesh water filter specifically designed to remove bacteria, or treated with chemical water purifiers.

10

Wi-Fi   See "Internet & Wi-Fi," earlier in this section.

Index

See also Accommodations and Restaurant indexes, below.

General Index

Restaurants

Map List

Photo Credits

Frommer's Yellowstone & Grand Teton National Parks, 9th edition

Published by
FROMMER MEDIA LLC

Copyright © 2017 by Frommer Media LLC. All rights reserved. No part of this publication may be reproduced, stored in a retrieval system, or transmitted in any form or by any means, electronic, mechanical, photocopying, recording, scanning or otherwise, except as permitted under Sections 107 or 108 of the 1976 United States Copyright Act, without the prior written permission of the Publisher. Requests to the Publisher for permission should be addressed to the support@frommermedia.com.

Frommer's is a registered trademark of Arthur Frommer. Frommer Media LLC is not associated with any product or vendor mentioned in this book.

ISBN 978-1-62887-334-4 (paper), 978-1-62887-335-1 (e-book)

Editorial Director: Pauline Frommer
Editor: Elizabeth Heath
Production Editor: Heather Wilcox
Cartographer: Roberta Stockwell
Cover Design: David Riedy

For information on our other products or services, see www.frommers.com.

Frommer Media LLC also publishes its books in a variety of electronic formats. Some content that appears in print may not be available in electronic formats.

Manufactured in the United States of America

5 4 3 2 1

ABOUT THE AUTHOR

Elisabeth Kwak-Hefferan is a freelance writer and editor who specializes in the outdoors, environment, travel, health, food, culture, and science. Her work has appeared in *Backpacker, Grist, Organic Life, Women's Adventure, 5280* (Denver's city magazine), and more.

She is *Backpacker's* Rocky Mountain Editor and a contributing writer for Grist.org. Elisabeth lives in Missoula, Montana, where the spectacular natural beauty is second in renown only to the staggeringly high craft brewery-per-capita ratio (beer of choice: Kettlehouse Cold Smoke, if you're buying).

ABOUT THE FROMMER TRAVEL GUIDES

For most of the past 50 years, Frommer's has been the leading series of travel guides in North America, accounting for as many as 24% of all guidebooks sold. I think I know why.

Though we hope our books are entertaining, we nevertheless deal with travel in a serious fashion. Our guidebooks have never looked on such journeys as a mere recreation, but as a far more important human function, a time of learning and introspection, an essential part of a civilized life. We stress the culture, lifestyle, history, and beliefs of the destinations we cover, and urge our readers to seek out people and new ideas as the chief rewards of travel.

We have never shied from controversy. We have, from the beginning, encouraged our authors to be intensely judgmental, critical—both pro and con—in their comments, and wholly independent. Our only clients are our readers, and we have triggered the ire of countless prominent sorts, from a tourist newspaper we called "practically worthless" (it unsuccessfully sued us) to the many rip-offs we've condemned.

And because we believe that travel should be available to everyone regardless of their incomes, we have always been cost-conscious at every level of expenditure. Though we have broadened our recommendations beyond the budget category, we insist that every lodging we include be sensibly priced. We use every form of media to assist our readers, and are particularly proud of our feisty daily website, the award-winning Frommers.com.

I have high hopes for the future of Frommer's. May these guidebooks, in all the years ahead, continue to reflect the joy of travel and the freedom that travel represents. May they always pursue a cost-conscious path, so that people of all incomes can enjoy the rewards of travel. And may they create, for both the traveler and the persons among whom we travel, a community of friends, where all human beings live in harmony and peace.

Arthur Frommer